An Emerging Non-Regular Labour Force in Japan

Like many industrialised nations, the current employment trend in Japan centres on diversification of the labour market with an increased use of temporary labour. Among a wide range of non-regular labour arrangements, *haken* are a newly legalised category of non-regular workers who are typically employed by the employment agency while working at the facilities of and being under the authority of the client firm. They have recently expanded exponentially under the state's deregulation policy and assumed considerable significance in political debate, especially with regard to the nation's 'widening gaps' known as *kakusa*.

This is the first anthropological study of *haken* and temporary agency work (TAW) in Japan which combines both macro- and micro-level analyses. At the macro-level, *haken* are explored from a historical perspective with a view to showing the changing state policy and public perception of *haken*. At the micro-level, how TAW is experienced by real people in concrete situations is extremely varied and complex, often depending on intersecting structural variables including gender, age and class. The book therefore provides insight into the gap between powerful discourses and everyday life, as well as a better understanding of personhood in Japan's shifting landscape of employment.

This book will be of interest to students and scholars of Japanese Studies, Japanese Business, Asian Business and Asian Anthropology.

Huiyan Fu is a Visiting Professor in the International Business Department, Aalen University of Applied Sciences, Germany.

The Nissan Institute/Routledge Japanese Studies Series

Editorial Board

Roger Goodman, Nissan Professor of Modern Japanese Studies, University of Oxford, Fellow, St Antony's College; J.A.A. Stockwin, formerly Nissan Professor of Modern Japanese Studies and former Director of the Nissan Institute of Japanese Studies, University of Oxford, Emeritus Fellow, St Antony's College; Alan Rix, Executive Dean, Faculty of Arts, The University of Queensland; Junji Banno, formerly Professor of the University of Tokyo, now Professor, Chiba University; Leonard Schoppa, Associate Professor, Department of Government and Foreign Affairs, and Director of the East Asia Center, University of Virginia

An Emerging Non-Regular Labour Force in Japan

The dignity of dispatched workers

Huiyan Fu

Routledge
Taylor & Francis Group

LONDON AND NEW YORK

First published 2012
by Routledge
2 Park Square, Milton Park, Abingdon, Oxfordshire OX14 4RN

Simultaneously published in the USA and Canada
by Routledge
711 Third Avenue, New York, NY 10017
First issued in paperback 2014

*Routledge is an imprint of the Taylor & Francis Group, an informa
business*

British Library Cataloguing in Publication Data
A catalogue record for this book is available from the British Library

Library of Congress Cataloging in Publication Data
Fu, Huiyan, 1974–
    An emerging non-regular labour force in Japan: the dignity of
    dispatched workers/Huiyan Fu.
    p. cm.—(The Nissan Institute/Routledge Japanese studies series)
    Includes bibliographical references and index.
    1. Temporary employment—Japan. 2. Part-time employment—Japan.
    3. Contract system (Labor)—Japan. I. Title.
    HD5854.2.J3F8 2011
    331.25'7270952—dc22
    2011004619

ISBN 978-0-415-66434-9 (hbk)
ISBN 978-1-138-85818-3 (pbk)
ISBN 978-0-203-80686-9 (ebk)

Typeset in Times New Roman
by Book Now Ltd, London

To Michael

Contents

Illustrations

Figures

Tables

Series editors' preface

For many years, the Japanese labour market has been characterised by duality; while the majority of employees were hired on permanent or semi-permanent contracts, a substantial minority were involved in a complex variety of temporary, casual and part-time arrangements. The former were regarded as a kind of labour aristocracy, benefiting from superior wages, bonuses and other perquisites of their status, whereas the latter, though often required to work as hard as the former, were less privileged, received fewer benefits and most crucially were relatively easy to dismiss (or not re-hire) at times of economic downturn or reduced fortunes on the part of the particular firm concerned. To a very considerable extent, duality in the labour market also reflected duality in the economy as a whole, between a relatively small number of enormous and prestigious companies and a myriad of firms in the small and medium sector. A further salient difference between the two types of employee was that whereas the former were overwhelmingly male, a high proportion of the latter were female, resulting in extensive gender discrimination in the workforce that in turn reflected (or was seen to reflect) embedded cultural norms of Japanese society.

The central position of permanently contracted workers in the Japanese labour market after the Second World War led to the widely publicised image of the 'salaryman': an individual dedicated to loyal service for the company, sacrificing personal and family interests to the corporate interest, working assiduously for long hours during the day then socialising with colleagues (and sometimes also clients) until late at night in what need to be seen as long-term bonding exercises designed to cement and perpetuate company esprit de corps.

Over the past 20 years, there has been a gradual blurring of the previous clear lines of duality. In part, this has been because social values in Japan have gradually been evolving from those appropriate to a developing economy to those expected of a developed economy whose population has become used to relative affluence; formerly prevalent ideas of self-sacrifice to the interests of an organisation have been progressively overlaid by values emphasising personal satisfaction and individual advancement. In part, the blurring of the duality has been due to 20 years of economic stagnation since the bursting of the 'bubble' at the end of the 1980s; corporations and employers have been experimenting with a variety of labour practices which give them maximal flexibility in an increasingly globalised economy.

Huiyan Fu, who has Chinese nationality and speaks fluent Japanese, examines an interesting manifestation of this gradual change, namely the phenomenon of *haken* or 'despatched' workers as a particular form of non-permanent labour. She was herself a *haken* worker in the mid-2000s, working successively in two large companies where she undertook her anthropological fieldwork. Her analysis is therefore enriched by personal experience of this type of employment. The employment of *haken* workers has become regularised since changes in the law dating from the 1980s. They are 'despatched' to receiving firms on limited-term contracts (normally of a few months), by *haken* companies, which in aggregate constitute an important and influential industry in contemporary Japan. Even though *haken* workers remain a fairly small percentage of the total workforce, they have been granted much prominence in the mass media, and have become symbolic of a new type of employee, often but not only female, who is more concerned with self than with organisation, but more positively, brings new ideas and an innovative perspective to the work environment. Indeed, the analysis presented here suggests that the image of the *'salaryman'* has become significantly tarnished, as such permanently employed 'shock troops' have become perceived by some commentators as complacent and risk-averse.

The Nissan Institute/Routledge Japanese Studies series – which has now been running for over 25 years and produced over 80 volumes – seeks to foster an informed, balanced, but not uncritical understanding of Japan. The present volume adds substantially to one of the most important areas which the series has covered during its history. It not only illuminates many aspects of the Japanese labour market, its historical background, changing legal basis as well as economic and sociological effects but also brings an interesting anthropological angle to these debates by laying out from the experience and perspective of the front-line workers the gradual changes that have been taking place in the field of Japanese employment in recent years.

Roger Goodman
J. A. A. Stockwin

Acknowledgements

'Teachers open the door. You enter by yourself.' This old Chinese proverb immediately springs to mind, when I look back on my student life at the University of Oxford. I want to thank, first and very much foremost, my supervisor Prof. Roger Goodman, who not only opened the door to an enthralling world but has always been a strict but caring mentor with unfailing support and tolerance throughout my entire anthropological training and research from 2004 to 2009. I am grateful to him both for having learned and benefited greatly from his scholarly insights and professional efficiency and for his profound influence in transforming me in such compelling fashion into a passionate devotee of anthropology.

This book, based on my PhD research, was made possible by the generosity of Oxford University Sasakawa Fund, Oxford University Pembroke College TEPCo Senior Studentship and the Japan Foundation Endowment Committee. It would have never borne fruit without many people who have kindly helped me in various ways. For amiable participation and cooperation, I am deeply indebted to friends and acquaintances in Japan – particularly so to Masafumi Morimoto, Miyuki Adachi, Hiromi Yamamoto, Ikuko Yamaguchi and Mayumi Adachi, who responded to my requests actively and allowed me to become, even if temporarily, part of their lives. Their and other anonymous informants' generous sharing of everyday life narratives and realities, which I draw on extensively in this study with awe and respect, could not be more appreciated. For stimulating inspiration and discussion, my gratitude goes to a number of individuals from different walks of life, whose perspicacious remarks, critical encouragement and sometimes much-needed comforting words have kept my spirits from flagging at crucial moments and sustained me through the trying times of fieldwork and writing. Those whose helpfulness merits special mention include Prof. David Parkin, Prof. David Gellner, Dr. Louella Matsunaga, Prof. Arthur Stockwin, Prof. Ian Neary, Prof. David H. Slater, Zaozao (Joey) Li and Yoshio Hori.

In addition to those wonderful people, whom it is my extremely good fortune to have met in my life, I would like to thank my families in China for their continuing support and love, which has made this book more important than it actually is!

Note on transliteration and romanisation

To facilitate communication and emphasise nuanced meanings, a number of Japanese terms are introduced in this book. As is common practice, all Japanese words are italicized, often in parentheses following an English translation. For a list of key Japanese words pertinent to the topic under discussion, an effort was made to provide explanations and references that were as detailed as possible. The romanisation of Japanese terms follows the Hepburn style, with the macron or elongation mark indicating long vowels.

Abbreviations

CIETT   Confederation Internationale des Entreprises de Travail Temporaire (*Kokusai Jinzai Haken Jigyō Dantai Rengō*)

EFILWC   European Foundation for the Improvement of Living and Working Conditions

ILO   International Labour Organisation

JASSA   Japan Staffing Services Association

JCGF   Japan Corporate Governance Forum

JCUF   Japan Community Union Federation (*Zenkoku Yunion*)

JILPT   Japan Institute for Labour Policy and Training

MHLW   Ministry of Health, Labour, and Welfare

MIC   Japanese Ministry of Internal Affairs and Communications

MOL   Ministry of Labour (replaced by MHLW in 2001)

NHK   Nihon Hōsō Kyōkai (Japan's public broadcasting organization)

TAW   Temporary Agency Work

1 Introduction

As in all modern societies, fundamental issues in Japan are normally first given explicit voice through the mass media. Indeed, it is often fictional drama of the soap-opera variety that has the freedom to venture into serious matters affecting many people in a population. I present as an opening entrée into the theoretical problem of this book, discussion of a very popular Japanese TV drama series, *Haken's Dignity* (*Haken no Hinkaku*). It was broadcast between January and March 2007 by NTV (Nihon Television), one of the major Japanese commercial television stations, in the wake of a Japanese government report on changing labour conditions published in October 2006. The Japanese term, *haken*, is an abbreviation for 'dispatched workers' (*haken shain*), referring to a specific category of non-regular workers who are involved in a triangular relationship with both employment agencies and client firms. While being typically employed and dispatched by employment agencies, *haken* workers are working at the facilities of and under the authority of client firms. Until the first enforcement of *Haken* Law in 1986, such labour leasing in the private sector was legally banned during post-war Japan.

The TV drama begins to unfold against a background of social changes in its first episode 'To work is to live … Super *haken* arrives'.

Location: Tokyo downtown
Narration: Winter, 2007.

The long-considered 'immortal' (*eikyū fumetsu*) life-time employment and the Japanese style of seniority promotion are on the verge of collapsing.

[1986: *Haken* Law passed (occupations/industries are limited)][1]
[1991~: Bursting of Bubble Economy]
[1997~1998: Major financial institutions bankrupt one after another]

The prolonged recession has pushed firms to slim down by fostering labour outsourcing.

[1999: *Haken* Law amended (most clerical jobs are free of restriction)]

As a result, non-regular workers, especially those called '*Haken* People' (*Haken Jinrui*), have increased exponentially.
The current population of *haken* is estimated at around 3 million.

[2000: University graduates' employment hit record low]
[2004: Amended *Haken* law took effect (jobs are expanded further in manufacturing industries)]

However
Haken workers are paid by the hour, with no bonus.
Transportation expenses are not paid.
Contracts are normally renewed every three months.
Their working environment is 'unstable' (*fuantei*) and 'harsh' (*kibishī*).

[2005: *Haken* market sales top 4 trillion Yen]

Treading such 'a thorny path' (*bara no michi*) are brave *haken* workers …

Prior to its legalisation, *haken* employment was largely associated with exploitative images and illegal labour supply practices. However, it has assumed considerable importance in the state's sweeping labour market reforms under a new slogan 'deregulation' (*kiseikanwa*) since the end of 1990s. The subsequent radical legal revisions have lifted many occupational and industrial restrictions, thus permitting the use of *haken* workers in most of the labour market. With its increasing business expansion, *haken*, as a newly developed non-regular employment, has received great attention. In particular, the dramatising effects of *Haken's Dignity* have made *haken* an emerging 'social phenomenon' (*shakai genshō*), being widely discussed and fiercely debated. The award-winning TV drama is composed of 10 episodes and its average viewing figure is over 20 per cent. The popularity has something to do with the starring of Ryōko Shinohara, a popular actress famous for excellent performance, and Kōtarō Koizumi, the former prime minister's son, as well as with the absorbing plot, witty puns and comic characters. Nevertheless, when it comes to wider social impact, much of the success of *Haken's Dignity* can be attributed to the first vivid representation, albeit in a sensational way, of *haken* life in the Japanese workplace – something, for many, widely known in everyday experience yet hardly defined in any compelling fashion.[2]

The heroine, Haruko, is featured as a 'super *haken*' who commands a very high hourly wage of 3,000 yen; the average level of *haken* workers was around 1,500 yen in 2006, according to a government report (MHLW 2007a). She has the most impressive assemblage of occupational certificates ranging from clerical and sales skills, midwife practice, the operation of heavy machinery, Russian language, to professional seafood preparation. Her talents are so sharply developed that client firms ask for her by name. In every episode, the long-established Japanese food-service firm where she is currently contracted to is rescued by her from crisis. Haruko is 'super' also in personality; she never cracks a smile or minces words and leaves the office on the dot. She desires no part of what the TV drama terms 'cumbersome human relations' (*wazurawashī ningen kankei*) and enjoys being a part-time flamenco dancer at night in a bar.[3] She is described as 'a nonconformist who saves the day' (*The Japan Times*, 4 Feb, 2007), a refreshingly radical figure in the Japanese workplace who acts out her strong personality flamboyantly whilst performing her professional duty superbly.

Yet, throughout her superheroic deeds, Haruko is in constant conflict with regular workers, known as Japanese salarymen/women, who are portrayed as lacking in both job competence and proper respect for *haken* workers. The tension between Haruko and regular workers is a key thread running through the entire TV drama series, which highlights the sharp division between regular and non-regular employment in Japan, an argument that has been simmering since the late 1990s. A Japanese economist, who was inspired by *Haken's Dignity* and published a book on *haken* workers, comments that the ironic contrast between super Haruko and unproductive regular workers gives the viewers 'a thrilling impression' (*tsūkai na inshō*) (Kadokura 2007: 4). An article in *Nikkei Business* (2 April, 2007) derides regular workers as the soulless, like 'dead skins' (*nukegara*) with no substance inside, who 'rest on their laurels' (*agura wo kaku*). At the same time, the growing reliance on *haken* and other non-regular labour on the part of Japanese firms has engendered considerable controversy; there have emerged divergent views on the changing relationship between workers and firms. Perhaps more striking is the fact that Haruko, as a super *haken* of extraordinary abilities, refracts the harsh reality of ordinary *haken* workers who are susceptible to employment insecurity, lower income and fewer benefits, compared to their regular counterparts. Along with those who promote and celebrate *haken* as a flexible and fashionable way of working, there are a chorus of voices worrying about Japan's *kakusa* or widening gaps between regular and non-regular workers, which could pose a threat to the coherence and integrity of Japanese society. As a consequence, whether *haken* should be evaluated positively or negatively is a highly contentious issue. It is from this discursive debate, triggered and intensified by media representation, that *haken* workers and what they stand for have emerged as an important symbol of contemporary Japanese society.

The changing discourse of Japanese personhood

In the TV drama, the depiction of *haken* workers accentuates their personal attributes and professional abilities, which figure more importantly than belonging to a corporate family – the key factor in the identity-making of the post-war Japanese salaried workers. This reflects a growing trend towards individuality and self-development in contemporary Japan, which is coupled with the declining importance of group-oriented corporate norms and conventions. The trend has pertinence to the understanding of Japanese personhood, which, from an anthropological perspective, is concerned with the shifting relationship between self and social roles, or '*moi*' and 'persona', according to Marcel Mauss's seminal work (1985).

To be sure, every person in everyday practice is composed of, or indeed capable of exercising, both autonomous self and socially imposed roles. As David Pocock (1971: 114) stresses, to understand humanity as social products is to 'effect the union of individual and society whose interaction is the object of study'. In contrast to this generic feature of personhood, what constitutes the ideal person as described in an ideology differs greatly from society to society and changes over time, depending on the varying construction of self and roles. We therefore should be sensitised to the danger of confusing ideology with real people in real situations. This is particularly true of the Japanese construction of person-hood, which values a complementary, rather than oppositional, relationship between self and roles, with precedence given to the fulfilling of a role without the negation of self. To be a respectable adult person, the Japanese from childhood have to learn '*kejime*' or 'differentiation', referring to the knowledge and ability needed to move fluidly between spontaneous/intimate self and disciplined/distant persona in various spheres of life (Tobin 1992; Bachnik 1992). As a result, the Japanese appear situational, if not 'chameleon-like' (Wolferen 1989), shifting in accordance with different contexts characterised by different rules of *kejime*. The changeability, multiplicity and inconsistency contrasts interestingly with the *conflation* of self and roles in such ideologies as 'individualism'[4] and 'socialism'. For example, while American society tends to romanticise self, emphasising the individualised perfor-mance of a role, Chinese society often extols the utopian ideal of performing a role so devotedly that self is essentially non-existent.[5] What becomes further clear from the comparison is that the ideological making of personhood in Japan has a much more pragmatic sense of the individual in society, but requires instead a strict obser-vance of *kejime*, a complex of values that prescribe how one should allocate self and roles separately and properly in different dimensions and stages of life.

Work, as a pivotal part of life, provides an important context in which to exam-ine the salient features of Japanese personhood. Given Japan's reputation as a corporate nation known as 'Japan inc.',[6] perhaps nowhere is the importance accorded to *kejime* more paramount than in the Japanese workplace. As mentioned earlier, the representation of *Haken's Dignity* signals the reinterpretation of *kejime*, with self being increasingly valued in fulfilling one's duty to work as 'a person of society' (*shakaijin*). The changing balance is in tune with a long-existing trend in post-growth Japan towards the emphasis on *kosei* or 'individuality', a Japanese term that distinguishes it from *kojinshugi* or 'individualism' (Hendry 1992). While individuality has been, in the words of Joy Hendry (2003: 58), 'sought in the pur-suit of personal interests and achievements, perfectly acceptable as long as they do not interfere with one's obligations to others', the Japanese translation for indi-vidualism is a derogatory term often used to refer to an immature, child-like person who, as Walter Edwards describes (1989: 126), 'is by definition *wagamama* – selfish, heedless of his interdependence with others, unwilling to recognise and accede to the constraints that social relations invariably entail'. Nevertheless, the western egoistical notion of solid self devoid of social ties, together with its 'inevitable companion of capitalism' (Moeran 1984: 263), has smuggled new meanings into the Japanese perception of self. For example, the notion of 'freedom' *(jiyū)* influ-enced by individualism has become something which people enjoy through the emancipation of their personal desires – instead of something to be pursued as a normative goal – in the post-industrial era when consumption-oriented mass cul-ture has replaced protestant asceticism (Ishida 1986: 12).

Recent years have seen growing attention to the importance of individuality in the Japanese business world, epitomised by the promotion of such fashionable concepts as 'creativity' (*sōzōsei*), 'innovation' (*kakushin*), 'diversity' (*tayōsei*) and 'uniqueness' (*dokutokusei*). Under the state's deregulation policies which emphasise the flexibilisation of work and the diversification of labour, *haken* and other non-regular workers have acquired fresh features, being portrayed as a new generation of self-activating individuals emerging from Japan's shifting national and international conditions. In many ways, *Haken's Dignity* successfully captures this transformation by questioning the conventional Japanese employment system as well as the hitherto taken-for-granted corporate values where personal needs and ambitions should be subjugated to group goals. The gap between the TV drama and the reality notwithstanding, there are signs of changes along these lines in the formalisation of political rhetoric brought about by the *haken* phenomenon.

The analysis of political rhetoric has a long chequered history in anthropology. More than half a century ago, Edmund Leach, in his classic account of Kachin in Burma (1954), pointed to the importance of studying symbolic statements and actions in terms of socio-political relations. However, the primary focus of interest had diverged, with some anthropologists concentrating on the interpretation of symbols and others power relations and struggles between individuals and groups.[7] Sherry Ortner (1984), for example, identifies the two major trends, contrasting the Geertzian enthusiasm for the 'cultural meanings' of symbols with Turnerian pragmatic view of symbols as 'active force' (see Geertz 1973; Turner 1967, 1969). It is now evident that these two variables are inseparable, constituting a collective concern in the area of semantic/linguistic anthropology or discourse analysis (Bourdieu 1991; Parkin 1978, 1982, 1984). Influenced by Michel Foucault's pioneering works, anthropologists have now proposed the term 'discourse', with its implicit connotations of power and possible contestation, as an alternative to traditional anthropological notions of culture (Lindstorm 2002: 162). The purpose is to accentuate the importance to grasp the heterogeneous and dynamic character of language use and the key role it plays in the social construction of reality, what Richard Bauman and Charles Briggs (1990) describe as the critical linkage between 'poetics' and 'performance'. Thus, while reflecting culture-specific meanings or values ascribed to various forms of linguistic symbols, all discourse 'embodies hegemonic aspects, in the combined sense of *shaping* and *dominating* other's wills' (Parkin 1984: 360, my italics).

The concern with discourse analysis for exploring societal change has only recently entered the anthropological study of Japan. Brian Moeran (1984) shows how the 'good' side of 'individualism' is adopted and adapted into Japanese context, being used to challenge the meaning of 'selflessness' in certain popular words. In his discussion of western concepts of 'freedom' and 'rights', Takeshi Ishida (1986) explains how some aspects of those foreign concepts were interpreted differently at different times by political activists and distinguished intellectuals in Japan, thus leading to internal political tensions as well as changes in popular attitudes. The contributors to Hiroshi Mannari and Harumi Befu's volume on *The Challenge of Japanese Internationalization* (1983) examine how '*kokusaika*', a new political rhetoric for the 'internationalisation' of Japan emerging from the later 1970s, was invoked as a means of reinforcing the earlier ideas of nationalism embodied in the old slogan of 'modernisation' (*kindaika*). At the same time, however, the newly formalised language of internationalisation also prompts 'a faction which defines the idea in a more idealistic global sense', as Roger Goodman (1990: 222–224) points out in his account of *kikokushijyo*, a small group of returnee children who were problematised and became an important symbol in the internationalisation debate. In 'symbolic competition' with mainstream society, the perceived positive values of such children arising from the debate bore importantly on the changing idea of education, work, youth and gender (ibid.: 226–231). The discursive power of symbols is perhaps most subtly felt in the modern construction of sexuality and procreation. Beverly Yamamoto (1999), Sabine Frühstück (2003) and Hiroko Takeda (2005) show how the policy-making elite draw on, for example, the powerful notion of 'science' to normalise sex, gender and sexuality aimed at improving both the quality and the quantity of the Japanese 'race'.

If 'ideological discourse in action' (Parkin 1984: 361) provides an analytical window onto the transformation of society, then personhood is one of the key areas in which to investigate such dynamics. What it means to be the ideal Japanese person has been a prominent theme in the anthropology of Japan, probably because the relationship between self and roles serves as a fundamental criterion by which 'western' or 'capitalist' societies might be distinguished from all the others, 'non-western' or 'pre-capitalist'. The early description of Japanese personhood in English can be found in Ruth Benedict's classic of *The Chrysanthemum and the Sword* (1946: 184, my italics below):

> Educated Japanese are thoroughly aware that English and Americans see immorality and obscenity where they do not, but they are not as conscious of the chasm between our conventional attitudes and their tenet that *'human feelings'* should not intrude upon *serious affairs of life*. It is, however, a major source of our difficulty in understanding Japanese attitudes about love and erotic pleasure. They fence off one province which belongs to the wife from another which belongs to erotic pleasure. Both provinces arc cqually opcn and aboveboard. The two are not divided from each other as in American life by the fact that one is what a man admits to the public and the other is surreptitious. They are separate because one is in the circle of a man's *major obligations* and the other in the circle of *minor relaxation*. This way of mapping out 'proper place' to each area makes the two as separate for the ideal father of a family as it does for the man about town.

The above reference to 'human feelings'/'minor relaxation' in contradistinction with 'serious affairs of life'/'major obligation' illustrates the specific relationship between self and roles in the Japanese man's pursuits of sexual pleasure and family life. The relationship is variously expressed in paired indigenous terms, such as *honne* and *tatemae* (real intention and professed intention), *ninjyo* and *giri* (human feelings and obligation) and *uchi* and *soto* (inside and outside).[8] In her comparative analysis of teenager sexuality in Japan and the United States, Merry White (1993: 179, 189) adds a contemporary flavour:

> Remember that in Japan the basic dilemma in teenage sexuality is between physical and social, rather than physical and moral, dimensions of sex. … like all *tatemae-honne* contrasts, these are both viable if they are kept in balance, in parallel, and in their place … it is not sexual activity per se that is the problem; public rampant display of sexuality is a problem.

The fact that Japanese personhood is not based on a *core* of ideological values emphasising either self – 'individualism' – or roles – 'socialism' – has stimulated a wide range of research interests. The 'relational' and 'multifaceted' person shifting between the self and the social in various dimensions of life receives detailed exposition in a collection edited by Nancy Rosenberger (1992). In addressing this layered changeability of Japanese personhood, Fiona Graham makes the following interesting observations (2003: 235–236):

> Any two people will, at some level, be members of the same group, and, at lower levels, members of different groups. Inasmuch as they share a group, they may discuss it in terms of what the members of the group actually believe about it, or their personal meaning (*honne*); inasmuch as they are members of different groups, they may present the ideal picture of their own group (*tatemae*). Two people from different nations share only the most general groups (for example, the group of humanity); two people from the same family share very small groups (from the group of humanity, through the group of that nation, down to the group of people from the same town and from the same family) … the more groups two people share, the more they are likely to share *honne* and the lower the line between *honne* and *tatemae* will be.

Accordingly, the same individual may draw the line of *kejime* at different points when talking to different people, or even at different times when talking to the same person. In her view, the variability of *kejime* indicates the difference in the level of group with which the individual associates himself or herself.

Such features show a marked contrast to the so-called 'western assumptions' that presuppose the opposition between the self and the social. The contrast is explicated powerfully in Dorinne Kondo's *Crafting Selves* (1990), a vivid account of everyday life in a small family-owned Japanese factory. It is worth noting that, although Marcel Mauss's personhood theory is not a central subject for Kondo, her work moves beyond the *emic* or culturally specific explanations that tend to reinforce the ideological imposition of Japanese personhood. What emerges from her nuanced analysis is multiple and gendered individuals, whose narratives and realities often contradict stereotypes about the Japanese way of work and life. Another volume edited by Jane Bachnik and Charles Quinn (1994), again, focuses on the 'situated', 'contextual' or 'indexical' meaning of Japanese personhood, yet it also takes into consideration the strategy of individuals in manipulating culturally internalised rules. The active role of individual agency has particular significance in Dolores P. Martinez's (2004) ethnographic depiction of the people in a Japanese diving village where diverse experiences of personhood and nationality in concrete situations call into question the 'totalising' ideological construction.

From static, structure-focused analysis to dynamic, actor-centred perspectives, and from arguing against western assumptions to deconstructing ideological discourse, the above studies contribute cumulatively to the anthropological understanding of Japanese personhood. By no accident is this development mirrored in the history of anthropology; the discipline itself spent a difficult time wrestling with the perennial problem of how individual and society are interconnected in mutual regulation. It is obvious that Geertz's interpretative approach has a strong influence on many of the existing works concerning Japanese personhood. The actor-centred, liberating view of culture as a web of negotiated meanings brings a new focus on symbols and thus stimulates new lines of thought on the dynamic nature of society. Yet, as many have pointed out, it lacks a systematic or sociological analysis of actors or practice from a political angle (Ortner 1984). That is, there are invariably inequalities in means and ability to define, impose, maintain and transform the meaning of symbols. Thus, to counteract Geerz's intimation of 'universal' intepretivism, it is important to revisit the asymmetrical power relations inherent in discourse.

Amid increasingly intensified global–local interactions, there has been an accelerated interest in social change. If, as David Pocock (1971: 112) suggests, we must devise a language which enables us to best conceive the constant interplay between individual and society, that is, society in transition, then 'society as discourse', following David Parkin's (1984) proposal, might prove to be most relevant to the study of a given society at a specific point of time. At the core of this approach is the view of political discourse – often referred to by several interchangeable terms including ideology, state policy and other variants of powerful public rhetoric – as a process of production and consumption. On the one hand, the role of political discourse in controlling and shaping thought and behaviour merits close investigation. Much has been made of the 'mystifying' effects of ideology with reference to the Marxist formula of base and superstructure. Ideology, as Maurice Bloch (1977) would argue, is (mis)represented 'reality' aimed at legitimising and obscuring power inequity, as distinct from how things 'really are' in everyday life. Such a viewpoint, as Talal Asad (1987: 605) criticises, postulates a simplistic relationship between 'deceiver and deceived'. A more complex phenomenon is that ideology, as revealed by *The Invention of Tradition* (Hobsbawm and Ranger 1983), is not constructed out of nothing, but rather entails *shared* historical values. On the other hand, however, the fact that symbols are malleable for interpretation is bound to create multiplicity, contradiction and complexity at both macro and micro levels, thereby constantly forming and deforming the hegemony of ideology. We may then ask: to what extent is the dominant discourse 'totalising'?; what are the complications involved in the implementation of that discourse?; how is the imposed discourse actually consumed by real people in real situations? and what are the factors that are important in distinguishing some individuals from others when it comes to perceptions and decisions in everyday life?

It is from this discursive approach that I set out to examine *haken*, an emerging non-regular labour force. Despite the fact that non-regular workers have a long history, *haken* employment embodies novel features and connotations pertaining to shifting economic, political and socio-cultural conditions in contemporary Japan. It is a key concept that has triggered off what David Parkin (1978) describes as 'internal cultural debate'. Such debate takes the form of a processual discourse among different interest groups and powerful actors on a variety of values ranging from social divide to the meaning of work and personhood. Together, those factors have implications for the changing relationship of labour to the state, to firms, to entrepreneurial opportunities and to the wider world. They indicate the deconstruction of the post-war Japanese employment system sustained by the 'firm-as-family' ideology, as well as ushering in fresh ideas about a new Japan where hitherto unsuccessful or spurned individuals may increasingly come to take centre stage. All those issues are to be discussed with reference to participatory experience of a year-long fieldwork in Japan where I worked as a *haken* employee myself, to which I now turn.

Encounter with *haken*: fieldwork experience

It is quite common that an 'immersed' fieldworker often stumbles across something more fascinating than what he or she is supposed to focus on. My encounter with *haken* was a serendipitous discovery. As already a fluent Japanese speaker, I embarked on my fieldwork in Tokyo in November 2006 with the aim of studying the changing images and practices of the dominant masculinity model, that is, the Japanese salaryman. In my search for fieldsite(s), an old Japanese friend recommended that I work as a *haken* instead of being introduced into a firm as a 'suspicious' researcher. I was told that although *haken* workers were different from regular workers I could work full-time just like a normal white-collar office worker – which would be a perfectly natural entrée into the Japanese society. Weighing up the benefits of standing on my own feet against the disadvantages of the dubious or forced entry aided by some powerful Japanese figure, I decided to become an ordinary *haken* worker myself, thinking that my Chinese nationality might at first give me a bumpy ride before being able to ensconce myself in such an employment position. After all, in many cases, 'for the ethnographer, adaptability to the circumstances is essential' (Gellner and Hirsch 2001: 5).

In fact, the new twist to my original plan had made the following year-long stay in Japan grippingly eventful, leading to a vast array of raw, thought-provoking material. Whether it is directly related to my central interest or not, every single detail of fieldwork is all grist to the mill of understanding a specific context in which any research project is embedded. To be sure, 'detail is often the clue to implicit worlds', which enables the fieldworker to address the obvious and think explicitly (Dresch and James 2000: 10). From the beginning of job-searching to actually working as a *haken* inside a Japanese firm, I staunchly followed those myriad minute details arising from everyday life, constantly being fascinated, enlightened or annoyed by them. As an ordinary *haken* worker, I was able to engage with Japanese people closely, listening to, observing and empathising with them in a systematic and cumulative manner. As E. E. Evans-Pritchard wrote a long time ago (1951: 78–79):

> … the anthropologist will not produce a good account of the people he is studying unless he can put himself in a position which enables him to establish ties of intimacy with them, and to observe their daily activities from within, and not from without, their community life. … He then not only sees and hears what goes on in the normal everyday life of the people as well as less common events, such as ceremonies and legal cases, but by taking part in those activities in which he can appropriately engage, he learns through action as well as by ear and eye what goes on around him …
>
> What is perhaps even more important for his work is the fact that he is all alone, cut off from the companionship of his own race and culture, and is dependent on the natives around him for company, friendship and human understanding. An anthropologist has failed unless, when he says goodbye to the natives, there is on both sides the sorrow of parting. It is evident that he can only establish this intimacy if he makes himself in some degree a member of their society and lives, thinks, and feels in their culture…

This 'intimacy' derived from physical proximity and dependency was indeed crucial to my evolving understanding of *haken*. By throwing myself into the *haken* world over a continuous period of time, I had great opportunities of interacting with a number of *haken* agencies, client firms, fellow *haken* and regular workers. As regards fieldsites, overall I had work contracts with two client firms, which were mediated by two different *haken* agencies. Most *haken* workers are registered with more than one agency in order to find suitable jobs as soon as possible. In my case, I attended registration sessions with six different agencies in total. My first *haken* job was concerned with an India–Japan joint IT project which required me to work inside the building of a big Japanese finance firm, which I shall call 'Miracle'. This was followed by a second one in a long-established Japanese manufacturing conglomerate, which I shall call 'Vision'. I worked at Miracle for less than two months and Vision for five months. Both are large and famous firms in Japan; Vision especially has earned a reputation for its products across the world. They fit coincidently into two characteristic categories, that is, long-established traditional manufacturing firms and emerging knowledge-intensive or service-focused enterprises. The white-collar office *haken* workers I met in the two firms were dominated by females and they differed considerably in occupational abilities as well as personality traits. Almost every *haken* at Miracle had what the current labour market considers as highly in demand job skills such as English and IT competency, whereas the majority at Vision were responsible for relatively unskilled clerical or secretarial work – the so-called *jimukei* which constitutes a staple part of the *haken* industry. The two groups of *haken* individuals, therefore, exhibited quite contrasting features in terms of pay and attitudes towards work.

It is important to point out here that *haken* workers are employed by almost all kinds of firms in Japan; small or mid-size firms or factories are said to be more likely to rely on flexible, low-cost non-regular labour than big firms. Moreover, with its rapid industrial growth and expansion in recent years, *haken* has become a wide-ranging employment prevalent among both white-collar and blue-collar workers including manufacturing assembly line workers. It is therefore reasonable to infer that many may have quite different perceptions and experiences from the white-collar *haken* workers at Miracle and Vision, with whom this study is mainly concerned. However, insofar as I am interested in the *process* – that is, the production and consumption – of political discourse, I consider my interactions with fellow *haken* workers play an important role in understanding how real people consume imposed policies and popular discourses in real situations, especially those 'muted groups' who are directly affected but not given the political space to articulate their feelings (Goodman 2002: 12). This actor-centred, micro-level perspective thus makes it possible to draw heuristic comparisons between explosive forces of ideological discourse and more mundane forms of everyday life.

For the same reason, I will focus mainly on the narratives and realties of *haken* and regular workers behind official policies and rhetoric, rather than dwelling on the details of organisational life at Vision and Miracle. There is an enormous literature on the Japanese company and its salarymen/women. Early ethnographic writings began with Vogel (1963), Nakane (1970), Dore (1973), Rohlen (1974), Clark (1979) and others. The interest has been kept alive over the past two decades by a number of authors including Kondo (1990), Hamabata (1990), Lo (1990), Allison (1994), Ogasawa (1998), Matsunaga (2000) and Graham (2003, 2004). An overview of the existing literature reveals not only what it is like to work at a Japanese company but also how the Japanese company, as well as the view of it on the part of scholars, has changed over time. An informative summation of such transition can be found in the introduction of Louella Matsunaga's account (2000).

Despite the fact that doing fieldwork has become a shared practice among many disciplines in social science, there is an enduring ethical issue that makes cross-cultural ethnographic research controversial. Nowadays, the 'arrival story' of an ethnographer in a host society has become an increasingly ritualistic process in the construction of anthropological monographs in the Anglo-Saxon anthropological community (Goodman 2006: 29). The implication is that fieldwork essentially involves unequal relationship and that the individual researcher is an indispensable part of his or her research project – a message sent perhaps too strongly by the discussion among anthropologists in the 1980s of the poetics and politics of representation often referred to as the post-modern reflexive, interlocutory or autobiographic turn (Clifford and Marcus 1986; Okely and Callaway 1992). While the exposure of one's personal traits is necessary, it should not be taken to such extremes that the central concern of anthropology seems to be how to make ethnographic accounts 'subjectively objective' to the eyes of the reader, that is, the striving for an element of objectivity by bringing sufficient subjective material about the researcher and the way in which he or she affected the studied people (Goodman 2006: 22–23). A balance needs to be struck between, to use David Pocock (1971, 1994)'s terms, 'a personal anthropology' and 'the formal anthropology'. Like the Japanese concept of *kejime* which makes self and roles complementary and in their proper place, it might be important to cogitate upon where the same sort of line should be drawn so that the consideration of indi-vidual traits does not deflect attention away from what fieldwork-based research can contribute to the discipline of anthropology as a knowledge-building enter-prise, rather than the exhaustive, 'scientific' understanding of humanity.

The fact that I am a Chinese national may have something that interests the reader since the anthropological study of Japan is largely concentrated in the circles of American, European and indigenous scholars. There are an increasing number of Japanese academics who study China, yet the trend certainly has not provoked much interest in Japanese studies among their Chinese counterparts who tend to address issues arising from their own country. In retrospect, I realise how being Chinese brought about my focus on personhood throughout my anthropological research on Japan and how this very fact inevitably bore on the way in which I interacted with Japanese people.

My learning about Japan began at a university in Shanghai where I studied Japanese language. Upon graduation I embarked on my first job in a Japan–China joint firm in Shanghai. I initially worked as an interpreter to the Japanese president of the firm and my responsibility involved daily cross-cultural communication and interpretation in executive meetings. I was later responsible for marketing strate-gies and client relationship management. Both roles entailed a huge amount of time working with a group of Japanese managers and employees from different kinds of firms such as 'manufacturers' (*mēkā*) and 'trading firms' (*shōsha*) – apparently, there was an underlying divide between the two; conflicts frequently arose as to how business should be done in the Japanese way. I was often impressed by their hard work and dogged perseverance. Yet, this impression was also dented by their bewildering after-work socialisation, which exhibited a sharp contrast with the decent-looking, neatly-dressed and gentlemanly behaved businessmen whom I knew at the office. It was a period when feelings of sympathy or disgust overrode empathy. Nevertheless, it is well worth reflecting on this previous experience, especially in comparison with the recently conducted fieldwork. Prior to my post-graduate studies at the University of Oxford, I had studied and lived in Japan for more than four years during which I took up several part-time jobs of interpretation and consultation regarding Japan–China joint business ventures. Perhaps due to this background, I landed in Japan for my first fieldwork with no unexpected events and had few barriers thereafter to gaining access to fieldsites. I also man-aged to integrate into various informally organised groups among both *haken* and regular workers such as 'drinking friends' (*nomi nakama*) who bonded regularly through after-work drinking sessions and 'Saturday-or-Sunday lunch gathering' (*donichi ranchi kai*) which was especially popular with my female informants.

The lack of a dramatic landing story, however, does not mean I was well prepared for the ethnographic research. From the first day when I set foot in a familiar place, I was constantly confronted by an unfamiliar feeling that all my interactions with Japanese people seemed to be mission-centred and driven by ulterior motives. For the sake of intellectual capital, a fieldworker would be proportionally rewarded by being a 'nosy parker' with 'prying' eyes and an 'inquisitive' mind. That is easier said than done; writing may be allowed relatively free flow and play, doing fieldwork is apparently always likely to be hedged about by rule-governed expectations which affect individual researchers in various different ways. In my case, I sometimes did not really know whether I was genuinely taking delight in sharing lives with my informants or exchanging their kindness and trust for my intellectual gains, as the boundaries in my conscience often became too entangled to be clearly drawn. One might feel a deep sense of release if the informants were *thoroughly* informed as to how and what *exactly* they are studied as subjects. Yet, in real fieldwork situations, I found that 'candour' or 'integrity' was either superficial, impractical or posing a serious impediment to any substantial research – albeit one should, I would agree, strive to 'come clean' as much as possible.

The ethical issue regarding the relationship between the researcher and the studied people is an unsettling one; how to deal with it may to a great degree depend on the discretion of the researcher. One of my personal therapeutic practices was gift-giving or treats of meals or drinks in gratitude for my informants' sharing, giving and more often than not, friendship – yes, one had better have a good budget for fieldwork! This sort of exchange and reciprocity is widely acceptable and pragmatically viable in Japan. Despite those small efforts in one way or another, ethical struggles continued throughout my fieldwork. I, therefore, feel compelled to put them down because they made up an unavoidable, if not significant, part of my research project. This what John Van Maanen (1988) describes as 'confessional tale' is subject to the judgement of readers in the hope of contributing to the open-ended debate on fieldwork ethics.

Clearly, there has always been an element of 'me', whose Chinese-born and other acquired personal traits must have some effect upon my relationship with the studied Japanese people, thus affecting the way in which Japan is approached in this study. Nevertheless, this 'soft subjectivity', which tends to blur the fieldwork account, does not necessarily present researchers with 'intractable dilemmas facing their craft' (Van Maanen 1988: 91, 96). As I stressed earlier, this self-revelation act should be treated as a personal flavour only being added in a proper dose to, rather than deflecting attention away from, what anthropological methodology and theories can contribute to the understanding of *haken* in what I am to recount.

The direction and the structure of the book

When I was conducting fieldwork in Tokyo, many of my informants talked a great deal about TV programmes. During the time when *Haken's Dignity* was on air, I was virtually forced to watch it so as to play a part in their conversation.

Television, as Marie Gillespie (1995: 56) argues, 'forms a nexus between language and the social world' and acts as 'a form of social lubrication, easing social interaction and sustaining it in countless everyday circumstances'. Indeed, it stimulates the art of conversation and creates chat-up lines that help overcome social inhibition and reserve – like the weather as a facilitator of social interaction among the English (see Fox 2004). More importantly, such media talk can often provide a revealing insight into how public representation impinges on and is interacted in private forms of social life.

My interest in *haken* has been driven by a research puzzle: why has *haken* become such a powerful representative symbol of the non-regular labour force as a whole, given its relatively small proportion especially compared with part-timers, by far the largest and most long-standing non-regular group in Japan? While political debates in the mass media play a significant role in bringing *haken* to prominence, the emergence of *haken* is also intertwined with other factors such as, historical controversy, legislative development and institutional structure. It is, therefore, 'a total social phenomenon' – to use Marcel Mauss's term (1967) – which entails explanations emanating from a nexus of political, economic and socio-cultural elements, macro and micro concerns and global and local forces. This holistic framework is fundamental to my approach to the *haken* project.

The next three chapters are designed to understand *haken* as both a cultural phenomenon and a historical construct. Chapter 2 provides an overview of *haken* in contemporary context as a distinct category of non-regular workers and a fast-growing industry. *Haken* is characteristic of a triangular employment structure where workers carry out their job assignments at the facilities of and under the authority of the client firm while being typically employed and dispatched by the *haken* agency. This newly legalised institution, combined with other related social factors, distinguishes *haken* from other varied non-regular arrangements. To get a practical sense of how the tripartite system works in concrete situations, Chapter 3 turns to an ethnographic account based on my own experience of working as a *haken* in Tokyo in 2007. This is followed by Chapter 4, which sets out a broader, historical context in which to examine the role of state policy in transforming *haken* from an exploitative and illegal form of labour supply with a fairly unsavoury past to a useful and fashionable way of non-regular working. Such a radical metamorphosis has much to do with the shifting national and international environment in Japan. To account for the effects of globalising processes, Chapter 4 also consists of a general study of temporary agency work in global terms, with particular reference to the ideology of neoliberalism which has a strong influence upon the flexibilisation of work across many parts of the world.

As a newly developed and fast-growing category of non-regular employment, *haken* has attracted a great deal of public attention in contemporary Japan. The aim of Chapter 5 is to investigate how *haken* has become involved in a 'gap-widening boom' (*kakusa būmu*) where a surge of interest in Japan's widening gaps has divided the country into two contrasting groups: regular workers (*seiki shain*) and non-regular workers (*hiseiki shain*). The importance of the Japanese mass media cannot be overemphasised here; they not only galvanise the public into political sympathy or repulsion by discovering, measuring, and embellishing hitherto unnoticed social problems, but also act collectively as a multi-voiced discursive space for diverse, often contradictory, opinions. Drawing extensively on a variety of materials presented in TV channels, magazines, newspapers and Internet forums, this chapter focuses on a number of *haken*-related phenomena including 'working poor' (*wākingu pua*), illegal labour dispatch and various perceived *kakusa* or differences between *haken* and regular workers.

It may be superfluous to claim that life as lived is full of equivocations, discontinuities and contradictions. Yet, the complexity of everyday life would not have been conveyed to the same degree had the examination of *haken* been limited to macro-level analyses. In contrast to the glut of official discourses that purport to confer an objective point of view of social reality, the voices of those targeted are often silenced, ignored or reduced to simplistic assumptions. To flesh out the impersonalised skeleton of much-represented *haken*, Chapter 6 provides an intimate look at individual *haken* workers, examining the different ways in which they consume *haken* employment in more mundane situations of life. By delving into the minute details of ethnographic examples, the chapter also attempts to address the Japanese perpetual search for meaningful work, which is concerned with the reconstruction of *kejime*, that is, the changing balance between self and roles, as evidenced by a trend characterised by the increasing emphasis on self-development and individuality and the declining importance of corporate belongingness and group-oriented values.

In the light of the above discussion based on multiple sources of data including *haken*'s triangular employment system in both the present and the past, media representation and individual experiences of *haken* work in everyday life, Chapter 7 takes as its central subject the *haken* debate. The content analysis of the debate shows how *haken*'s 'symbolic values' are brought to the public's attention by a number of powerful groups and actors with different political agendas. Significantly, there are forces of both change and continuity, which focus on either the promotion or the denigration of *haken* employment. The corollary is that *haken* is invested with a blend of positive and negative values portrayed as benefiting or besetting the Japanese way of life, which in turn bear importantly on the shifting ideology, as well as ordinary people's perceptions and practices about their work, life and identity. Such dynamics have implications for the theoretical saliency of political discourse and personhood in anthropology, providing significant clues to the understanding of an ever-changing Japan resulting from ongoing interaction between individual and society.

It is my aim that this book will be read as a general ethnography of *haken* workers by those who are interested in the changes taking place in Japan today. More broadly, because of the light it cases on the ways in which the relationship between individual and society is being constructed and reconstructed, the book will also be of interest to anyone who is concerned with recent developments in post-industrial economies in the context of the wider global discourse of neoliberalism. Finally, there are two specific issues I would like to clarify with regard to my holistic approach to *haken* workers. Firstly, empirical material is used separately, rather than being grouped together, in Chapter 3, which focuses on the triangular *haken* employment system, and Chapter 6, which depicts individual *haken* workers' diverse experiences. The purpose is to provide the reader with a better understanding of the *haken* way of work in Japan, which has become very complex in recent years. Secondly, although the holistic framework may invariably make it difficult to have a single theoretical thread running logically throughout the book, as I mentioned earlier, two major themes, political discourse and personhood, are central to my argument and emphasised repeatedly in some of the chapters. The conclusion chapter summarises the key ideas with a view to showing the theoretical significance of the emerging of *haken*, a non-regular labour force in Japan.

2 *Haken*

A new non-regular labour force and a booming industry

Introduction

The word *haken* made its first appearance in official discourse when labour leasing in the private sector – or temporary agency work in global terms – was discussed around the early 1980s. Since the legislation of *haken* was enforced in 1986, the term had gradually been recognised but hadn't reached a position of prominence in the public arena until the broadcast of a TV drama series between January and March 2007 called *Haken's Dignity*. The highly acclaimed drama with an average viewing figure of over 20 per cent has made *haken* one of the most popular buzzwords in recent years.

In Japanese, *haken* literally means 'dispatch'. It is commonly used as an abbreviation to describe 'dispatched employees', 'dispatch firms' or 'dispatch employment'. As those verbal compounds indicate, the concept of *haken* refers to a type of non-regular workers, a group of intermediary employment agencies who dispatch workers to client firms, and a triangular system which entails a relationship among the three parties. To understand these different dimensions of meaning, a general background is necessary. The aim of this chapter is to set up a relevant context in which to examine *haken* as a distinct category of non-regular workers and as a booming personnel business in contemporary Japan. How the tripartite employment system actually works in everyday practice will be discussed in the next chapter by drawing on my fieldwork experience of working as a *haken* in Tokyo from November 2006 to September 2007.

Haken: a new breed of non-regular workers[1]

Just as the word 'dispatch' denotes 'transmitting', *haken* workers are on the move. They are a specific type of non-regular workers who are institutionally designed to be mobile and flexible. In his study of Japanese day labourers, Tom Gill (2003: 144–145) argues that mobility in Japan is an escapist fantasy, as portrayed in the romanticised movie series of Tora-san, a loveable vagabond who wanders freely around the country, ageing through the decades but always unmarried. Few perhaps would disagree that the Japanese salaryman model 'has undoubtedly dominated images of Japan out of all proportion to his role in real-life society', yet 'imposed immobility and involuntary mobility are facts of life for most men in regular employment, whatever the colour of their collar' (ibid.: 145). While the permanent is still much valued over the temporary, the meanings attached to the salaryman figure in steady employment have transformed from everyday and desired to mundane and derided. Indeed, even the word 'salaryman' (*sararīman*) itself has assumed derogatory connotations among young people in Japan today. The alluring freedom from the shackles of mainstream life is a fashionable topic in Japanese popular culture, as well attested to by the enduring popularity of Tora-san movie series. Nonetheless, for non-fictional Japanese people, the detachment from a web of family/work connections often comes at a high price. As Tom Gill (2003: 157) observes, there were a number of serious problems faced by male-dominated day labourers who not only suffered from 'the darkness of the choice' but were also susceptible to 'social opprobrium and/or personal feelings of guilt' because of their rejection of or failure to achieve expected masculine roles in the Japanese household and workplace.

If day labourers and life-time salarymen represent two extremes of a mobility-stasis spectrum, then *haken* workers stand in the middle of the spectrum since their protean character common to all casual workers is circumscribed by a legally stipulated tripartite employment contract under which they are both protected and restricted to a certain extent. Unlike day labourers, the majority of *haken* workers do not work by the day[2]; nor can they completely dissociate themselves from organisational obligations and duties. While being typically employed and dispatched by staffing or employment agencies, *haken* are working at the facilities of and under the authority of client firms. Like many other non-regular workers, they do not normally have a stable and long-term corporate membership and are generally considered as being deprived of a number of corporate entitlements ranging from bonus payments to holiday allowances.[3] But when they are working on a job assignment, *haken* workers are involved in a more prescriptive employment relationship, being affiliated with two employers of different kind for the contract length of the assignment. The *haken* agency, or the middle man, acts as the primary employer who negotiates with the client employer on *haken* workers' behalf over a wide range of issues including pay rises, complaints about working conditions and contract renewal or termination. Perhaps more significantly, the agency is held accountable by *Haken* Law for workers' enrolment in national social security schemes. This highly institutionalised structure is a key element that distinguishes *haken* from other non-regular workers, especially part-timers who are by far the largest group (Table 2.1).

There are other related social factors which make *haken* workers stand out from the existing casual labour in Japan. First of all, people who engage in *haken* employment are neither conceived as remiss, indolent or self-absorbed, nor do they pose any threat to the nation's strong work ethic. On the contrary, political and commercial discourses often portray *haken* as a useful and fashionable way of working where individuals can develop their own career paths and lifestyles. Even among those who disapprove of *haken* employment, *haken* workers are

Table 2.1 Types of non-regular employment in Japan[a]

Part-time (*pāto)*	*Pāto* workers have scheduled working hours, usually 30 or more hours a week, which are designed to be less than those of regular workers in the same workplace. The number of *pāto* has increased considerably since the 1970s in many sectors of the economy, especially in wholesale and retail (Matsunaga 2000: 19). Many *pāto* workers are married or older women and the so-called 'veterans', who show considerable involvement in and long-term commitment to the company (ibid.: 139).
Part-time (*arubaito*)	The Japanese term *arubaito* is derived from the German *arbeit*. Compared with *pāto*, *arubaito* shows a much more even gender split and accounts for a much lower percentage of the workforce (Matsunaga 2000: 22). This category is particularly popular with students who often work less scheduled and shorter hours and are 'a floating element of the workforce' (ibid.).
Contract (*keiyaku*)	Contract workers commonly have special skills and work on fixed-term contracts which are made directly with employers.
Entrusted (*shokutaku*)	Entrusted workers are similar to contract workers, but the term *shokutaku* is often used to refer to those who are rehired after mandatory retirement.
Others	There are other temporary workers traditionally known as 'seasonal workers' (*kisetsukō*), 'emergency workers' (*rinjikō*) and 'day labourers' (*hiyatoi rōdōsha*) who are hired for a specifically limited duration. Official statistics sometimes make a distinction between those working on a contract between 1 month and 1 year and those working on a daily basis.
Haken	*Haken* workers are employed and dispatched by *haken* agencies to work at the facilities of client firms. They are remunerated by *haken* agencies but receive day-to-day job supervision from client firms.

Note: [a]Non-regular employment in Japan takes a bewildering variety of forms, which are not defined consistently and cannot always be distinguishable in practice. For instance, *pāto* and *arubaito* can be used casually in everyday conversation to refer to all kinds of temporary jobs.

perceived as the victims of Japan's economic downturn, changing corporate hiring practices, or money-grubbing *haken* agencies. In other words, the controversy doesn't contain direct charges levelled against *haken* workers themselves; many of them belong to Japan's younger generation who are described as being either enticed or forced into the *haken* way of work.

Such compassionate views make an interesting contrast with public denunciation of the 'problematic' young people such as *'freeters'* (*furītā*) who hop from one temporary job to another and 'NEETs' (*nīto*) who are Not in Employment, Education or Training. The term *freeter* is a combination of the English 'free' and the German *'arbeiter'* created in the late 1980s by Recruit, a well-known

Japanese information service provider, in order to capture the phenomenon of young people postponing their entry into the regular labour market and instead engaging in temporary jobs after leaving school (Smith 2006; Hook and Takeda 2007). NEET is originally coined by the Social Exclusion Unit of the British cabinet in 1999 and it is used in particular for 16- to 18-year olds in the British context (Lunsing 2007). In Japan, both NEETs and *freeters* are applied to a much broader age bracket usually from 15- to 34-year olds and they share in common the condition that neither has regular employment. While NEETs fall into the category of 'a dormant or non-functioning labour force' (*hirōdōryoku*) in official terms, *freeters* refer to those who switch casually between part-time jobs – students and professional housewives are not included in government statistics. The labels as such carry with them the premise that those who become NEETs or *freeters* are a cohort of ne'er-do-wells, contributing to the creation of problems and illnesses afflicting the Japanese society. As Wim Lunsing (2007) points out, an overly hasty publication of academic books has subsequently emerged in an attempt to investigate and remedy young people's 'maladies' without, however, engaging closely with those concerned; in so doing, those volumes play an important role in justifying and reinforcing what regulatory authorities supposedly want the younger generation to do.[4]

Despite the apparent difference in official classification, *freeters* are not so easily distinguishable from *haken* workers in everyday life. Whether those who hop from one *haken* job to another are considered to be *freeters* is a bone of contention even within the government.[5] It should be noted here that, when it first appeared in the mass media during the time of the buoyant economy, the concept of *freeter* was used to depict 'a hip, urban image of young people who were pursuing artistic and other creative activities with the free time enabled by part-time jobs' (Smith 2006: 56). Being a *freeter* was then interpreted as voluntarily choosing one's own lifestyles based on 'self-responsibility', an alternative, avant-garde style of working 'to the mainstream idea of elite employment in post-war Japan – that is being employed by a company immediately after graduation, trained by the employer and remaining with the same firm for the rest of one's working life, only exercising "responsibility" and facing risk regarding employment within the context of Japan's "enterprise-ism" (*kaishashugi*)' (Hook and Takeda 2007: 114–115). However, from the late 1990s when Japan witnessed a series of youth-related social panics and crises amid the prolonged post-bubble economic recession, the increased number of *freeters* has turned into a serious cause for concern. As Colin Smith (2006: 57) explains, the intense media reaction against *freeters* was triggered off by the portrayal of young adults as 'parasite singles', a neologism coined by Yamada Masahiro (1999), a famous sociologist in Japan. Indeed, the stinging phrase has since become a powerful symbol for the irresponsible, self-indulgent and unproductive young generation who evade or delay adult commitment by scrounging off their parents' largesse.

For the policy-making elite, *freeters* and NEETs have been related to a host of economic anxieties with respect to social welfare and the labour market. The trend that more and more young people who are approaching their early 30s or

40s remain unmarried and in low-paying temporary jobs has raised widespread concern about family breakdown, declining fertility rates and employment instability. As Glenn Hook and Hiroko Takeda (2007) point out, the existence of this 'irresponsible' type of Japanese citizen is extremely costly for the Japanese state as it poses a serious internal risk by creating a deficit in the social security budget. A school of Japanese academics fuels the sense of crisis by describing *freeters* as 'non-performing loans' of Japanese society (Yamada 2004) – like the bad bank loans that caused bankruptcy in the aftermath of the bursting of the bubble economy – or as an alarming liability that will lead to 'national ruin' in the future (Maruyama 2004). Their argument is apparently empowered by neoliberalism, a new global paradigm of ideology that entails contradictory statements about human dignity and freedom.[6] On the one hand, there is approval for individual exercise of free choice and self-responsibility in line with so-called 'free-market' principles. On the other hand, however, the ideology subtly pushes forward a message that to be a responsible citizen of society is to place priority on the market that requires individual improvement on competence, employability and consumption. In the Japanese context, such recalibrated citizenship is embodied in the state's enunciation of 'productive self' (Hook and Takeda 2007) in response to the assumed risks posed by those 'degenerate' or 'parasitic' young people.

By contrast, *haken* are spared from the same public bashing as meted out to freeters and NEETs who tend to arouse the ire of the older generation. Although the boundary between *haken* and *freeters* is ambiguous in definition and permeable in practice, *haken*, as a newly developed concept, has assumed connotations of skills and professionalism. Far from being a bunch of hedonistic dreamers and loafers, *haken* are often referred to by political and economic leaders as a useful human resource supplemental to the core salaried workers. Compared to the majority of non-regular workers who concentrate on service or retail sectors, *haken* workers penetrate almost all kinds of industries and companies and, generally speaking, receive better remuneration and higher social status. In particular, white-collar *haken* are increasingly replacing regular employees on the Japanese 'auxiliary employment track' (*ippanshoku*) usually reserved for female workers, as opposed to the male-dominated 'general or comprehensive employment track' (*sōgōshoku*) (Keizer 2007). While clerical or secretarial jobs remain a staple part of *haken* work, the fact that there is an increasing number of *haken* professionals and specialists who are popular with companies makes it hard to classify *haken* as an unequivocally low-class labour force or 'a group of losers' (*makegumi*). From the employers' point of view, *haken* are not only just-in-time and low-cost but also the most institutionally organised, professional and reliable type of flexible workers among the wide and varied non-regular labour pool in Japan. For some individual workers, white-collar *haken* experience with large companies can improve their curriculum vitae and, to some extent, can appeal to employers when it comes to corporate regular hiring. This makes a striking contrast with *freeters* whose part-time work is often dismissed as not 'real' work experience or something that young people should 'graduate' from (Smith 2006: 177).

Nevertheless, both *haken* and *freeters* have a similar role in the reorganisation of work taking place in contemporary Japan. As a new generation of non-regular workers, their unconventional work patterns and life paths provide important clues to the ever-changing Japanese society. Growing up with Japan's affluence, today's young people are increasingly seen to be apathetic about, alienated from or railing against the post-war salaryman and office lady lifestyle. The popular political and commercial discourses that promote flexibility and individuality in the workplace are influential in forming and reforming social reality where young people constantly negotiate imposed social roles with their self-driven personal dreams. Colin Smith's account describes how *freeters* appropriate shifting popular discourses to explore new ideas of work and identity even at the risk of exposing themselves to insecurity, exploitation and impoverishment (2006: 174–175):

> By redefining the meaning of work and living out new lifestyles they act as agents of the reorganization of work and the production of culture. Their lifestyles stand in contrast to that of *salaryman*. The image of the *salaryman* is losing its organizing force in society. Its power as a marker of Japanese identity and pride has waned. In many cases, the decision to become a freeter is also influenced by a matter of truly finding working as a *salaryman* or office lady an unappealing proposition …
>
> But this is not to say they are rejecting the notion of full-time employment. Just because freeters are rejecting the salaryman path, it doesn't mean they want to stay in part-time jobs or become freelancers. Many see themselves either going into career track jobs or returning to them. They do want the security that it provides, but they are willing to risk it until they can find meaningful work that is also stable and secure. What is different is the way in which their identity is connected to their work. Not only is the line of work more important than identifying with a particular organization, but the work is often related to fashion, entertainment, design, and other expressive and consumer culture fields in some way. Work for them is another means of the kind of self-fashioning performed through consumption of goods and styles. They see it as a period of experimentation and self reflection where they are trying to figure out what they want to do. Others see it as a period of training or a stage they have to go through before they can get full time jobs …
>
> In a way, we can think of them as experimenting with, taking advantage of, or testing the limits of, the contradictions of both the postwar social formation and the new one that is emerging through neoliberalization.

Like *freeters*, *haken* do not follow the standardised steady career path; their triangular non-regular working presents a distinct, if not diametrical, antithesis to the ideal salaryman person whose corporate affiliation informs much of self-worth, social status and private life. The fact that *haken* workers do not necessarily incur public wrath or criticism puts them in a better position of compromising or transgressing the taken-for-granted social norms. While the legitimacy and

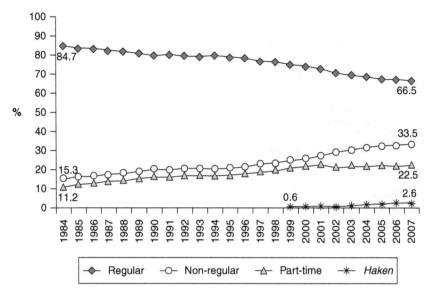

Figure 2.1 Percentage of non-executive employees in total employment.

Source: 2007 Labour Force Survey (*Rōdōryoku Chōsa*), MIC.

popularity of 'company person' (*kaisha ningen*) in Japan have been on the wane, the emergence of *haken* as a new breed of mobile workers heralds a new era of company–worker relationships in which hitherto unsuccessful or spurned individuals have increasingly made inroads into the salaryman territory.

The official profile of *haken*

Many scholars have observed that the growth in non-regular workers along with the decrease in regular workers is the single most important change that is taking place in the Japanese labour market (Rebick 2005; Imai and Shire 2006). The latest figure shows that one out of three in Japan's national workforce is identified as a non-regular worker (Figure 2.1).[7] The swelling 'peripheral' labour as opposed to the shrinking 'core' labour has recently attracted great attention, although the dual employment structure is in fact a long-existing trend that can be traced back to as early as the beginning of the high-growth era (Gordon 1985). Since the burst of the bubble economy in the early 1990s, Japan has been mired in its worst post-war economic recession. Faced with the ever-rising unemployment and the prolonged economic stagnation, the government has put forward a series of deregulation policies aimed at steering the national economy in a new direction that shows increasing congruence with global trends. In the process of reforming the labour market, *haken* employment has assumed considerable importance in the government deregulation agenda. In 1986, *Haken* Law

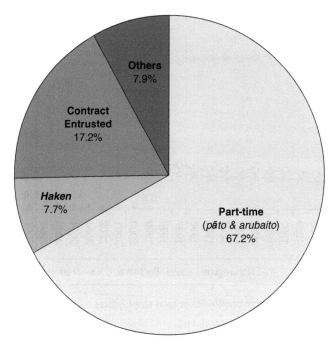

Figure 2.2 Composition of non-regular labour force in Japan.

Source: Labour Force Survey 2007 (*Rōdōryoku Chōsa*), MIC.

was put into force, which for the first time in Japan's post-war history lifted the ban on labour-leasing business that used to be associated with exploitative or unlawful activities in the past. The subsequent revisions of the law, especially from the late 1990s, have allowed *haken* to be used in a wide range of occupations and industrial areas with few restrictions. As a result, the drastic liberalisation of *haken* has led to not only the rapid growth of *haken* business but also to a social phenomenon where *haken* finds itself becoming the most powerful symbol of non-regular working in contemporary Japan.

   In contrast to their received prominence in the public arena, the number of *haken* workers appears to be negligible. According to a recent government survey, *haken* constitutes 2.6 per cent of the total employment (Figure 2.1) and 7.7 per cent of the entire non-regular population (Figure 2.2). The small proportion of *haken* workers becomes even more striking when compared with part-timers who account for the overwhelming majority of non-regular workers. It is noteworthy that official figures do not normally include those 'dormant' *haken* who hadn't been active in the past 1 year at the time when surveys were conducted. Moreover, the estimated number of *haken* is often calculated based on a certain standard of working hours pertinent to the employed type of *haken* – which explains why people who engage in *haken* in different ways outnumber the 'statistical' employed *haken* by more than 2 to 1 (Table 2.2).

Table 2.2 Number of *haken* workers by type of employment and agencies

General *haken* agencies	(1) Employed *haken*	645,767
	(2) Registered *haken* that can be calculated as employed type by dividing their total annual working hours by an average annual working hours per employed *haken*	651,687
	(3) Registered *haken*	2,343,967
Special *haken* agencies	(4) Employed *haken*	220,734
Number of *haken*	(1) + (3) + (4) Total	3,210,468
	(1) + (2) + (4) 'Statistical' employed type	1,518,188

Source: Haken *Business Report* 2006 (*Rōdōsha Haken Jigyō Hōkoku*), MHLW.

There are two major groups of *haken*: 'the registered type' (*tōroku gata*) and 'the employed type' (*jyōyō koyō gata*). While the registered groups are *haken* agencies' contingent registrants who are only considered as *haken* when actually working on a job assignment that involves a triangular employment contract, the employed groups are *full-time* workers of *haken* agencies. To put it another way, employed *haken* are a special category of regular workers in non-regular employment due to the middleman nature of their employers. To add a further element of complexity, there are two types of *haken* agencies operating in Japan. One is 'general *haken* agencies' (*ippan haken gaisha*), which are allowed to hire both registered and employed *haken* and require the sanction of MHLW for business start-up – the so-called 'licence system' (*kyokasei*). The other is 'special *haken* agencies ' (*tokutei haken gaisha*) agencies, which are restricted to the management of only employed *haken* and can be easily established provided that they submit a notification to MHLW – the so-called 'report system' (*todokesei*).

As shown in the latest annual *Haken Business Report*[8] issued by MHLW, more than 70 per cent of *haken* employees in the fiscal year of 2006 are registered *haken*, numbering 2.34 million out of the total 3.21 million *haken* (Table 2.2). Registered *haken* usually work for a contract term of less than 3 months, compared to most of the employed *haken* who are relatively evenly distributed among different terms of contract ranging from less than 3 months to 1–3 years (Table 2.3). It is, therefore, reasonable to infer that registered *haken* move from one contract or workplace to another with higher frequency and that they are likely to be out of employment for a longer time between different job assignments. Unlike registered *haken*, employed *haken* are paid a monthly salary and have pay increases, bonuses and other corporate benefits that regular employees are usually entitled to. More importantly, they still get paid during the in-between period when shifting from one *haken* assignment to another, albeit on the condition that they must come to their agency's office and stay standing by. In addition to the two major categories, recent years have seen the growing popularity of 'temp-to-perm *haken*' (*shōkai yotei haken*), which provides a screening period for both workers and client firms as a step towards permanent employment. As large *haken* agencies expand their

Table 2.3 Contract length of *haken* workers by type of agencies

	Less than 3 months (%)	3–6 months (%)	6–9 months (%)	9–12 months (%)	1–3 years (%)	Other (%)
General *haken* agencies	81.8	12.4	2.9	1.0	1.7	0.1
Special *haken* agencies	17.7	25.5	20.4	11.0	22.1	3.3
Total	80.4	12.7	3.3	1.2	2.2	0.2

Source: Haken *Business Report* 2006 (*Rōdōsha Haken Jigyō Hōkoku*), MHLW.

business across borders, there has also emerged a type of 'overseas *haken*' (*kaigai haken*), which dispatches workers to firms operating abroad.

With *haken* becoming a widespread and wide-ranging employment in the Japanese workplace, the state is keen to 'measure' *haken*, an emerging labour force deemed a positive contribution to employment stability and national economy. The measurement is carried out through surveys and questionnaires and legitimised by a multiplicity of quantitative data. As Roger Goodman (2002: 9, my italics) puts it:

> Statistics seems to be particularly widely used in official documents in Japan, perhaps because of the high general level of numeracy in the population and the general respect for 'fact' over interpretation. Indeed, it is unusual to be able to think of a statistic in Japan that might exist but that has not been collected ... the study of official statistics in any society is also the study of the people who collect those statistics, the questions they use to collect them, the labels they put on the tables to present them, and the conclusion they draw from them; these questions, labels and conclusions often provide a fascinating insight into the assumptions that the researcher bring to their projects, which in themselves are often *a reflection of wider views about the issue under study*.

Given the great degree to which official statistics are invoked, respected and accepted in Japan, the main purpose of presenting a number of statistics conducted by government ministries or think-tank researchers here is to provide a general perception of *haken* imposed on the wider populace, rather than justifying or reinforcing what those statistics are supposed to tell. This is particularly worth stressing as there is tendency among researchers to confuse official profiles with real people in real situations.

In 2004, MHLW (2005) conducted a first comprehensive *haken* survey following several drastic legislative revisions of *haken* between 1999 and 2003. Based on data collected from questionnaires, the survey describes the 'realities' (*jittai*)

Table 2.4 *Haken*'s age distribution

| Sex | Haken total (%) | Age brackets (%) | | | | | | | | | | | Average age |
		15–19	20–24	25–29	30–34	35–39	40–44	45–49	50–54	55–59	60–64	65–	
Total	100.0	0.8	10.0	25.5	24.5	13.2	8.4	5.9	3.7	3.6	2.8	1.7	35.1
Male	100.0	1.2	13.3	21.7	19.0	11.6	8.0	5.5	4.2	6.5	5.4	3.6	37.0
Female	100.0	0.5	8.0	27.8	27.7	14.2	8.6	6.1	3.4	2.0	1.3	0.5	33.9

Source: *Haken* Survey 2004 (*Haken Rōdōsha Jittai Chōsa*), MHLW.

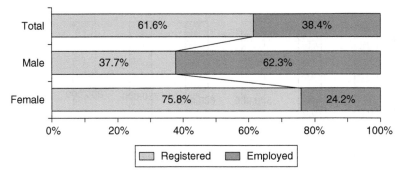

Figure 2.3 *Haken*'s sex ratio by employment type.

Source: *Haken* Survey 2004 (*Haken Rōdōsha Jittai Chōsa*), MHLW.

or 'attributes' (*zokusei*) of *haken* workers by referring to such differentials as gender, age, employment type and education attainment. First, *haken* employment appears to attract people who are young or in their prime of work. Table 2.4 shows that more than 70 per cent come from the age bracket of 20–39, with those aged 25–34 making up 50 per cent of the total *haken* population. Second, in terms of employment type, employed *haken* are heavily outnumbered by registered *haken* (Figure 2.3). However, the trend differs greatly in gender; nearly 76 per cent women, as opposed to 38 per cent men, fall into the registered type. In other words, employed *haken*, or full-time employees of *haken* agencies, seem to be much more common among male *haken* than female *haken*. The same survey also includes *haken*'s educational background (Table 2.5). Senior high school stands at the top, but a good proportion of *haken* have higher education qualifications from vocational or 2-year colleges and universities.

   The above statistics suggest that gender is a salient feature of *haken* work, which intersects with other important variables including age, employment type and education. Indeed, women comprise the bulk of *haken* agencies' rosters; as Jun Imai (2004: 38) says, *haken* is a predominantly female employment, although the ratio

Table 2.5 Haken's education attainment

Sex	Haken total (%)	Education attainment (%)				
		Junior high school	Senior high school	Vocational college	Two-year college	University and above
Total	100.0	5.4	38.4	10.9	20.6	24.6
Male	100.0	11.5	44.4	11.5	4.9	27.7
Female	100.0	1.9	34.9	10.5	30.0	22.7

Source: *Haken* Survey 2004 (*Haken Rōdōsha Jittai Chōsa*), MHLW.

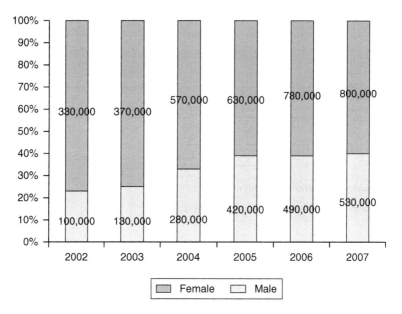

Figure 2.4 Haken's changing gender ratio.

Source: Labour Force Survey 2007 (*Rōdōryoku Chōsa*), Statistics Bureau, MIC.

of men to women has been improving over the past few years (Figure 2.4). The saliency of gender is manifested in *haken* occupations as well. Women remain dominant in clerical or secretarial office work, whereas men are seen to increasingly concentrate in manufacturing and construction jobs, with a sharp rise from 26.4 per cent in 1997 to 63.1 per cent in 2007 (Table 2.6). This is primarily because the government in 2003 lifted the ban on the use of *haken* on manufacturing assembly lines. The same deregulation measure also explains why the proportion of female *haken* who engage in manufacturing and construction jobs has grown to 25.2 per cent in 2007, compared to 6.9 per cent in 1997.

Table 2.6 Haken occupation by gender (unit: 1,000 people)

Occupation	1997			2002			2007		
	Total	Male	Female	Total	Male	Female	Total	Male	Female
Specialist and Technical	30 11.7%	20 37.7%	10 4.9%	44 6.1%	23 11.3%	21 4.1%	76 4.7%	41 6.7%	35 3.5%
Clerical	180 70.0%	14 26.4%	166 81.4%	360 49.9%	29 14.2%	331 64.0%	588 36.6%	58 9.5%	530 53.1%
Sales	4 1.6%	1 1.9%	3 1.5%	48 6.7%	11 5.4%	37 7.2%	91 5.7%	26 4.3%	65 6.5%
Service	10 3.9%	2 3.8%	8 3.9%	43 6.0%	9 4.4%	34 6.6%	72 4.5%	20 3.3%	52 5.2%
Agriculture, forestry and fisheries	0 0.0%	0 0.0%	0 0.0%	1 0.1%	1 0.5%	0 0.0%	4 0.2%	3 0.5%	1 0.1%
Transportation and communication	4 1.6%	1 1.9%	3 1.5%	11 1.5%	9 4.4%	2 0.4%	31 1.9%	26 4.3%	5 0.5%
Manufacturing and construction	28 10.9%	14 26.4%	14 6.9%	192 26.6%	113 55.4%	79 15.3%	636 39.6%	385 63.1%	251 25.2%
Unclassified	0 0.0%	0 0.0%	0 0.0%	21 2.9%	8 3.9%	13 2.5%	110 6.8%	51 8.4%	59 5.9%
Total	257 100%	53 100%	204 100%	721 100%	204 100%	517 100%	1608 100%	610 100%	998 100%

Source: Employment Structure Survey (Shūgyō Kōzō Kihon Chōsa), Statistics Bureau, MIC.

Note:
The survey is conducted by the Japanese government every 5 years.

Table 2.7 Annual income distribution of regular and non-regular workers

Annual income (10,000 yen)	Regular workers		Non-regular workers	
	Male (%)	Female (%)	Male (%)	Female (%)
~ 100	1.2	5.6	27.5	49.0
100–199	5.7	21.0	29.6	36.9
200–299	14.8	28.6	20.8	10.0
300–399	19.6	19.5	11.1	2.8
400–499	17.4	11.0	5.0	0.7
500–699	21.1	9.6	3.4	0.4
700–999	15.5	4.2	2.1	0.1
1000–1499	4.1	0.5	0.4	0.0
1500–	0.7	0.1	0.2	0.0
Total	100.0	100.0	100.0	100.0

Source: Labour Force Survey 2007 (*Rōdōryoku Chōsa*), Statistics Bureau, MIC.

The occupational and industrial diversity makes it difficult to generalise the income level of *haken* workers. Indeed, *haken*'s well-being is a constant source of controversy, especially in relation to a 'gap-widening boom' (*kakusa būmu*) – a media-generated phenomenon which highlights the *kakusa* or widening gaps between regular and non-regular workers that has recently gripped the country (see Chapter 5). It is widely acknowledged that the majority of non-regular workers are worse off than regular workers in annual pay. While 49 per cent of the non-regular women earn less than 1 million yen and 37 per cent of those earn 1–1.99 million yen, only 26.6 per cent of the regular women earn less than 2 million yen and around 48 per cent of those earn 2–3.99 million yen (Table 2.7). The difference within the male group is equally striking; 77.9 per cent of the non-regular men are distributed relatively evenly on three low-income levels: less than 1 million yen, 1–1.99 million yen and 2–2.99 million yen, compared to 58.1 per cent of the regular men who are paid between 3 and 6.99 million yen. Much of media coverage draws attention to 'working poor' (*wākingu pua*), a *kakusa*-related buzzword referring to a state of perpetuated desperation from which those non-regular workers in low social strata are unable to escape, no matter how much effort they have invested in improving their standard of life (see Chapter 5). However, when it comes to the pay issue of *haken*, opinions tend to diverge. As Table 2.8 suggests, there is a discernible polarisation between those who earn below 2 million yen, which form 46.2 per cent, and those who earn between 2 and 3.99 million yen, which form 50.8 per cent. In addition, there is a growing minority of professional *haken*, who take well-paid, high-demand jobs and are often invoked as the envy of regular workers.

Table 2.8 Annual income distribution of *haken* workers

Annual income (10,000 yen)	Male haken		Female haken		Total	
~50	17,300	2.9%	45,100	4.6%	62,400	3.9%
50–99	35,800	6.0%	121,400	12.3%	157,200	9.9%
100–149	54,700	9.1%	168,200	17.0%	222,900	14.0%
150–199	94,400	15.7%	197,600	20.0%	292,000	18.4%
200–249	151,900	25.3%	249,600	25.2%	401,500	25.2%
250–299	105,600	17.6%	122,900	12.4%	228,500	14.4%
300–399	100,300	16.7%	77,200	7.8%	177,500	11.2%
500–699	28,800	4.8%	4,600	0.5%	33,400	2.1%
700–	12,700	2.1%	3,100	0.3%	15,800	1.0%
Total	601,500	100%	989,700	100%	1,591,200	100%

Source: Employment Structure Survey 2007 (*Shūgyō Kōzō Kihon Chōsa*), Statistics Bureau, MIC.

Apparently, occupational specialisation and employment status are two elements that contribute most importantly to the internal pay variance of *haken* (Table 2.9). The average hourly wage varies considerably between technical and professional assignments such as those concerning IT software development, mechanical design and corporate project operation and relatively low-skilled manual labour such as building cleaning. The income polarisation might be greater, if taking into account, for example, 'day *haken* labourers' (*hiyatoi haken*) who are dispatched to client firms on a daily basis. Furthermore, the employed *haken* who have the safety net of regular employment are likely to benefit from thicker remuneration packages than their registered counterparts.

Haken: a booming industry

If the government deregulation policy has instigated the emergence of a hitherto prohibited category of non-regular workers, *haken* agencies are the linchpin of *haken*'s development, a key actor transforming official guidelines into strategic practices. They are a distinct group of employers whose business relies on their intermediary role in leasing or exchanging labour as commodities. As Table 2.9 shows, *haken* agencies' revenues come from commission, that is the profit margin of dispatching fees which is commonly around 30 per cent. Although *haken* workers occupy only a small percentage of the entire non-regular legion, the rate at which they have increased over the past few years is unprecedented. The reported number of *haken* workers has tripled from 1999 to 2006; there are now more than 3 million Japanese (out of a total population of about 128 million) who are actively taking part in the *haken* employment (Figure 2.5). Perhaps more striking is the exponential growth of *haken* agencies as an emerging industry in Japan. The

Table 2.9 Haken daily wages and dispatching fees by occupation and employment type

Occupation	Haken employees number and average daily wages[a]				Haken agencies average dispatching fees[a]			
					Registered		Employed	
	Number	%	Registered yen	Employed yen	Yen	Margin (%)	Yen	Margin (%)
Total average (all occupations)			10,571	14,156	15,577		22,948	
26 designated occupations[a]	883,454	100	11,777	13,899	16,946	30	22,076	36
1. Software development	60,740	6.9	15,118	17,166	23,321	35	30,576	44
2. Mechanical design	61,576	7.0	13,590	16,258	20,836	35	26,675	39
3. Operation of broadcasting machines	4,515	0.5	12,570	14,922	18,030	30	22,689	34
4. Broadcasting programmes production	3,796	0.4	12,870	15,503	17,814	28	22,338	31
5. Operation of office machines	378,889	42.9	10,060	11,752	14,479	31	18,828	38
6. Interpretation, translation, stenography	5,705	0.6	14,446	14,434	20,535	30	23,371	38
7. Secretary	5,338	0.6	11,749	11,759	16,392	28	17,249	32
8. Filing	38,214	4.3	9,172	10,818	13,372	31	16,120	33
9. Investigation	8,182	0.9	11,795	15,753	16,599	29	26,089	40
10. Financial transactions/documents	80,698	9.1	10,776	11,954	15,106	29	18,085	34
11. Transaction documents drafting	49,469	5.6	11,328	13,889	15,915	29	21,055	34
12. Sales demonstration	10,546	1.2	11,173	13,407	15,899	30	23,779	44

Occupation	Haken employees number and average daily wages[a]				Haken agencies average dispatching fees[a]			
	Number	%	Registered yen	Employed yen	Registered		Employed	
					Yen	Margin (%)	Yen	Margin (%)
13. Tour guide	6,246	0.7	10,266	9,886	13,927	26	13,875	29
14. Building cleaning	4,623	0.5	6,995	8,074	11,303	38	11,833	32
15. Building maintenance	6,538	0.7	11,863	13,732	17,276	31	21,254	35
16. Receptionist	36,696	4.2	9,168	9,502	13,526	32	14,119	33
17. Research and development	38,489	4.4	11,898	14,975	18,078	34	26,736	44
18. Project operation planning	3,220	0.4	15,296	20,373	21,772	30	33,148	39
19. Editorial staff	4,364	0.5	11,624	13,618	16,310	29	22,376	39
20. Advertising design	2,994	0.3	12,080	13,801	17,111	29	20,984	34
21. Interior decorator/designer	2,011	0.2	10,889	15,053	15,386	29	22,174	32
22. Media announcer/presenter	167	0.0	14,338	16,141	20,640	31	23,608	32
23. OA instruction	6,760	0.8	12,636	13,894	17,924	30	25,116	45
24. Tele-marketing	56,050	6.3	10,310	11,661	14,350	28	19,072	39
25. Sales	6,038	0.7	13,467	17,208	19,154	30	29,470	42
26. Broadcasting stage preparation	1,590	0.2	10,716	15,842	15,531	31	23,353	32

Source: *Haken* Business Report 2006 (*Rōdōsha Haken Jigyō Hōkoku*), MHLW (2007a).

Notes

a 1. Average daily wages and dispatching fees are based on eight working hours per day, which exclude costs incurred by employment and health insurance and pension schemes.

2. The 26 designated occupations (*Seirei 26 Gyōmu*) are only part of *haken* occupations that are generally perceived as more professional and specialised than others (see *haken*'s legislation changes in Chapter 4). Those who are involved in other areas including day *haken* and recently permitted manufacturing assembly lines are therefore not represented in the table.

34   Haken

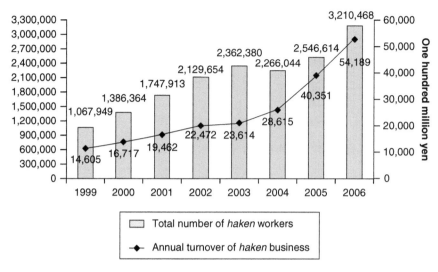

Figure 2.5 Growth of *haken* workers and *haken* business.

Source: *Haken* Business Report 2006 (*Rōdōsha Haken Jigyō Hōkoku*), MHLW (2007a).

haken market is dominated by several large agencies, for example, Pasona, Adecco, Recruit staffing, Manpower and Staff Service. The business is indeed thriving, as evidenced by its annual turnover in 2006 which tops 5.4 trillion yen (approximately 54 billion US$), compared to 1.5 trillion yen in 1999.

The industrial spokesman for *haken* agencies is Japan Staffing Services Association (JASSA), which was officially founded in 1986 – the same year when the first *Haken* Law was put into force. In 1994, JASSA joined CIETT (Confederation Internationale des Entreprises de Travail Temporaire or *Kokusai Jinzai Haken Jigyō Dantai Rengō*) and subsequently hosted the 2006 international private employment agencies' annual conference in Tokyo. It has also become an official member of Japan Business Federation known as *Keidanren* (*Nihon Keizai Dantai Renmei*), the most powerful business association formed by large companies. With the continuing business expansion, the membership of JASSA increased to 787 as of April 2008. In addition to being a source of information, JASSA has played an active role in supporting, promoting and more recently defending the *haken* employment in response to adverse criticism. As illustrated by the latest message from Chairman Kazuhiko Kamata published in JASSA's official website:

> The Japanese labour market is facing rapid changes and challenges due to the diversification of individual perception of work and the unbalanced labour structure of companies. JASSA has been dedicated to the improvement of *haken* workers' skills development and working conditions as well as the adjustment to companies' changing employment environment. As a result, *haken* has established itself as an industry.

However, our industry has been increasingly subject to criticism in relation to social disparity, working poor and internal scandals. With the introduction of the revised guidance on day *haken* labourers in February 2008 and the recent heated debate over *haken*'s legislative review, the environment surrounding *haken* is going through a major transformation.

JASSA will continue to facilitate its members' professional responsibility and the appropriate management of *haken* business as a whole. To achieve such goals, the association will issue and effectively enforce relevant directives including 'the establishment of legal compliance and high ethical standards', 'the career formation of *haken* workers' and 'the enrolment of the social insurance system'.

JASSA's members account for 10 per cent of the agencies in Japan and generate 60 per cent of the total sales of general agencies. The association is committed to further industrial cohesion, the improvement of social contribution and reliability and the sound development of *haken* industry.

Many of *haken* agencies' commercial and political discourses focus on the creation of fashionable values about *haken* work. In particular, *haken* agencies draw attention to their bridge-building role in bringing benefits to both client firms and workers. On the one hand, they provide client firms with a cost-effective, flexible and institutionally organised workforce – it is said that the existence of *haken* agencies proves a boon especially to middle-size and small firms which find it difficult to secure the right people in the right place at the right time. On the other hand, *haken* agencies lay emphasis on the diversification of work and life, often presenting themselves as sympathetic to a variety of individual choices and needs. Popular concepts such as 'individuality' (*kosei*), 'self-development' (*jikokeihatsu*) and 'diversity' (*tayōsei*) feature prominently in large agencies' advertising campaigns. Such attractive images are influential in making *haken* more desirable, respectable and meaningful than other various kinds of non-regular employment, as well as challenging the legitimacy and dominance of the salaryman style of work. The goal of *haken* industry is to become the so-called 'comprehensive personnel services business' (*sōgōteki na jinzai bijinesu gyō*), which deals with not only labour dispatch services but also a wide range of labour market issues including job placement services. To achieve such an ambitious goal, *haken* agencies are strategic and imaginative in their implementation of government policies, while lobbying the policy-making elite for further legal deregulation on *haken*.

One of the key strategies for *haken* agencies is to attract and secure as many registrants as possible. There is a widely shared sentiment that contemporary Japan is faced with an imminent labour shortage resulting from an unfortunate combination of falling fertility rates and a rapidly ageing population. Much has been discussed about 'ageing society' (*kōreika shakai*) and 'low-birth rate society' (*shōshika shakai*), as well as adverse economic effects those trends have on Japan's future (Roberts 2002). Amid speculations over the implications of Japan's population crisis, the number of *haken* registrants is estimated to fall considerably over the medium and long terms. This sense of labour crisis is further fuelled by the recent massive retirement of Japan's baby boomers – those who were born between 1947 and 1949. It is against this backdrop of widespread demographic concerns, together with increasingly intense internal competition, that leading *haken* agencies have appeared to change their focus of strategies from client firms to workers. Instead of catering mainly to the needs of client firms, they have attached greater importance to the acquisition and retention of workers from the dwindling labour pool in Japan.

Japanese newspapers often feature how leading agencies strive to gain their competitive edge by taking it upon themselves to improve both the quantity and the quality of *haken* workers on their rolls.[9] For instance, in fighting demographics, some have stepped up efforts to tap potential labour sources in collaboration with the government's so-called 'second-chance measures' which are aimed at enhancing the employability of inexperienced or 'problematic' youth, women and elderly people. As a result, innovative schemes on the part of *haken* agencies have been introduced to integrate *freeters*, NEETs, housewives and retirees into the national workforce. In addition, with demand outstripping supply for specialists in certain knowledge-intensive areas such as IT engineering development, the *haken* industry has explored further afield, looking for talents in emerging nations such as China and India as well as providing services to the local units of Japanese companies operating abroad. It is small wonder that it supports a liberal approach to immigration in a country which has the lowest proportion of immigrant workers among major industrialised economies. Kazuo Miura, one of the chief editors of a major *haken* magazine, *Monthly Personnel Business*, points out that the development of *haken* industry in the future decade hinges on 'guest workers' (22 February, 2008)[10]:

> I had a talk with a senior LDP member of the Diet the other day. The main point is that against the current declining trend of population it is imperative to take prompt measures to meet labour demands. One measure, which has been discussed, is to introduce new legislation on the acceptance of foreign workers …

> The growth of clerical *haken* work has already shown signs of slowing down. Given the predicted difficulty in securing labour, the growth rate of manufacturing work in the future will not be the same as in the past. Hence, the possibility of filling the gap caused by the population decrease rests on foreign workers. The number of foreign workers required is projected to be more than 1 million.

> It could be said that 'the wind of the times is directed at guest workers' (*Jidai no kaze wa* Guest Worker *ni mukatteiru*).

Although worker dispatching for office auxiliary work remains a major contribution to their sales, *haken* agencies have diversified their services in a number of new fields and regions. With the full-scale introduction of a government-initiated scheme called 'marketisation of public services' in 2007, *haken* agencies have begun to seek gains from local and central governments by participating in some public employment services such as Hello Work operations.[11] They have also found a host of new incentives to expand their business such that some dispatch doctors to rural areas where the shortage of medical professionals is acute and others create new jobs in agriculture where labour mobility is low. Their ambition of moving into uncharted territory is also manifested in the transformation of novices into professionals. Amid growing demands for highly knowledgeable and skilled labour, it is now common for top players in the industry to train and professionalise their registered workers by offering a diversity of career development programmes. For example, some give free classes for learning Japanese business manners, interviewing skills and basic levels of computer software operation; others team up with educational institutions and training firms to help registrants acquire specialist qualifications. To attract new registrants and secure those already on their rosters, *haken* agencies are also bending over backwards to create new ways of appealing to various individuals, such as widening options to choose workplaces, issuing point cards based on working hours that can be cashed in or traded for travel and providing after-work culture schools aimed at enriching *haken* workers' social life.

Despite the patina of success especially in terms of industrial expansion, *haken* agencies are often exposed to controversy. The recent debate over Japan's *kakusa* or widening gap between regular and non-regular workers has made *haken* agencies a prime target for strong criticism. This is particularly the case when a growing number of corporate scandals turn the spotlight on the ills of *haken* business. Many of those scandals are concerned with illegal labour dispatch such as 'disguised *ukeoi*' (*gisō ukeoi*) and 'double *haken*' (*nijyū haken*); the former refers to a widespread practice of disguising *haken* as *ukeoi*, a long-existing type of outsourcing workers, and the latter means that *haken* workers are re-dispatched by the client firm to a third party. Disguised *ukeoi* is especially rampant in Japanese manufacturing firms, which has become a social problem in recent years due to a large volume of media disclosure (see Chapter 5). For laymen, it might be difficult to distinguish between *haken* and *ukeoi* as both workers are dispatched to work in the facilities of client firms. The only difference, according to the law, is that *haken* workers are defined to work under the direct instruction and supervision of their client firms whereas *ukeoi* workers are prohibited from taking orders from client firms and are only subject to the authority of their own employers, that is, dispatch firms. However, the advantage of disguising *haken* as *ukeoi* on the part of client firms becomes clear when *Haken* Law is taken into account. Unlike *haken*, the employment of *ukeoi* does not require client firms to abide by regulations concerning the payment of health and safety insurance and the obligation to directly employ workers after a certain period.[12] The illegal practice of disguised *ukeoi* has a long historical entanglement with today's *haken* and is likely to take place among 'group companies' (*keiretsu gaisha*) which operate under the umbrella of a Japanese brand name (see Chapter 4). It is noteworthy that a number of Japanese conglomerates have set up their internal or in-house *haken* agencies which dispatch workers mainly to their own group companies. Such a practice not only has consequences for *haken* workers (see Chapters 3 and 6), but also is conducive to having regular workers retire before being rehired as workers of *haken* agencies at lower wages, according to some opinion leaders (*The Japan Times* 30 July, 2008, 5 November, 2008).

Following a series of high-profile scandals involving, for example, Canon and Matsushita Electric, which were found guilty of utilising disguised *ukeoi*, there has been widespread public condemnation towards the mishandling of workers by *haken* agencies and client firms (*Asahi Shimbun* 2007). In June 2008, Goodwill, a problem-laden large staffing agency announced its decision to sell its 'day *haken* business' (*hiyatoi haken*), the largest of its kind in the *haken* industry, after the Tokyo Summary Court ordered 1 million yen in fines for its illegal labour supply including double *haken* and dispatching day *haken* labourers to prohibited fields including stevedoring and construction (*The Japan Times* 26 June, 2008). The misconduct of Goodwill and another well-known agency Fullcast has triggered off a new wave of opposition to *haken* agencies which put profit-making before *haken* workers' interest. Strong criticisms are particularly levelled against the dispatch of *haken* workers on a daily basis. As a result, the latest legal revision banned *haken* agencies from dispatching workers on a contract term of less than 30 days for relatively low-skilled occupations (*The Japan Times* 30 July, 2008, 5 November, 2008; MHLW 2008).

Conclusion

In this chapter, I have provided a wide context in contemporary Japan in which to study *haken* as a new breed of non-regular workers and as a booming industry composed of *haken* agencies, a group of intermediary employers.

Haken employment shares generic features of non-regular work; it is an unconventional way of working which presents an antithesis of the post-war salaryman model. Yet, there are several factors which distinguish *haken* from other categories of non-regular workers. In addition to the highly institutionalised and legalised structure which involves a triangular employment relationship, *haken* workers are exempt from the opprobrium heaped upon 'problematic' young people such as *freeters* and NEETs deemed 'malfunctioning' or 'non-performing'. They are generally considered by the policy-making elite as a useful labour force contributing to employment stability and economic development. In popular discourse, *haken* work has also assumed a veneer of liberated spirit and professional flair; not only does it emphasise individuality in pursuing meaningful work and life, but also provide different ways of advancing one's career. Within the *haken* population, there are a number of variables such as age, gender, employment type and occupation, which differentiate among *haken* workers themselves. The general view is that *haken* employment is common to young people in their 20s and 30s and is dominated by female *haken* who are involved in clerical or *jimukei* jobs across almost all kinds of industries and companies.

The existence of intermediary agencies is perhaps the most distinctive feature that sets *haken* apart from other casual labour in Japan. In recent years, *haken* agencies have grown exponentially and expanded their services in a variety of new fields. They are an increasingly powerful industry which plays a vital role in promoting *haken* work and a proliferation of fashionable values associated with it. However, the rapid development of *haken* is often clouded by scandals in connection with illegal dispatch activities, which have exposed *haken* agencies to controversy and criticism.

In the light of *haken*'s salient features as a labour force and an industry, I shall in the next chapter describe how the distinct tripartite employment system works in concrete situations by drawing on my own experience of working as a *haken* in Japan.

3 Working as a *haken* in a triangular employment relationship

Introduction

Arguably, controversy over non-regular work in contemporary Japan is at its most acute in the case of *haken*. This has much to do with *haken*'s triangular employment relationship where workers are typically employed and dispatched by agencies while working at the facilities of and under the authority of client firms (Figure 3.1). The tripartite structure is not entirely new during the post-war development of Japanese employment practices; internal and external labour adjustments such as *shukkō* and *ukeoi* have been widely used by firms to whittle down the workforce, which subject a great many workers, regular or non-regular, to dual-employer situations outside the (full) protection of the much-touted Japanese life-time employment (see Chapter 4).

What is new about *haken*, however, is the special attention it has received in the state's post-bubble deregulation reforms. The legalisation and liberation of *haken* over the past two decades has not only conferred a legitimate status upon the generalised private labour leasing, but also significantly transformed what it means to be working in contemporary Japan. With its growing penetration into the Japanese workplace, *haken* heralds a new era of employer–employee relationship that contrasts sharply with the post-war salaryman or company-as-family model. The role of *haken* agencies is particularly important here, as it is frequently offered up to the public as that of an active link between companies and workers and an equal benefit to both. Such a triangular employment relationship entails a complex combination of different expectations and practices from three parties, which merits empirical investigation. Drawing on my fieldwork experience of working as a *haken*, this chapter sets out to provide a practical sense of *haken* work with the view to revealing some features that are often unstated or hidden in official profiles and discourses.

Registrations with *haken* agencies

Like many first-time ethnographers, I embarked on my fieldwork in Tokyo in November 2007 in high spirits, determining to immerse myself in the Japanese way of life. My original research focus was on the salaryman model, exploring the

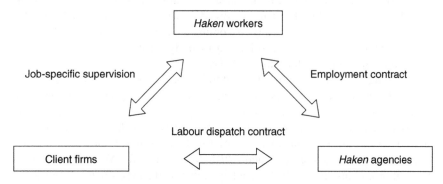

Figure 3.1 Haken's triangular employment relationship.

changing Japanese hegemonic masculinity. However, the importance of depending on the studied people for company, friendship and human understanding, as E.E. Evans-Pritchard (1951: 79) stresses, often brings about serendipitous discoveries. In my search for Japanese firms as fieldsites, an old friend, who was a senior director of a mid-size family-run firm, recommended that I should work as a *haken* myself instead of being introduced into an organisation as an outside researcher. As he put it:

> Nowadays *compliance* (*konpuraiansu*) assumes great importance in Japan, which means Japanese companies are extremely sensitive about potential whistle-blowers. If you enter into a company as an Oxford researcher, I do not think it is easy for you to integrate with the everyday life of ordinary Japanese employees. People would look at you differently. Some perhaps would be very cautious about what they have to talk to you. This is particularly a problem when it comes to big companies where rules and regulations are much more rigid than small and mid-size companies. …
>
> Given your situation, why do not you work as an office *haken*? *Haken* workers are everywhere now and they work just like normal regular workers. My company hires about 20 *haken* workers, working at both the office and the factory. … *Haken* workers are different from part-timers; they are screened, dispatched, and paid by *haken* agencies. My company usually does business with 2 or 3 agencies. … *Haken* workers are not necessarily cheap; insurance and overtime fees have to be paid properly according to the law. In a sense, they are better off than regular workers who have to put up with a lot of 'unpaid overtime work' (*sābisu zangyō*). But, the merit for companies is for sure; it is very 'convenient' (*benri*) to hire and fire workers via intermediary agencies in line with changing business conditions. In Japan, the dismissal of regular workers is very complicated and costly, but companies can easily terminate *haken* contracts if job opportunities are decreasing.

I was immediately fascinated by his idea. My curiosity about *haken*, combined with the need to adapt to the actual fieldwork circumstances, prompted me to try a new entrée into Japanese society: becoming a *haken* myself. Little did I know that this change of plan would result in a grippingly eventful year, leading eventually to a doctoral project focusing on *haken*.

Becoming a *haken* in Japan turned out to be not as difficult as I had expected – despite being a fluent Japanese speaker, I was a little apprehensive about my Chinese nationality which might cause some problems. One can respond to job advertisements in newspapers, magazines, bulletins and perhaps most commonly and effectively, over the Internet. I started looking for *haken* jobs from popular recruitment websites such as Yahoo *Riku Nabi* (short for Yahoo Recruitment Navigation). Many listed jobs have a tag 'welcome the inexperienced' (*mikeiken kangei*). There are a vast array of choices and options with which one can browse jobs. Some choices are generic ones such as employment type, occupation, industry, length of assignment and location. Others, however, are particular or, as Yahoo *Riku Nabi* puts it, 'individualised preferences' (*kodawari jyōken*), for example:

- Making good use of English language (*eigoryoku wo ikasu*)
- Starting work after 10 am (10 *ji igo shussha* OK)
- Leaving work before 4 pm (16 *ji mae taisha* OK)
- Fashion and cosmetic areas (*fasshon kosume kanren*)
- Within five minutes walk to stations (*eki toho 5fun inai*)
- Having a company cafeteria (*shain shokudō ari*)
- Less than 20 hours overtime (*zangyō 20 jikan miman*)
- Having days off during weekdays (*heijitsu yasumi ari*)
- Free dress code (*fukusō jiyū*)
- Foreign-affiliated companies (*gaishi kei*)
- No-smoking office or having the separation of space for non-smokers (*ofisu kinen bunen*)

After repeating a process of filling in an online form of CV for each selected job, I was then contacted by different *haken* agencies within one to two working days. All asked me politely to book a registration session with them as soon as possible in order to be an eligible candidate for the jobs they advertised. The registration is basically a screening process in which *haken* agencies gauge how registrants' skills and competence match up with job categories, as well as gathering information about their personal backgrounds and preferences. During my fieldwork at different points of time, I registered with a total of six *haken* agencies, which I shall name A *sha*, B *sha*, C *sha*, D *sha*, E *sha* and F *sha* – I was told by my informants that the more *haken* agencies I registered with the more likely it was that I could come across my favourite jobs. Those agencies varied considerably in size, market share, client portfolios and business practice. A *sha*, B *sha* and C *sha* were among those big names in the *haken* industry whereas E *sha* was a tiny agency run mainly by one person, that is, the president, with the aid of three or four part-timers. *D sha* was a middle-size agency famous for its specialisation in high-demand and well-paid IT engineering jobs, which were generally considered as the top echelons of *haken* occupations. Perhaps more interesting was F *sha*, which was one of the internal or in-house agencies founded by Vision, a long-established Japanese manufacturing conglomerate. As distinct from other independent agencies, F *sha* committed itself to dispatching *haken* workers mainly within the Vision group companies including a large number of branches and subcontractors.

All registration sessions I attended followed more or less a similar pattern, although bigger agencies had much more rigorous and consequently longer screening processes than smaller ones. My first experience was with A *sha*, a well-known agency which offered a rich variety of jobs in large and especially foreign-affiliated firms that many young people found attractive. I was hoping to get an A *sha*'s multi-lingual job concerning international sales in a major Japanese TV corporation. Below is an account of how I got on with A *sha*'s registration.

It was a drizzly February afternoon when I entered a skyscraper near *Shinjuku* station where one of A *sha*'s registration centres was located. The registration session I booked began at 1:00pm; there were normally several sessions per day with one overlapping with another such as at 1:00pm, then at 2:00pm. A middle-aged woman assembled six of us ranging from early 20s to late 30s, among whom only one was male. She began the registration by showing a 10-minute video which gave a brief overview of A *sha* and the *haken* system, especially the triangular employment relationship and pay-receiving procedures. We were then instructed to enter personal information into the computer in front of each of us and to fill in two forms: one was a bank account for future payment and the other was a legal acknowledgement of the employment relationship between the registrant and the *haken* agency. After the paperwork, we were divided into separate small booths where we started our individual screening under the supervision of an A *sha*'s staff. In my booth, I met a woman in her late 30s, who introduced herself with impeccable professional manners. First, she interviewed me for about 20 minutes, asking questions about my education background, work experience and job preferences in terms of occupation, industry, and length of assignments. Following the interview, she commented that I was the ideal candidate for the job I applied for earlier online. She then explained the job in further details, trying to make sure if it was the job I was really interested in.

In the next stage, I was left alone for about one and an half hours to carry out several computer-based competence tests, which included Japanese language, numeracy, typing, and personality aptitude. Those tests were not difficult and I was particularly amused by the personality test which contained more than 200 questions that you had to answer by ticking either Yes or No. For example:

- Do you often stick to your own opinion?

- Do you often get stressed?

- Are you afraid of moving forward because of the previous mistakes you have made?

- Do you tend to agree with others at the expense of your own point of view?

Since I was interested in the TV international sales job, I tried to adjust my answers to what might be required of an ideal candidate for that job. My efforts paid off; the result at the end of the test was just as I expected[1]:

You are a type of person who is reform-oriented and diplomatic. You are cheerful, positive, and tactful in dealing with people. You enjoy interacting with a large number of people. You are keen to learn by keeping abreast of the latest information. You use leadership and are interested in pioneering new areas of work. Suitable jobs: Management, Sales, Consultant

As the last part of the competence tests, I had a 10-minute chat over the phone with a native English speaker who was responsible for checking my speaking English. After that, the woman who interviewed me was back in my booth and seemed pleased with the result of my tests. She told me that she would immediately transfer my registration report to the sales department where a relevant person would then contact me about the job. Before leaving the small, stuffy booth where I stayed two and an half hours, I had to fill in a feedback survey. When I finally left the registration centre with an A *sha*'s paper bag full of leaflets, guidebooks and small gifts, it was already 4pm – a total of three hours for the entire registration session.

The next day a salesman did ring me up, saying apologetically that the job I applied for had already been secured by an applicant from one of A *sha*'s competitors. He added that it was quite common that the client firm approached several *haken* at the same time in order to find the most appropriate person for the job. He assured me that they had all my registration details and would contact me as soon as other suitable jobs became available.

Although I didn't get the job I initially applied for, the registration enabled me to log into A *sha*'s website, making it easy to apply for other jobs – it was actually through A *sha* that I embarked on my first *haken* job. My later registrations with B *sha* and C *sha*, which were A *sha*'s major competitors, had similar processes, but neither had the English-speaking skill test. Compared to large agencies, registration with mid-size and small agencies was more relaxed and less time-consuming. D *sha*, whose major business focus was on the attraction of people with IT engineering qualifications, only required registrants to bring ID documents and fill in several forms; there were no individual interviews and competence tests. Probably due to D *sha*'s occupational specialisation, its registration session was dominated by young men; the ratio of female to male registrants was around 1:10 whereas other agencies' registrations were the other way around.

I personally enjoyed the registration with the smallest agency, E *sha*, which took place in a small office. Unlike other sessions which were organised in groups, I was the only registrant on the day supervised by an E *sha*'s female part-timer. After filling in a two-page form and a short interview, I ended up having a long chat with the woman who had a family history straddling Japan and China and was curious about my background. By the time when I registered with the last agency, F *sha*, in the hope of getting my second *haken* job in F *sha*'s parent company, Vision, I had become a veteran who could casually walk into a registration centre without any preparation.

Interviews with client firms

Being registered with several *haken* agencies is only the first step towards potential job assignments. It usually takes some time to come across a job opportunity that meets the requirements of both the candidate and the agency. Before approaching the client firm on its registrant's behalf, the agency will make sure that he or she fully understands a potential job opportunity and is committed to attending the subsequent interview at the request of the client firm. This prior arrangement, however, could be easily thwarted by the fact, as I mentioned earlier, that the client firm frequently relies on multiple agencies to select the most suitable person. There are two resulting consequences: one is that the vacancy has already been filled, of which not all the contending agencies is informed; the second is that the client firm may reject the recommended candidate based on the candidate's CV sent by the agency. If the candidate is successful in passing the first CV screening, then the next step is to be interviewed by the client firm, often in competition with other shortlisted candidates mediated by different agencies.

The selecting practice on the part of the client firm is, however, illegal – a fact that I didn't know until I finished my fieldwork and that I believe many of my fellow *haken* workers were unaware of. The law doesn't allow the client firm to select *haken* workers by requesting CVs, let alone holding a round of interviews. The main aim of such prohibition is to prevent employment discrimination on the grounds of gender, age and race. Violations can be reported to the regional government labour bureau, which under the aegis of MHLW is responsible for investigating allegations and issuing the law-breaking firms a 'Rectifying Advice Sheet' (*Zesei Shidō Hyō*). In retrospect, I realised that the agencies never used the exact term of 'interview' (*mensetsu*); instead they came up with a number of alternative indigenous expressions such as 'face-to-face meeting' (*kao awase*) and or 'a tour around the firm' (*kaisha kengaku*). The defensive view on the part of *haken* agencies is that the ban on 'ex-ante interviews' (*jizen mensetsu*) is not necessary and should be repealed, as JASSA, the Japanese employer organisation of *haken* agencies, states (2006a):

- For a renewable *haken* assignment, ex-ante interviews should be allowed if demanded by both or either of the client firm and the job candidate.

- Ex-ante interviews are used to confirm the job candidate's aptitude and ability.
- Ex-ante interviews must be carried out in accordance with the prevention of sex/age discrimination, plural candidates by a single agency, and individual data leakage.
- Ex-ante interviews do not in any way reduce *haken* agencies' responsibility for matching people to jobs.
- Ex-ante interviews are useful in cases where an objective assessment is difficult to make, thus contributing to the avoidance of mismatch.

Despite being outlawed by *Haken* Law, interviews with client firms are a widely accepted norm in the *haken* industry. According to Charles Weathers (2001: 208), most coordinators and managers of *haken* agencies believe the interviewing process is useful because workers usually want to get a feel for where they might work, and might feel uneasy about walking into a client firm about which they know nothing; some were quoted as saying that interviewing allows both sides to meet, thereby reducing the risk of bad matches. Once an interview schedule is decided, an agency person in the sales department will meet the candidate in advance, usually at the nearby station or the reception area of the client firm, and accompany him or her throughout the interview. At this stage, team spirit is easily established; the agency person will spend 10–30 minutes providing moral support and coaching the candidate on how to deal with certain situations so as to clinch the deal that will benefit both. Once the interview begins, the agency side, although being present, has to depend on the candidate alone to directly interact with the client firm. The interviewing process usually lasts between 30 and 60 minutes and is generally similar, consisting of introduction, answering questions and job explanation – occasionally the candidate might be asked to conduct a short test such as English–Japanese translation if he or she is applying for a bilingual job. After the interview, it normally takes 1–3 days for the result to be confirmed. Sometimes, the client firm hires the candidate on the day shortly after the interview – as in the case of my first *haken* job via A *sha*. However, I also came across a client firm which for some reason couldn't make a decision within a week. The agency person, a confident young man of A *sha*, was clearly annoyed, complaining of the client firm's 'awful' (*hidoi*) and 'unreasonable' (*wake no wakaranai*) personnel management.

During my fieldwork, I had six interviews with various client firms ranging from foreign-affiliated firms to long-established Japanese manufacturers. Among them, three interviews were mediated by E *sha*; unfortunately none of them was successful. E *sha*'s president Mr. Yamaguchi, who was also responsible for sales, went to those interviews with me. Because of its small size, E *sha* didn't have a rich client base and it introduced mainly clerical or secretarial jobs (*jimukei*) – which constitute a staple part of *haken* work. There were indeed very few jobs to choose from; Mr. Yamaguchi rang me up whenever a new job became available. Compared with top player such as A *sha*, B *sha* and C *sha*, E *sha* was clearly at a disadvantage; not only did it lack job varieties to attract registrants, it was also in need of a well-established reputation that would play an important role in convincing client firms that its candidates were more rigorously selected and thus more reliable than others. Nevertheless, Mr. Yamaguchi, who was a cheerful middle-aged man, remained optimistic about his business:

> I quit my salaryman life and started my own business five years ago. There is no point in staying in a Japanese company with security but without enjoying yourself. I am glad I did take the plunge. ... The *haken* business is not new; it has been around for a quite long time. But it is true that there are more competitors now than before. My agency firm has been making steady, if not rapid, progress and I am very hopeful about its future. ... I spend most of my time visiting client firms and building up connections so as to secure more jobs. And I am really grateful to my part-time staff who are working as hard as I am. I should turn them into regular staff as soon as possible, perhaps some time next year.

It was a shame that we had three consecutive failed interviews – Mr. Yamaguchi bought me a coffee every time after the interview. In the first two interviews, I was rejected by the client firm. The failure for the third time, however, was partly because I decided to withdraw immediately after the interview, which was a truly memorable experience. The third interview was for a secretarial job in a mid-size manufacturer which required the *haken* to assist a female senior executive, who was said to be the most powerful person in the firm, in day-to-day office tasks such as filing, making documents and phone calls, and a small amount of English or Chinese translation. Given the nature of the job, I was astonished by the number of representatives from the client firm at the interview: there were eight people including various levels of managers and the female executive herself, each of whom asked me a couple of questions. Mr. Yamaguchi, who was sitting next to me, kept his head low throughout; he seemed to be much more nervous than I was. During the first half of the interview, I answered questions with ease, thinking that I might be getting the job this time. But things took a sudden turn for the worse when the female executive started to grill me about my motivation and commitment, as she put it:

> I can't understand. Shouldn't you look for more 'serious' (*mattō na*) jobs that you could make good use of your education and experience than this? Why do you choose *haken*? ... I have to warn you that this is a very low-profile job and I do not like the person for this position to be 'obtrusive' (*deshabari*). ... Are you married? Do you have children? ... This job requires considerable commitment and sometimes you have to work overtime. This is not a kind of job you can play around. And how long can you work for us? It would be very troubling to us if you quit after two or three months.

As the female boss continued to ask questions that took me by surprise, I stumbled over my words a couple of times. When the interview finally ended, both

Mr. Yamaguchi and I felt so relieved. Perhaps for fear of being bullied by the future boss, I told Mr. Yamaguchi on the way home that I had to withdraw even if the client firm decided to offer me the job. Mr. Yamaguchi didn't seem to be very surprised, commenting that:

> What a horrible 'battleaxe' (*gamigami onna*)! I couldn't believe what she just said. This is beyond common sense; I haven't met this kind of situation since I started my own *haken* business. *Haken* employment is designed to work short-term, usually on a renewable three-month contract; of course, there are variations depending on the compatibility between the *haken* worker and the client firm. How could they expect *haken* to work very long for them? They'd better hire a regular employee instead!

In describing the interview process and the relatively long assessment involved in *haken* employment, Charles Weathers (2001: 209) argues that Japanese employers play less emphasis on short-term flexibility than American employers in hiring agency workers; while American workers are frequently under pressure to be able to report to assignments on very short notice, in Japan it generally takes 7–10 days to get a *haken* into a job after it is posted. From *haken* workers' point of view, as many of my informants remarked, the whole process was not only time-consuming but also fraught with frustration; few would relish the prospect of going through several interviews and ending up with nothing.

Working inside client firms

I eventually succeeded in passing other interviews and secured my first *haken* job through A *sha* and second through F *sha*. A *sha*'s assignment was concerned with an Indian-Japanese joint IT project which required me to work inside a major Japanese finance firm, Miracle. My responsibilities included communication and coordination between Indian and Japanese teams. I stayed with Miracle for a trial period of one and a half months before declining a renewable three-month contract. This was followed by a marketing research job in Vision, a well-known Japanese manufacturing conglomerate, which was assigned by F *sha*, one of Vision's internal or in-house agencies. I worked inside Vision for a two-month trial period plus a three-month contract. As with the first job at Miracle, I decided to leave before being offered another contract by Vision – I was told that many Vision's *haken* were working on a one-year contract following an initial three-month contract. Both jobs were relatively well paid, compared to an average hourly wage of between 1,200 and 1,500 yen for office clerical or secretarial jobs (*jimukei*). Probably because Miracle's project was involved in finance and IT software, A *sha*'s pay was about one-third higher than that of F *sha*. Both Miracle and Vision are brand names in their respective financial and manufacturing industries; Vision, in particular, has earned a worldwide reputation for its electrical and high-tech products. The two groups of fellow *haken* workers I met in each firm exhibited quite contrasting features; while every *haken* in Miracle was fluent in

English and some had very impressive work experience across a number of industries, those in Vision were more or less the rank and file of the *haken* worker force, that is, clerical or secretarial workers. Overall, female *haken* in their 20s and 30s were in the majority; I only interacted with two young male *haken* while working inside Vision.

In her account of the changing face of Japanese retail, Louella Matsunaga (2000) provides an intimate look at employment in retail and service industries by focusing on a case study of a retail company where a large proportion of its employees are female part-timers. It is widely acknowledged that most, if not all, sectors are affected by a structural change in employment practices, which has resulted in the growing ratio of non-regular/periphery to regular/core workers. The developments in retail and restaurant industries are particularly striking, as evidenced by the widespread phenomenon of 'core part-timers' or 'pseudo-part-timers' – non-regular employees who are classified as part-timers but work about the same number of hours as full-time employees (Keizer 2007). In other words, for those industries the line of demarcation between core and periphery workers doesn't coincide with that between regular and non-regular workers. Moreover, the importance and character of non-regular employment differs considerably among different sizes of companies. For instance, the rise in non-regular employment was less drastic in such big firms as Miracle and Vision, which continued to depend on regular employment. However, it is in those typical Japanese companies that white-collar *haken* workers tend to assume great importance in public discourse, who are increasingly replacing regular (female) workers allocated in the 'auxiliary employment track' (*ippanshoku*), as opposed to the 'general or comprehensive employment track' (*sōgōshoku*) which leads to positions in management and is very much a male domain (Keizer 2007). With the ideal of life-time employment coming under considerable strain over the post-bubble years, the prevalence and expansion of *haken* has attracted widespread attention in the Japanese mass media (see Chapter 5). The emergence of *haken* has raised important questions about the post-war 'firm-as-family' ideology, the changing Japanese company and the notion of meaningful work in today's Japan (see Chapter 6).

Everyday life inside the Japanese company is a well-documented subject. There is an enormous literature ranging from earlier ethnographic writings of Vogel (1963), Nakane (1970), Dore (1973), Rohlen (1974) and Clark (1979) to more recent accounts of Kondo (1990), Hamabata (1990), Ogasawa (1998) and Graham (2003, 2004) – to name but a few. Despite variations in understanding, what becomes irrefutable is that the company-family analogy is a constantly evolving construct subject to the changing politic economy in Japan; it is in essence an invented powerful ideal that impinges on people's perceptions, but hardly reflects the complexity of everyday practice. As Louella Matsunaga puts it (2000: 8):

> The idea of the Japanese company as community thus appears problematic for two principle reasons. First, the boundaries of the corporate community are not fixed, and second the company means different things to different people. … The company's public face, at least in certain contexts, will tend

to show the company in simple terms – the ideal, or normative, model of Japanese company life. From this viewpoint, the idea of the company as a bounded community may seem unproblematic. However, the private face shows a more complex and varied picture. This also accords well with the important emic categories in Japan of inside and outside (*uchi* and *soto*), and the linked pairs of *honne* (how things 'really' are – the unofficial and private realm) and *tatemae* (how things are supposed to be – the official or public realm), and *ura* (backstage – that which lies beneath the surface) and *omote* (surface)…

In the case of *haken*, the difference between the public face and the private face can be recast as that between the production and the consumption of political and commercial discourses regarding *haken*. It is, therefore, imperative to investigate both the shifting construction of the company–employee relationship at the macro-level of the society and the narratives and realties of *haken* workers at the micro-level of the individual. Those issues and their theoretical implications are addressed in the following chapters. Here I shall focus on some specific aspects that concern *haken* workers most when working on job assignments inside the client firms.

What struck me as particularly interesting from my own experience was concerned with the differentiation and relationship between *haken* and regular employees. To outsiders, it was difficult to tell *haken* from regular workers as neither initial introduction sessions nor physical appearance, such as outfits and ID cards worn around the neck, could provide obvious clues to the employment status of workers. Within Miracle and Vision, at first glance, *haken* workers blended in with their regular counterparts in fairly invisible ways. The identification of people's employment status usually was not an easy topic to bring up in everyday conversation. This was particularly true when I was working in Vision where the atmosphere at the office was sometimes very tense. However, there was a simple method of finding the truth: everybody was given an organisational seat chart which showed all employees' name, position, extension number and 'belonging' (*shozoku*). The belonging part was indicated by various abbreviations, but it didn't take me a long time to figure out their meanings. There were approximately 100 people at the open, gigantic office where I was working and about ten people – two of them were male – were dispatched by several different *haken* agencies including both internal and external ones. By contrast, the differentiation between *haken* and regular workers was more easily made at Miracle's relatively smaller office: all female workers were *haken*. Perhaps due to the fact that Miracle's job was concerned with a cross-border project between Japanese and Indian teams, issues about *haken* employment were sometimes openly discussed among *haken* workers even during the office hours.

The relationship between *haken* and non-regular employees at both Miracle and Vision was not as 'dramatic' as, for example, depicted in the popular drama *Haken's Dignity* in which the heroine Haruko, a super *haken* with extraordinary skills and high devotion to her work, saves the client firm from all kinds of disaster in every sequel and yet often comes into conflict with regular workers who are not only unproductive but also hostile towards *haken* workers. On the contrary, the majority of my fellow *haken* workers tried to fit in with regular workers; for some this meant finding a tactful way of avoiding trouble even though they were lukewarm about establishing camaraderie in the client firm. Only on one occasion, a female *haken* at Miracle had a quarrel with a Japanese manager in front of everyone at the office, which was quite unusual. The *haken*–regular relationship at Vision was kept relatively a low-profile matter; in my observation, it was often overshadowed by gender,[2] a more noticeable controlling force than employment status. Vision's workforce was characterised by a predominance of male workers; the ratio of men to women, all included, stood at 9:1. From the first day, I was introduced into a female lunch group which was comprised of both regular and *haken* workers aged between twenties and fifties. Vision's office workers didn't normally go to lunch in mixed-sex groups; some commented that men's eating habits were naturally dissonant with those of women. Thanks to the lunch group, I quickly established a close rapport with other members. Some were very responsive to my questions concerning the difference between regular and *haken* workers within the firm, although much of our conversation focused on gossip about male workers, out-of-office activities, family stories and TV programmes.

As with employment status, gender is an important element that bears on everyday life of *haken* workers. Female non-regular workers in Japan are said to be particularly vulnerable to sexual harassment in the workplace, over and above discrimination on the basis of gender and age that often affects their employability (Weathers 2001; Rebick 2005). Amid recent public interest in Japan's gap-widening society that brings non-regular workers' predicament to the fore, topics regarding *haken* have been eagerly seized upon by the mass media (see Chapter 5). For example, an article in *Yomiuri Weekly* (27 January, 2008) features a number of problems faced by female *haken*, especially 'sexual harassment' (*seku hara*) and 'power harassment' (*pawā hara*) – an English word coined in Japan which refers to bullying behaviour or tactics by superiors and bosses in the workplace. During my *haken* work at Miracle and Vision, I didn't come cross any incidents that could be classified as sexual or power harassment. Vision was especially sensitised to such easily-hitting-the-headlines problems; on my first day, I was asked to read carefully two pieces of paper which contained preventive measures and guidance on how to deal with sexual or power harassment as well as law-breaking acts in the workplace. There were several occasions where a male manager at Vision was not friendly towards a male *haken* who asked him for help, but the manager was not kind to his regular subordinates either. Neither Miracle nor Vision required uniforms for either sex; a business casual code applied to most of the workers. The day-to-day working environment also showed some signs of relaxation in terms of hierarchical relations, which was most noticeable in the interaction between men and women. For example, elite young men at Vision including some senior managers in their 30s and 40s were very gentlemanly towards women, perhaps because many of them had international education background or extensive experience of working abroad. Some practiced the 'ladies first' principle to perfection;

others used carefully chosen polite words when conversing with women regardless of rank, employment status and age.

I surmise that it might be easier for sexual harassment to take place during after-work 'drinking sessions' (*nomikai*); I was once slightly annoyed by a drunken male employee at a Vision's dinner party. But, the after-work enforced socialisation (*tsukiai*) had decreased significantly during the past decade. Some Vision's sections only had group activities once or twice throughout the year; more and more people tended to socialise with their friends in contexts that were unrelated with work. Besides, compared to the regular members of client firms, *haken* workers under the distinct triangular employment relationship were less obligated to attend drinking parties and thus were more unlikely to be frowned upon when declining invitations. A dinner party plus drinking sessions in Tokyo cost around 10,000 yen a night; it was understandable why some *haken* workers at Vision tended to avoid such extra expenses, given their relatively low level of average earnings and benefits.

All in all, *haken*'s human relations in the workplace didn't stand out as a conspicuous matter during my fieldwork. In the case of Vision, this had something to do with diminishing communications among regular workers. I was surprised to find that some didn't even know each other's name, let alone making conversation, despite the fact that they had been sitting at the same office – for some virtually a few metres away – for years. An interesting episode pertinent to this was that when a regular employee was performing an induction ritual,[3] introducing a newly recruited *haken* to a neighbouring section, he added at the end in a self-mocking tone:

> By the way, I probably should have introduced myself first. I am really sorry that I haven't been known to many of you for a long time. My name is …

This brought about a sudden burst of laughter around the office. The indifference to other sections' business and people, according to a regular worker sitting opposite my desk, was quite prevalent among the younger generation of self-motivated individuals who adopted what he described as 'an American style of working'. The same trend was also reflected in the assertive behaviour of some *haken* workers at Vision. A young female *haken* in her 20s who was working in an accounting section was indifferent to human relations surrounding her and was rarely distracted from her work by others' whispering. I remember a time when two male superiors from other sections came to her and asked politely for help, she didn't even raise her eyes from her computer and refused abruptly, saying that she was too busy to look into their business matter. The two men were left standing there awkwardly with a bitter smile.

Nevertheless, it would be indeed erroneous to assume that the majority of *haken* workers could afford to be nonconformist without constraint when working inside the client firm. Some of my fellow *haken* workers, especially those in Vision who were responsible for office back-up work, did suffer from stress because of heavy workloads or troubles with getting along with colleagues and superiors. One possible remedy was to consult with the *haken* agency whose intermediary role could sometimes make a difference. It is incumbent upon the *haken* agency, which acts as the primary employer, to deal with work-related problems affecting their *haken* workers and negotiate with the client firm on their behalf, whether it be complaints about human relations or requirement of a pay rise. From my own experience, *haken* workers were encouraged to report any problems to their agency's coordinators; both A *sha* and F *sha* showed a willingness to listen to my feedback on the client firm's working conditions. In a sense, the triangular employment system makes it easier for *haken* workers to air their grievances against the client firm, although the end result could vary considerably, depending on the individual case and the bargaining power of the *haken* agency. Some critics point out that the *Haken* Law doesn't clarify the responsibilities of either *haken* agencies or client firms for *haken* workers, leaving them vulnerable to harassment and arbitrary firings (Weathers 2001: 209). The issue concerning the dual-employer responsibilities assumes greater significance when it comes to workers' remuneration and benefits and contract renewal or termination, to which I now turn.

Contract renewal or termination

Along with the nature of job assignments and client firms, the choice of *haken* agencies sometimes has a noticeable effect on *haken* worker's well-being. For example, the hourly wage of Miracle's female *haken* workers differs from agency to agency, despite the fact that we all played a same role in the same project. According to one of A *sha*'s rules, *haken* workers should refrain from revealing their hourly pay to either the client firm or other agencies' *haken* co-workers in the same workplace.[4] Perhaps more importantly, large *haken* agencies not only have a rich variety of job opportunities but also offer various training opportunities, for example, free seminars or classes and partial sponsorship of courses for a specific qualification, which are designed to help their registrants improve employability. Small and mid-size *haken* agencies, however, focus mainly on dispatch services, which lack variety in job categories. The difference among *haken* agencies themselves also has pertinence to legal compliance with the law concerning *haken* workers' welfare; not all *haken* agencies are devoted to having their workers join the prescribed insurance and pension schemes. In an attempt to rectify the situation, JASSA (2008) states:

> The *haken* industry must follow procedures for employment insurance and social insurance (health and welfare pension) relevant to the eligible *haken* workers. Needless to say, workers' accident compensation insurance applies to everyone. Because of *haken*'s diversified working conditions and labour mobility that result in a large quantity of complicated processes pertaining to acquisition and loss, the enrolment level has not reached 100%, to our disappointment. However, in order to ensure *haken* workers' safety net that contributes to their life stability, it is the *haken* industry's obligation to maintain an ever-near 100% enrolment rate.

It is evident that the majority of *haken* workers do not have bonuses, travel allowances and other benefits that are available to regular workers and that the coverage of basic insurance schemes is short of universal (Weathers 2001: 215). Moreover, my fieldwork experience suggests that there were discrepancies as to when *haken* workers began to receive insurance benefits. While A *sha* didn't have me join the employment and social insurance schemes during the first trial period, F *sha* required me to join all the mandatory schemes from the first day of my job assignment at Vision, which seemed to be exceptional within the *haken* industry. A well-informed young woman at Miracle who had a wide range of *haken* experiences once mentioned that:

> Every time we shift to a new *haken* job, we have to re-enrol in the insurance systems. To make matters worse, the re-enrolment won't take place until we finish the initial trial period which lasts between half a month and two months. *Haken* agencies, as well as client firms, are making good profits out of those non-protection periods at the expense of our interests.

Another phenomenon that is peculiar to the *haken* industry is the existence of internal or in-house agencies, such as F *sha*, as opposed to external or independent agencies. Since the legalisation of *haken*, many Japanese conglomerates have set up their internal agencies, which dispatch workers mostly within the network of their own 'group companies' (*keiretsu gaisha*) including subsidiaries or subcontractors. In the past, similar practices fell within the remit of internal labour arrangements by firms, known as different names such as *shukkō* and *ukeoi* which contributed to the uneven application of life-time employment (see Chapter 4). In recent years, large Japanese firms' in-house *haken* agencies have been involved in a number of corporate scandals in connection with illegal labour supply. A government research panel stresses that the in-house agencies are also used as a means of cutting down the regular workforce as firms frequently have regular workers retire before being rehired as workers of an internal agency at lower wages (*The Japan Times* 30 July 2008; *Nikkei* 29 July 2008). For *haken* workers, however, this new corporate strategy has a profound impact on their chance of being directly employed as regular workers by client firms.

The contract renewal of *haken* employment normally occurs on a three-month basis. The *Haken* Law stipulates that client firms are 'obligated' to offer regular employment status to *haken* workers who have worked on the same job assignment for three consecutive years – with some exceptions for a few specialised occupations such as engineering and interpretation which are allowed longer length of contract terms. Yet, there are various ways of circumventing the obligation. Two practices are particularly prevalent among client firms; one is to simply alter the job's title so as to make it look like a different *haken* job and the other is to move the *haken* worker to different divisions or branches within the client firm before the obligation of direct employment comes into effect

(Kadokura 2007). Both are more easily to take place in large Japanese firm such as Vision, which utilise in-house *haken* agencies as a better substitute for previous internal labour arrangements, since *haken* workers can be released rapidly in response to business fluctuations. I met some *haken* workers who had been working within various parts of the wide Vision network for as long as 8 years; like many long-serving, veteran part-timers (Matsunaga 2000), they were a kind of long-term non-regular worker, who played a vital part in corporate policies on flexible and low-cost personnel management but were vulnerable to forced dismissal.

Termination by client firms before the expiry of a contract is not unusual in the *haken* industry.[5] In principle client firms are required to provide one month's notice of dismissal to workers or to pay one month's wages to prematurely terminated workers, but they can avoid doing so by justifying the dismissal such that the *haken* worker's skills are not commensurate with the position (Weathers 2001: 212). The contract I signed with F *sha* regarding the job assignment at Vision wrote that if the assignment was terminated due to the circumstances of the client firm, then the client firm had 'an obligation' to find alternative assignments for the *haken* worker concerned. It should be noted that Vision had a high-profile reputation in Japan for its commitment of corporate social responsibility. I was frequently told that Vision and its internal agencies were more *haken*-friendly than other firms and agencies. Not only did F *sha*, which was located inside the Vision's high-rise building where I worked, allow its *haken* workers to use Vision's cafeterias and some health facilities and holiday resorts at reduced prices, it also offered paid holidays under certain conditions. However, the other side of the coin was perhaps more striking. There was a civil group organised by Vision's present and former workers whose cause was to promote human rights in the workplace and protest against unfair treatment of workers especially *haken* and other non-regular workers. The civil group regularly held demonstrations near Vision's workplaces in Tokyo and nearby cities, distributing fliers that revealed various scandals inside Vision and other large Japanese firms, for example, unjustified dismissal, illegal dispatch and management exploitation. Because of their non-regular employment status, *haken* workers are not entitled to join corporate unions which commit themselves mainly to the job security of regular workers. Hence, the protection of non-regular workers depends much on alternative voice mechanisms such as civil societies, NGO groups and new forms of unions such as Japan Community Union Federation (JCUF, *Zenkoku Yunion*).[6]

Contract renewal or termination is of course not solely controlled by client firms. *Haken* workers have a right of their own to decide whether the job assignment and the client firm are suitable for them. Among my fellow *haken* workers, there were more cases of early quitting or refusal of contract renewal than those of contract terminations by client firms. Individual reasons were extremely complex and varied (see Chapter 6); for example, some were bored with the current unfulfilling job and moved onto the better ones while others were disappointed by the client firm's working conditions or human relations. Many of us, however, shared a view that quitting was made easier because of the intermediary of *haken* agencies which were answerable to client firms for their *haken* workers' actions and decisions.

Conclusion

From registrations with *haken* agencies and interviews with client firms to the undertaking and termination of a job assignment, *haken*'s triangular employment relationship is not as simple as it might appear to be at first glance. For many of my fellow *haken* workers, the process of securing a favourite *haken* job was often time-consuming and frustration-laden. Moreover, the *haken* industry is fraught with problems, despite its rapid expansion. The ambiguous regulatory framework, combined with the lax enforcement, has resulted in a widely observed gap between official prohibitions and customary practices. Such a gap is likely to put *haken* workers at a disadvantage, not least when it comes to employment equality, insurance and pension benefits, transformation to regular employment and dismissal.

My fieldwork experience provides some clues to the understanding of the intermediary role of *haken* agencies, which not only distinguishes *haken* workers from other long-standing non-regular arrangements, but also has significant implications for the changing Japanese firm, as well as social norms that guide human relations in the workplace. With their growing importance and expertise in dealing with various personnel issues, leading *haken* agencies are developing strategies and operations that could reshape client firms' human resources management and workers' career patterns. By purporting to connect the paired parties in mutually beneficial ways, *haken* agencies act as the key actor of the tripartite *haken* employment, which has a powerful impact on the transformation of the notion of meaningful work and the ideal worker in contemporary Japan.

4   *Haken* in historical perspective

Introduction

Chapter 2 has profiled *haken* as a new breed of non-regular workers and as a fast-growing industry, with the view to highlighting some specific features which distinguish *haken* from other categories of non-regular workers/work in contemporary Japan. This is followed by Chapter 3, which has turned to an empirical delineation of *haken*'s triangular employment relationship by drawing on my fieldwork experience of working as a *haken* in Tokyo in 2007. To complete *haken*'s general background, this chapter sets out to chart the diachrony of *haken*, examining the changing state policy on labour over a relatively long period of time primarily in post-war Japan. The purpose is to provide a broader context in which to explore how and why the generalised private labour-leasing business has been legitimised and endorsed as a useful non-regular labour force supplemental to the nation's core salaried workers. Beginning with *haken*'s pre-legalisation forms tainted with feudal exploitation and illegal activities, the chapter focuses on forces of both stability and change taking place in the process of legalising *haken*, as well as the articulation of *haken*'s developmental dynamics with large-scale globalising processes.

Haken's development in national legislation

Beneath the patina of glamour in its revamped contemporary form, *haken* employment is associated with a murky past from which it has only recently begun to detach itself. The prototype of *haken* employment can be traced back to the late nineteenth century when the senior members of Meiji working-class society called *oyakata* or labour masters, rose as a much-needed solution to firm owners' frustration caused by workers' travelling and frequent job-switching customs. Like *haken* agencies in today's Japan, *oyakata* acted as an intermediary who organised workers and sent them to work for firms. As Andrew Gordon (1985: 36) describes:

> The oyakata were a varied lot. Some owned small machine shops or shipyards, some were independent labor bosses who would contract the services of their charges to various companies, some were labor bosses providing men

exclusively for a particularly large factory, and some were just powerful fore-men, unable to intervene between company and worker to the extent of set-ting work contracts but able, nonetheless, to exercise independent authority over hiring and wage decisions. Oyakata of all types were important. They exercised some control over wage payment to the workers, either through distribution of contract fees or by setting the rate at which the company was to pay each worker. They served to some extent as employers, either hiring their own apprentices and subordinate laborers or making hiring decisions on behalf of the company. They had some responsibility for the training of apprentices or new workers. The oyakata all occupied positions of more or less independence between the company and the rest of the workers.

By the early 1900s, a growing number of *oyakata* became more closely associated with a particular company and companies increasingly replaced *oyakata* with shop-floor foremen who were integrated into a management control system (ibid.: 37–46). Such a shift during the Meiji modernisation coincided with the beginning of a new era of industrial relationship where management took measures to draw mobile workers into a stable, direct and dependent relationship with a firm. Workers were promised a package of enticements including retirement or sever-ance compensation, tenure-related pay and bonuses and company-specific training and welfare benefits. In tandem with those incentives, the Japanese kinship values such as loyalty and benevolence were evoked to construct a new ideology later known as the Japanese firm-as-family model of management, which was used to keep workers loyal and counter union-led labour unrest (Clark 1979; Fruin 1980). This paved the way for the maturation of the so-called three pillars or jewels of Japanese firms: lifetime employment (*shūshin koyō*), seniority-based promotion/ remuneration (*nenkō jyoretsu*) and company unionism (*kigyō kumiai*).

It should be noted that the newly created employment principles, often embod-ied in the Japanese salaryman, carried on a key element similar to that of the labour-leasing business handled by *oyakata*, that is, 'the quasi-parent–children relationship' (*oyabun-kobun kankei*). Both controlling systems flourished by drawing on the fundamental values of the Japanese traditional family system called *ie*, which placed an emphasis on the benevolence of parents/masters vis-à-vis the loyalty of children/subordinates. Yet, while the Japanese firm was transformed into the Japanese family writ large for its employees, *oyakata* became a target for a lot of criticism in connection with the abusive use of the dependent quasi-kin relationship. As Imai Jun (2004: 2–3) records, labourers under the authority of labour masters during the feudal era suffered from exploitation and they were commonly engaged in the lowest rank of manual jobs in industries such as con-struction, mining and transportation which had poor working conditions (also see Takanashi 2001; Goka 1999; Yoroi, Wakita and Goka 2001). In stark contrast to *haken*'s popularity and fashionable images in today's Japan, the private labour-leasing business prior to the post-war legalisation was riddled with unsavoury narratives in which *oyakata* were often portrayed as manipulative villains, preying on the disadvantaged.

There was a surge of interest in the legislation of labour during the interwar period as Japan's capitalistic economy made marked progress (Dean 2002: 104). Yet, it was only after Second World War when Japan ushered in democratising reforms under the American occupation forces that fundamental changes took place in labour laws. The *oyakata*-mediated labour activities were condemned as remnants of a feudalistic past that were out of tune with democratic principles. Important labour laws such as Employment Security Law (*Shokugyō Antei Hō*) were enacted in 1947, which prohibited temporary labour dispatch as well as private job placement.[1] Instead, the state was to shoulder the major responsibility for job placement services. During Japan's double-digit economic growth from around 1950s until the Oil Shock in the 1970s, the government employment institution called *Shokugyō antei jo* played an important role in placing workers and school leavers in rapidly industrialised industries and regions across the nation (Kariya *et al.* 2000; Ujihara 1989).[2]

Despite being outlawed, private labour-leasing business persisted surreptitiously throughout Japan's post-war economic development in disguised forms that were embedded in customary practices.[3] The situation was in part related to the myth of lifetime employment. As many scholars have pointed out, the label of lifetime employment is misleading since it typically applies to regular employees in large companies, who only account for a small minority of the working population in Japan. Indeed, during and after the high-growth era, it was common for employers to extensively hire external non-regular workers as a means of reducing labour cost. The commitment of Japanese corporate unions to the job security of regular workers also played a part in the facilitation of the trend. In describing the consequence of the job settlement between labour and management, Andrew Gordon (1985: 386–411) writes that many firms hired a substantial number of temporary workers in expansionary periods in the 1950s and 1960s to serve as a buffer protecting the jobs of regular union members who would not tolerate lay-offs.[4] The centrality of job protection within a firm, that is, the prevention of dismissal, in the union movement also enabled managers to retain near total control over job transfers, an effective way of avoiding the cost of firing regular workers (ibid.).[5] *Tenseki* and *shukkō* are two widely observed internal labour adjustments whereby large companies transfer excess regular workers to their subsidiaries and subcontractors known as 'group companies' (*keiretsu gaisha*). While *tenseki* requires the permanent conversion of corporate membership to the transferred firm, *shukkō* allows workers to remain as official members of the original firm. The dual-employer situation of *shukkō* indicates a customary continuity with that of *haken*, although the former is operating within the 'zone' (*ken*) of the Japanese lifetime employment system (Imai 2004: 8, also see Inagami 1989; Hyōdō 1997). During Japan's post-war economic growth, *shukkō* was also used to allocate skilled personnel who could transfer their managerial and technological skills to branch companies, as well as contributing to the downsizing of the workforce. When the government set up a research committee to deliberate on the legalisation of *haken* in the late 1970s, *haken* was often referred to as a variant of *shukkō* and the newly introduced term *haken* or dispatch was to emphasise the special management of relatively skilled or experienced workers (Imai 2004: 7, also see Takanashi 1985, 2001).

Along with the extensive use of non-regular hirings and job transfers, *ukeoi* was another popular measure to reduce labour cost. *Ukeoi* can be translated as subcontracting, a common practice adopted by large companies to outsource tasks to their subcontractors (*shitauke gaisha*). *Ukeoi* workers were normally engaged in low-skilled jobs and were called 'outsiders' (*shagaikō*) by client firms. There are two types of *ukeoi*: 'off-the-premises' (*kōgai*) *ukeoi* and 'on-the-premises' (*kōnai*) *ukeoi*. Off-the-premises *ukeoi* means subcontractors carry out the contract independently and outside the client firm's premises, which is the standard form of subcontracting. By contrast, on-the-premises *ukeoi* means subcontractors send their workers to work inside the client firm's premises, which, to some extent, resemble the pre-war *oyakata*-controlled labour supply, thus often resulting in controversy. To regulate on-the-premises *ukeoi* and prevent it from being used against workers' interests, Labour Standards Law was revised in 1948 to clarify *ukeoi* (Imai 2004: 4):

1   *Ukeoi* firms or subcontractors as business proprietors must assume legal and financial responsibilities.
2   *Ukeoi* firms must instruct and supervise their own workers during the process of completing contracted tasks.
3   *Ukeoi* firms must assume employers' responsibility in compliance with employment regulations.
4   *Ukeoi* firms as business proprietors must possess the necessary facilities, machines and instruments, or use their own specialised procedures/techniques (/competence, added in 1952), to complete contracted tasks. They should not provide only the labour of their workers to client firms.

The need to stimulate the labour market, however, prompted the government in 1952 to add 'competence' or 'experience' (*keiken*) to the above paraphernalia that subcontractors could rely on to carry out contracted tasks. This change, combined with the lax legal enforcement, eventually created conditions where on-the-premises *ukeoi* could easily slip into the outlawed private labour-leasing, since the only differentiation was that *ukeoi* workers were prohibited from taking orders from client firms. The difficulty in detecting violations of the superintendence rule of *ukeoi* workers was one of the important causes of rampant illegal *ukeoi* (Takanashi 2001; Wakita 1995; Goka 1999). However, the problem in the legal framework of *ukeoi* only began to surface after the oil crisis in the 1970s when the government turned to a campaign for 'the rationalisation or downsizing of management' (*genryō keiei*) with the aim of providing incentives for firms to step up their efforts to whittle down the core workforce. In conjunction with job transfers and temporary employment, there was an intensified use of on-the-premises *ukeoi* by Japanese firms, which continued well into the 1990s. As a result, *ukeoi* not only was actively used for manufacturing assembly lines but also diversified into new occupational areas such as building maintenance, information technology and office clerical work (Imai 2004: 9). With the increasing expansion, the gravity of illegal *ukeoi*, which was relatively invisible and largely ignored during the period of rapid economic growth, started to attract the state's attention.

Thus, it was in the post-war form of on-the-premises *ukeoi* that the pre-war *oyakata* sort of labour supply survived, albeit in a surreptitious way. Prior to the government deliberations on the legalisation of *haken*, there was also a new type of business from outside which posed a more direct challenge to the legal ban on the generalised private labour leasing. In 1962, the American worker-dispatching agency, Manpower, opened its first Japanese branch called 'clerical services' (*jimushori sābisu*) and more Japanese firms began to join the same line of business in 1970s (JASSA 2002). The exogenous clerical services, like the indigenous on-the-premises *ukeoi*, thrived by taking advantage of the lax legal regulation; as long as it was the 'service' (*ekimu*), not the 'labour' (*rōdōryoku*), that was contracted and outsourced and workers were not found to be receiving orders from the client firm, both the agency and the client firm would not fall foul of the law. The continuing development of clerical services made office dispatched workers – who became known as '*haken*' instead of 'outsiders' (*shagaikō*) of the client firm – 'a symbolic phenomenon' of illegal labour leasing in Japan (Imai 2004: 9).

Facing the increasing unsustainability of the existing law, the Japanese government launched committees in the late 1970s to review the private labour leasing industry, which led to the first establishment of *Haken* Law in 1986. Under the new law, *haken* employment was allowed for a positive list of 13 relatively skilled and specialised occupations with restricted contract terms. Both the positive list and the term restriction were subsequently revised in line with the state's deregulation policies, which facilitated more rapid growth of *haken*. The 1999 and 2003 revisions were particularly radical. These not only removed most of restrictions but also ended the public monopoly on job placement services (Table 4.1).[6] The drastic liberalisation of *haken* is variously described as a turning point in the Japanese history of labour policy or a clear step towards the creation of an industry for private job placement and personnel services (Suwa 2000; Tsuchida 2000; Imai and Shire 2006). The result of the state's deregulation is indeed striking; the reported number of *haken* soared to 3.21 million in 2006, compared to 1.07 million in 1999, and the industry of *haken* agencies was worth 5.4 trillion yen in turnover in 2006, compared to 1.5 trillion yen in 1999 (see Figure 2.5 in Chapter 2).

From the feudal *oyakata* and the post-war illegalisation to the insidious *ukeoi* and the new legalisation, the historical development is perhaps the least savoury part of *haken*'s public profile in today's Japan. Despite the newly found prominence in the state policy and the mass media, *haken* is still haunted by its past, not least when it comes to the recent 'discovery' of illegal activities under the legal cover of *haken*. The media revelation of a series of high-profile scandals involving big agencies and client firms has drawn widespread condemnation of the mishandling of

Table 4.1 Changes in the legislation of *haken* (1985–2008)

1985	*Haken* Law (*Rōdōsha Haken Hō*), short for Law for Ensuring the Proper Operation of *Haken* Business and Improved Working Conditions for *Haken* Workers (*Rōdōsha Haken Jigyō no Tekisei na Unei no Kakuho oyobi Haken Rōdōsha no Shūgyō Jyōken no Seibi nado ni kansuru Hōritsu*): legalisation establishment for a positive list of 13 designated occupations with a limited contract term of 9 months to 1 year.
1986	July: Enforcement of *Haken* Law.
	October: Revision of *Haken* Law: extension of the positive list from 13 to 16 occupations.
1990	Revision of *Haken* Law: extension of the contract term for all occupations to 1 year.
1994	Revision of *Haken* Law for workers aged 60 and above: replacement of the positive list with a negative or prohibited list of occupations with the contract term up to 1 year in principle.
1996	Revision of *Haken* Law: extension of the positive list from 16 to 26 occupations; enforcement of a special *Haken* Law for workers taking child/family care leave.
1997	Revision of Employment Security Law (*Shokugyō Antei Hō*): relaxation of private job placement regarding occupation restrictions and conditions for the establishment of private firms.
1999	Revision of Labour Standards Law (*Rōdō Kijyun Hō*): legalisation of fixed-term contract work for most specialised occupations with an extended contract term of 3 years.
	Revision of *Haken* Law: replacement of the positive list with a negative or prohibited list; 1 year contract term for newly permitted occupations; extension of the contract term for the existing 26 occupations from 1 to 3 years ; repeal of special measures for elder workers aged 60 and above and workers taking child/family care leave.
	Revision of Employment Security Law: further relaxation of private job placement by removing all occupational restrictions except for jobs in stevedoring and construction areas.
2000	Enforcement of temp-to-perm *haken* (*Shōkai Yotei Haken*).
2002	Enforcement of a special law for workers aged 45 and above (valid until 31 March, 2005): extension of the contract term of *haken* from 1 to 3 years.
2003	Revision of Labour Standards Law: relaxation of fixed-term contract work by extending the contract term to 3 years for project-related work and 5 years for specialised work.
	Revision of *Haken* Law: abolition of the 3-year term restriction for the designated 26 occupations; extension of the term for other newly permitted occupations from 1 to 3 years; lifting of ban on manufacturing assembly lines with a limited term of 1 year; new obligation to directly employ *haken*; lifting of ban on the interview with client firms for temp-to-perm *haken*; lifting of ban on temp-to-perm *haken* in medical services.
	Revision of Employment Security Law: further relaxation of private job placement regarding the establishment of private firms and placement industries.

Continued

2006	Revision of *Haken* Law: lifting of ban on medical services in hospitals or clinics; partial permission of patent solicitors and chartered/certified accountants
2007	Revision of *Haken* Law: extension of the term for manufacturing assembly lines to 3 years.
2008	Revision of *Haken* Law: introduction of a ban on dispatching *haken* on a daily basis or for less than 30-day employment with the exception of 18 specialised occupations; restriction of the ratio of workers dispatched to group firms to below 80 per cent; obligation to reveal the profit margin and turn registered *haken* into employed *haken*; establishment of admonition rules to advice companies in violation of the law pertaining to *haken*'s direct employment.

Source: MHLW (2008), JASSA (2006a), Imai and Shire (2006), Imai (2004).

workers. As a consequence, the general public attitude towards *haken* is quite mixed. On the one hand, the policy-making elite promote contemporary *haken* as an effective means of boosting employment as well as taking up the slack where the 'traditional' style of personnel management fails to cope with new market pressures. On the other, however, there are a number of sceptics who contend that the problem-laden *haken* employment spawns young 'working-poor' and contributes to Japan's widening gaps between regular and non-regular workers (see Chapter 5). Such derogatory terms as 'the leasing of labour' (*ninpukashi*) and 'unscrupulous labour brokers' (*tehaishi*), which evoke exploitative *oyakata*, continue to have wide currency among those who disapprove of or abhor the kind of middleman-mediated labour supply. The fact that *haken* agencies gain profits from commission fees for dispatching workers is often referred to in everyday parlance as pocketing a 'rake-off' (*pinhane*) from hard-working, vulnerable *haken* workers.

The changing Japanese labour policy: continuing and renewed dualities

From the above *haken*'s legislative development, a curious paradox is thrown into relief: *haken* is as much new in the recently acquired legal form as old in the long-lasting customary practices – noticeably, the external hiring of low-skilled non-regular labour (*oyakata* and on-the-premises *ukeoi)* and the internal transfer of regular employees (*shukkō*). At the heart of such a paradox is the role of the state in the formulation and transformation of labour policies which affects the way in which *haken* and other non-regular arrangements are perceived and integrated into everyday life. While the relationship between state and citizenry in different countries shares generic features, it is often said that the state apparatus in Japan has its own peculiar style. Much has been made of the Japanese tripartite establishment: party officials, ministry bureaucrats and business leaders, which is one of the most distinguishing features that set Japan apart from other major democratic nations. The power triumvirate, which underlies the 'meaning construction'

(Just 1992) of Japan's legal and policy-making systems, is eloquently described by Karel van Wolferen (1989: 5):

> No one is ultimately in charge. These semi-autonomous components, each endowed with discretionary powers that undermine the authority of the state, are not represented by any central body that rules the roost.
>
> It is important to distinguish this situation from others where governments are besieged by special interest groups, or unable to make up their minds because of inter-departmental dispute. We are dealing not with lobbies but with a structural phenomenon unaccounted for in the categories of accepted political theory. There is, to be sure, a hierarchy or rather, a complex of hierarchies. But it has no peak; it is a truncated pyramid. There is no supreme institution with ultimate policy-making jurisdiction. Hence, there is no place where, as Harry Truman would have said, the buck stops. In Japan, the buck keeps circulating.

Arguably, this elusive power structure is more effective in making 'policies – and the iron laws they purport to rest upon – often function as a vehicle for distancing policy authors from the intended objects of policy' (Shore and Wright 1997: 11).

To a great degree, the evolving policy pertaining to *haken* and non-regular employment in general reflects the state's shifting discourse on the Japanese lifetime employment system. There is little doubt that non-regular employment has played an indispensable part in Japan's post-war economic development, and that it provides a flexible, disposable and low-cost labour force, functioning as a buffer against economic fluctuations and as a means of propping up regular employment. Indeed, the Japanese style of management is characterised by differential treatment with major fault lines between regular and non-regular workers, between those working for big firms and those working for small and medium-sized firms and between male and female workers. The perceived significance and intensity of non-regular employment, however, vary from time to time, depending on the changing political economy.

Until the end of the 1980s, lifetime employment, one of the key pillars of the Japanese firm-as-family or salaryman model, remained sacrosanct in official rhetoric. Non-regular workers, in spite of their long-serving nature and considerable contribution, were assumed as either 'a floating element of the workforce' (Matsunaga 2000: 174), secondary or supplementary income earners within a male-breadwinner model (Weathers 2001: 223), or, like on-the-premises *ukeoi*, out of place. To a great degree, the enactment of *Haken* Law in 1986 was aimed at curbing rampant illegal worker-dispatch services in order to defend the status quo of regular workers, albeit with some positive evaluations of *haken*'s role in the labour market. It is only during the post-bubble era, especially after the financial crisis in 1997, that the state policy has turned to a new direction of 'deregulation' (*kiseikanwa*) that embraces what is known as a global neoliberal regime which celebrates the withdrawal of state control, 'free-market' logic and individual entrepreneurship. In this connection, we can speak of 'a continuing and renewed duality' in Japanese labour policy (Keizer 2007).

Since the beginning of 1990s, Japan has been mired in a decade-long economic downturn often portrayed as 'the lost decade'. As John Crump (2003: 138) illustrates:

> Not only was Japan's economic performance from 1992 far inferior to its past record, but also it was uncharacteristically outclassed by its principal rivals within world capitalism. ... Whereas in 1974 it was the precipitous rise in the international price of oil that had disrupted the economy, the economic downturn from 1992 was primarily due to the reckless expansion in which many Japanese companies had engaged during the so-called 'bubble' years, 1987–90. ... As a result, the dilemma facing Japanese companies in the 1990s was that they were burdened with a level of productive capacity that was vastly in excess of what the markets could profitably absorb. ... From 1992 successive governments unleashed one fiscal package after another, running into trillions of yen, in an effort to reinvigorate the economy by means of tax reductions and public spending. While this policy had the effect of driving the level of government debt considerably higher than total GDP, it made little impression on the dead weight of overcapacity and failed in its purpose of ending the recession.

Against the background of the protracted sluggish economy, the Japanese government began to address non-regular employment agendas in a more positive and pronounced fashion. As with every kind of economic recession, job loss poses a major threat to the stability of society and thus is a big issue facing the state. To tackle the ever-rising level of unemployment that repeatedly broke post-war records,[7] the Japanese government, as shown in the 1995 Labour White Paper (MOL 1995),[8] mulled over a middle position between the approach of the United States and that of Europe; the former focused on high rates of labour flexibility and job creation which would lead to greater social inequalities, while the latter had relatively stringent labour protection which would cause long-term unemployment for low-skilled workers. Although the need to stimulate external labour markets was acknowledged, central to the government policy was the reinforcement of conventional internal arrangements on the part of firms like *shukkō*, together with public job placement services, as key measures to reduce the number of the jobless. A new twist to this official guidance was that employers turned unemployment and its threat into a potent rhetorical weapon to squeeze workers' wages and create more extensive stratification within the national workforce (Crump 2003: 144–149). *Nikkeiren*,[9] the most powerful employers' organisation, published 'Japanese-style Management for a New Era' (*Shinjidai no Nihon Keiei*) (1995), which proposed a 'flexible firm' model with a 'multi-track' personnel system' (also see Keizer 2007; *Keidanren* 2003). The proposal, which was aimed at limiting long-term security to a shrinking 'aristocracy of labour' and expanding peripheral, flexible strata, divided workers into three tracks (Crump 2003: 148):

1   A core or elite group of workers with secure tenure. This would be comprised of those such as managers, key technicians and workers with accumulated expertise. They would be on permanent contracts and would enjoy a range of benefits, such as generous bonuses, incremental salaries, company pensions and comprehensive welfare provision.
2   An intermediate stratum made up of those equipped with specialist skills which were currently in demand. They would be on fixed-term contracts, would not be provided with pensions and would have access to only limited welfare.
3   'Flexible' workforce. These workers would be on fixed-term contracts, would not be provided with pensions and would be treated as inferiors in various other ways. For example, their pay and welfare entitlements would be worse than those available to the specialist group, let alone the core group, and their wages would not rise incrementally.

The third track was reserved for the majority of non-regular workers including part-timers and *haken*. In spite of this flexible, multi-track model and some headline-grabbing lay-offs as a result of corporate restructuring, the political and economic policy during most of the 1990s acted to maintain the existing employment practices by reducing the number of new regular entrants and maximising the use of non-regular workers – not by making the core workers redundant. The effort to sustain the post-war ideology, however, became attenuated towards the end of the 1990s when Japan's unemployment rates climbed abruptly following the 1997 financial crisis and reached more than 4 per cent in 1998. In the 1999 Labour White Paper, the government for the first time admitted that although Japan's 'long-term employment custom' (*chōki koyō kanrei*) contributed to economic stability and keeping unemployment costs down, it could hinder a swift transformation in the industrial structure. In a similar vein, the government argued that the lifetime system gave workers and firms both advantages and disadvantages, as shown in Table 4.2.

In response to the 'gradual change' (*yuruyaka na henka*) taking place in the lifetime employment, the 1999 Labour White Paper proposed that the development of vocational abilities should be aimed at facilitating workers' 'employability' (*enpuroiabiriti*), rather than merely ensuring their proper function in a specific firm. Close cooperation between public and private job placement services was also necessary to establish efficient and effective labour markets. Such new language and guidelines reflected the state's determination to wrestle with unemployment issues, which eventually prompted the drastic liberalisation of *haken* beginning in 1999.

The revision of *Haken* Law in 1999, which unleashed most of the restrictions on *haken* and private job placement, heralded a new era of labour policies characterised by the slogan of 'deregulation' (*kiseikanwa*). In the process of revising

Table 4.2 The pros and cons of Japan's life-time employment

Firms	Pros	• Long-term vocational development and evaluation • Harmony and mutual trust between management and labour • Information sharing • Corporate belongingness and morale improvement • Flexible in the arrangement and transfer of positions • Cost reduction of recruiting, hiring and training
	Cons	• Potential obstruction in the ability of management and business to adapt to changing economic conditions • Rising cost of the seniority-based pay system because of the ageing population
Workers	Pros	• Life stability associated with employment security • Long-term life planning
	Cons	• Firm-specific vocational abilities unfavourable for re-employment in the case of job changes and redundancies • Long working hours and company centrism • Disadvantageous for female and elderly workers who are likely to be excluded from the long-term employment system

Source: MOL (1999).

haken, frequently invoked were market-oriented neoliberal principles, the intensified global economic competition and the ratification of the ILO (International Labour Organisation) Convention 181 which lifted the ban on private fee-charging employment services in 1997. Another pertinent fact was that the government deregulation committee was dominated by employers; labour unions were only occasionally represented (Imai and Shire 2006). The special deregulation attention *haken* received continued well into the first decade of the twentyfirst century, with further relaxation on occupations and contract terms (see Table 4.1). As a result, *haken* workers, though remaining a minority of the non-regular legion, became by far the fastest-growing group; not only has the number of *haken* workers soared but also the industry of *haken* agencies has grown exponentially over the past few years. At the same time, this deregulation has in turn affected other types of non-regular workers as well; for example, part-timers continued to increase at a much higher rate and were more prevalent across different sections of the population and industries than their counterparts in the United States (Houseman and Osawa 2003).

For Japanese companies, the growing reliance on non-regular employment accelerated by the government deregulation policies corresponded with a kind of paradigm shift in terms of corporate governance. Recent years have seen a surge of interest in corporate reforms, which has led to a burgeoning Japanese literature debating 'the new Japanese company'. The debate is partly inspired by the OECD's principles of corporate governance in 1998, or more generally, the neoliberal flexible, or 'post-bureaucratic', model of business and employment practice emerging from the Anglo-Saxon world, which is purportedly driven by the economic pressures of globalisation and predicated upon an information technology revolution (Aoki *et al.* 2007; Morris *et al.* 2006).[10] Influenced by this neoliberal model, large Japanese firms stepped up their efforts to slim down the core workforce, as well as increasing the salience of international standards (ibid.).

Consequently, the notion of 'lifetime employment' (*shushin koyō*) gradually fell into disuse in favour of 'long-term employment' (*chōki koyō*) or 'regular employment' (*seiki koyō*); seniority-based pay systems were increasingly overshadowed by merit-based or individualised pay systems known as *seikashugi*. With companies moving towards flatter, less hierarchical structures, those with specialised and market-demanding skills were perceived as more valuable than those generalists with firm-specific vocational skills. There was also a shift from the conventional annual hiring of new graduates of the same-age group to more flexible practices including non-regular and mid-career hires. In short, the new emphasis on deregulation brought about palpable changes in corporate human resources management, as well as increased supplies of *haken* and other non-regular workers in accordance with the so-called 'free-market' logic.

Certain qualifications, however, are necessary when it comes to the substantiation of those changes. To be sure, rarely does change occur in isolation from continuity. The enabling nature of state policies and legal reforms may increasingly diversify employment practices and corporate governance patterns, steering Japan to a market-oriented direction that appears to converge with the global or Anglo-Saxon model in format. Yet, as Ronald Dore (2007) points out, when it comes to meaning-interpretation of the format, large differences remain between Japan and other industrialised nations like the United States and United Kingdom; the current period of change that Japan is undergoing can be best understood in terms of emerging 'hybrid' forms that are unlike either the past Japanese model or the current global model. Indeed, many new trends do not exhibit a radical departure from previous practices; for example, the emerging merit-based pay systems which take into account individual performance and skills alongside a host of other factors are carried out by more or less overlaying the seniority-based pay systems with 'incremental modification' (Jackson 2007: 282–309) – the seniority-based pay systems are to some extent sacrificed to protect the all-important lifetime employment (Morris *et al.* 2006). Despite the fact that the number of regular employees has decreased and in some small and mid-sized firms even ceased to be a majority, the discursive power of lifetime employment remains relatively robust.

Closely related to this, as I mentioned earlier, are the extraordinary lengths to which management has gone during the post-bubble era to rely on 'benevolent' forms of downsizing and delayering, that is, internal job transfers and increased use of *haken* and other non-regular workers, rather than outright lay-offs of the existing regular employees of older generations. The effort to salvage the post-war ideology is reflected in the legal framework of *haken* as well. As Noriaki Kojima and Keiko Fujikawa (2003) point out, concerns over the job security of regular workers which would be undermined by *haken* workers are an important element that separates the regulation terms of *haken* in Japan from those in the United States. Careful examination of recent changes in official discourse also suggests that the renewed labour duality characterised by an increased ratio of non-regular to regular workers has been ascribed not only to economic factors but also to diversified individual choices. In the 2007 Labour Economy White Paper, the government featured 'work-life balance', along with a continued emphasis on the importance of maintaining the Japanese long-term employment (MHLW 2007b: 31):

> Companies continue to stress the customary long-term employment that recognises long-term service. Despite the steady development of 'the individualisation of labour relations' (*rōdō kankei kobetsuka*) and the incorporation of performance and ability into the pay systems, the seniority-based curve remains intact. ... And there is no change in the guidelines of corporate human resources management, which combine regular workers regarded as 'core labour' (*chūkakuteki na rōdōsha*) with the active use of non-regular workers. Thus, our country's employment system has reached a new stage where the long-term employment as a fundamental policy coexists with the increasing individualisation of labour relations. Key issues in the future should focus on the realisation of flexible working that will enable each and every worker to strike a good balance between work and life through a variety of combinations and choices.

The rhetorical trappings of 'individualised labour relations' (*rōdō kankei kobetsuka*) in the current labour dualism were further reinforced by the 2008 Labour Economy White Paper. Important issues concerning the Japanese employment practices were presented in a way that purported to sympathise with 'working people's way of thinking' (*hataraku hitobito no ishiki*) (MHLW 2008: 36):

> From a long-term perspective, the direct connection of income systems with workers' motivations should be reconsidered. As our society has accomplished advanced development, people's awareness has shifted from the pursuit of material affluence to the pursuit of 'the richness of mind' (*kokoro no yutakasa*). The issue arising from such a shift is how to encourage people whose work reflects a wide array of individualities. While those who are capable of high performance might wish to be proportionately rewarded by the company, careful consideration should be given to the fact that the success of any kind of work cannot be achieved without the assistance of a number of others. It is expected that the trend towards the clarification of job remit and roles will continue in order to respect the individuality of workers and to promote efficient personnel and career management. Yet, workers' incentives should be created in association with the content of work itself, rather than merely based on the amount of income. Company managers should strive to carry out an enterprise in a working environment where workers 'feel motivated' (*hatarakigai wo kanjiru*). To facilitate the meaning of work, it is of paramount importance to establish a corporate climate conducive to open and frank discussions between labour and management.

This evocation of the old languages such as human interconnectedness, together with the new ones such as 'individuality' (*kosei*) and 'the richness of mind' (*kokoro no yutakasa*), should be understood within a particular context where contemporary Japan is gripped by a heightened sense of social divide – one of the most noticeable by-products of the neoliberal regime (Harvey 2005). By constructing meaningful work in association with non-material pleasure, the government intended to deflect public attention from the controversial divide between regular and non-regular workers, between haves or have-nots, or between winners and losers. In other words, the difference in employment status and income had little to do with one's perception of meaningful work. However, such an imposition has met with resistance from opponents both within and outside the Japanese power triumvirate. To be sure, the process of state policy is by no means neat and lineal; there are complexities, contradictions and discontinuities in the infiltration of ideologies into institutions and practices of everyday life. The following chapters will demonstrate how policies pertaining to *haken* are subject to fragmentation at both the macro-level and the micro-level of discourse.

To summarise, the post-war development of the Japanese employment system is characterised by a continuing and renewed core-peripheral labour duality. The turn to deregulation during the post-bubble era plays a vital role in the liberalisation of *haken* as well as the rapid expansion of non-regular workers as a whole. By unpacking official language in policy documents, we can also discern that the formulation and transformation of labour policies is strongly influenced by the changing political economy in Japan.[11] With *haken* and other modes of non-regular employment being elevated to an increasingly important labour force contributing to the national economy, there has been a shift in the state stance on the traditional lifetime employment.

Haken: a global phenomenon

Despite its specific features that entail contextual exploration, *haken* is not a unique phenomenon in Japan; rather, it bears close resemblance to temporary agency work (TAW) in other industrialised nations. The development of *haken* corresponds with a global trend of employment changes over the past two decades. TAW was practically outlawed across the world during the 1950s, as stipulated by ILO Convention 96 which banned fee-charging private employment agencies. In a similar way to the past of *haken* in Japan, an undercurrent of resentment persisted towards making profits out of the labour-leasing business. However, the somewhat disturbing notion of 'labour as commodity' gradually paled in comparison with the importance of labour flexibility in an increasingly globalised economy. In recognising the role which private employment agencies might play in the functioning of labour markets, ILO Convention 181 lifted the ban on TAW in 1997. Recent years have seen growing acceptance of TAW in many parts of the world; as Chris Forde and Gary Slater (2004: 4) observe, 'from raising initial concerns about job quality and insecurity the expansion of agency work has come to be seen by some as a welcome (and inevitable) development'.

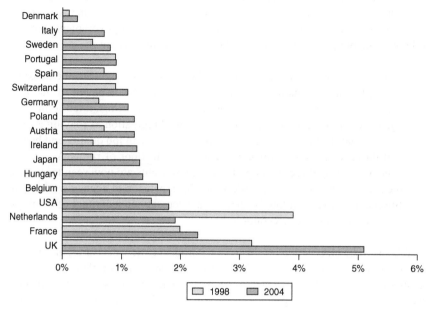

Figure 4.1 The ratio of TAW in total employment (1998 and 2004)[a].

Source: Graaf-Zijl and Berkhout (2007).

Note
[a] The Netherlands is an exception to the rising trend of TAW, which is said to be linked with the specific relationship between GDP and TAW (Graaf-Zijl and Berkhout 2007). The high ratio of TAW in the UK has much to do with the conspicuous lack of legal regulation on both the TAW industry and workers' occupation and length of assignments, as a result of the state reluctance to interfere in the 'free-market' mechanism (see Forde & Slater 2004; Morris 2004).

For example, in Europe, as diversification of the labour market has become the norm, not only is TAW widespread and wide-ranging, but also certain forms of private employment services are allowed, de facto or de jure (Blanpain 2004).

As a result, the TAW industry now virtually exists on all five continents, with the United States, Europe, Japan and Australia making up most of the global turnover (Denys 2004). Rapid expansion has occurred across many industrialised countries, although the proportion of TAW remains relatively small in total employment (Figure 4.1). The situation in the United Kingdom is particularly striking here; between 1992 and 2001 the number of people working through a temporary employment agency increased by some 346 per cent, to stand at 281,000 (Forde and Slater 2003: 7). The same pattern of growth is seen in the United States and Europe as well; while TAW has been characterised as one of the fastest growing sectors in the US economy, its expansion in Europe has extended into both countries where this form of employment has been long-established (such as France and the Netherlands) and countries where the legislation of TAW is newly introduced in the 1990s (such as Spain and Italy) (*ibid.*).

Similarly to *haken* in Japan, state policy regarding labour market regulation was a key element in the development of TAW. Indeed, variation between countries can be largely ascribed to the different ways in which governments see the role of regulation, as Chris Forde and Gary Slater (2004: 4) put it:

> Whilst the British government has tended to view any significant extension of employment rights as a potential fetter on the development of the new economy, recent European Union directives covering fixed-term and agency employment have, in contrast, viewed regulation as playing a supporting role. To be sure, there remains a concern with job quality and hence that these workers are protected by a minimum floor of rights. Yet in the agency working directive in particular, these rights are now seen more as a means to an end, namely to underwrite the expansion of agency working in Europe, an expansion that is seen as the necessary concomitant of employment in the knowledge economy.

Whether it be eliminating legal barriers, introducing new measures, or, like the United Kingdom, minimising the level of regulation, there is little disagreement among governments that the current economic climate requires greater adaptability which TAW is seen to provide. For employers, this means low labour costs, contributing to swift adjustment to changing business conditions. At the same time, however, the rapid expansion of TAW has sparked off oppositional movements which challenge the justifiability of the generalised labour leasing, especially in terms of workers' rights to equal treatment (Blanpain and Graham 2004; EFILWC 2006). It is widely observed that TAW is typically concentrated among the disadvantaged who are forced to engage in temporary assignments as a second choice to permanent work, rather than enjoying the 'freedom' conferred by TAW's flexible forms of working. For example, in the United Kingdom, despite the government's emphasis on the largely voluntary nature of TAW, that is, meeting the demands of particular groups for flexible work, particularly women, youngsters and those with children, only a tiny minority of TAW workers fits the popular description of 'free knowledge worker' in the new, 'knowledge' economy (Forde and Slater 2003: 22, 2004: 9, 12). The general view is that compared to regular or full-time workers, TAW workers are susceptible to employment insecurity, lower pay, fewer benefits and less access to training opportunities. Indeed, TAW remains a contentious issue with which the UK government and the EU employment committee have to grapple (*BBC News*, 22 February, 2008).

In many ways, the trend of TAW in Japan and other major industrialised nations speaks of the proliferating acceptance of 'neoliberalism', a new ideology of political economy often subsumed under the rubric of 'globalisation', as evidenced by the supposed link between TAW and the emergence of a knowledge-based global economy invoked by many governments. A burgeoning academic and popular literature has emerged since the late 1980s, in an attempt to highlight the sweeping transformation wrought by contemporary globalising processes and transnational interconnectedness. Within the discipline of anthropology, to what extent the current globalisation is 'new' forms a major focus for debate. For example, Thomas Eriksen (2003) remarks that many of the issues surrounding today's globalisation do not represent a drastic departure from those raised by earlier generations of anthropologists, although the need to *explicitly* articulate synchronic fieldwork and micro-historic analyses with large-scale processes at the macro-level seems to have gained wide currency in recent years.[12] To be sure, the world has not fundamentally changed as commonly assumed. Yet, in terms of degree of intensity and awareness, the present contrasts sharply with the past; today's globalisation is characterised by 'the dual character' (Eriksen 2007: 4): the intensified transnational or cross-border interconnectedness and the increased awareness of mutual exposure aided by advanced modern information technology – what David Harvey (1989) refers to as 'time-space compression'.

Along with the concept of globalisation, a neoliberal doctrine that celebrates the untrammelled 'free-market' has caused a flurry of excitement. It is worth mentioning that the turn of interest to global capitalist dominance has long been in the making, stimulated particularly by Immanuel Wallerstein's world-system theory (1974). Generally speaking, the world economy has passed through a globalising phase from approximately 1870 to 1914, a relatively deglobalising period from about 1930 to 1980 and a renewed era of globalisation since 1980 in parallel with the rise of neo-liberalism in political–economic practices and thinking (Edelman and Haugerud 2005: 23). The notion of neoliberalism is commonly used to mark a departure from classical liberal philosophy – or 'embedded liberalism' (Harvey 2005) – prior to the Keynesian era during which the 1944 Bretton Woods Agreement endorsed 'the intimate links between state and market' and 'the use of national controls on capital movements' until the early 1970s (ibid. 2005: 16, 17). There are obvious continuities between the two versions of liberalism, noticeably the reductionist modelling of the person anchored to Christianity-informed, rhetorically powerful values including human dignity, freedom and individualism.[13] Nevertheless, under the neoliberal regime the relationship between individual and society is reconstructed so as to fit in with the 'free-market' logic, as Chris Hann (2006: 7) explains:

Neoliberalism means first and foremost the implementation of an open economic logic based on global competition in place of the closed, primarily political logic of the developmental state, of which the socialist states were a major variant. Under contemporary conditions this cannot possibly be a return to pre-Keynesian liberalism. If the ultimate value in classical liberal thought was the liberty of the individual citizen, then under neoliberalism it is the innovative capacity of each individual entrepreneur. Every human being is assumed to think and act as an entrepreneur, with the result that the impersonal laws of the market are drawn into all areas of human capacity. In classic liberalism, property ownership was a marker of status as well as a guarantor of liberty. In the advanced economies of neoliberalism, access to goods and control over them through a proliferation of contracting often becomes more important than ownership per se. Nonetheless, for neoliberals it is axiomatic that making people owners is the best way to give them incentives to work harder and to invest more. An increase in the inequality of wealth distribution is justifiable as the price to be paid for an efficient economy, which is expected to raise the absolute living standard of all sections of the population.

In his account of 'a brief history of neoliberalism', David Harvey (2005) describes the years 1978–1980 as a revolutionary turning-point in the world's social and economic history, when Deng Xiaoping in China in 1978 adopted incrementalist policies aimed at opening up new markets for private consumption and Margaret Thacher in Britain in 1979 and Ronald Reagan in the United States in 1980 were elected on neoliberal platforms. From these several epicentres, neo-liberalism, as a hegemonic model of discourse, initiated the political ascendance of a new economic orthodoxy across much of the rest of the world. With the spread of market triumphalism intensified by today's information technology revolution, such a seismic shift on a global scale has informed almost every aspect of people's lives – what scholars in globalisation studies describe as 'unprece-dented extensity, intensity, velocity and impact' (Held *et al.* 1999) or 'ever-com-plex cultural process' (Hannerz 1992, 1996). In addition to the accelerated cross-border flows or connections of commodities, people, symbols, ideas and capital, a significant amount of attention is also drawn to differences, conflicts, disconnections, exclusion and dispossession. The latter receives a particular boost from those who stress the uneven recasting process and geographic development, for example, fragmental disjunctures between economic, cultural and political '-scapes' (Appadurai 1996) and the commitment to 'moral economy' in Eurasia as a counter-current to industrial capitalism (Hann 2006). Hence, the theme of global convergence–divergence is an enduring one. Indeed, the effects of globalisation are fraught with controversy; the neoliberal camp itself is not short of rival fac-tions, as Marc Edelman and Angelique Haugerud (2005: 26) point out[14]:

> (N)ew debates about alternatives are emerging in centrist as well as more Left-leaning circles ... critics and advocates remain profoundly divided about whether economic globalization writ large is a force for social good – whether it alleviates or causes poverty, and whether it improves or under-mines labor and environmental standards, health protections, gender equality, democracy, and human rights.

As mentioned earlier, the important role of anthropology that has come to play in addressing globalisation issues is not fundamentally different from the tradi-tional focus on synchronic, small-scale fieldwork and 'types of relationship between persons' (Firth 1967). There are indeed good reasons for anthropologists to see globalising processes as embodied specifically, if not explicitly, in the studied people. The work of Eric Wolf (1982) provides a good example of how the analysis of imperialism from the perspective of the conquered shed lights on a complex of external and internal forces instantiated by the indigenous people. Although a good grasp of macro-narratives is necessary, the actual realisation of globalisation effects is 'always local and embedded in locally constituted life-worlds and power relations' (Eriksen 2003: 4).

In the light of the above discussion, it is clear that the liberalisation of *haken* in contemporary Japan is closely linked with the global environment where neoliberal market exchange prefers more flexible and informal employment contracts. The assumed link between neoliberalism and short-term employment is reinforced by a new construction of the relationship of individuals with markets, employers and the state. In this regard, David Harvey (2005: 168) provides interesting observations:

> Neoliberalization seeks to strip away the protective coverings that embedded liberalism allowed and occasionally nurtured. … The powers of trade unions and other working-class institutions are curbed or dismantled within a particular state (by violence if necessary). Flexible labour markets are established. State withdrawal from social welfare provision and technologically induced shift in job structures that render large segments of the labour force redundant complete the domination of capital over labour in the market-place. The individualized and relatively powerless worker then confronts a labour market in which only short-term contracts are offered on a customized basis. Security of tenure becomes a thing of the past (Thatcher abolished it in universities, for example). A 'personal responsibility system' (how apt Deng's language was!) is substituted for social protections (pensions, health care, protections against injury) that were formerly an obligation of employers and the state. Individuals buy products in the markets that sell social protections instead. Individual security is therefore a matter of individual choice tied to the affordability of financial products embedded in risky financial markets.[15]

In Japan, similar trends are mirrored in recent structural changes, which are aimed at promoting deregulation and privatisation of employment services. Recent years have seen a growing tendency of the state to rely on discourses of 'self-responsibility' and 'productive self' that place the individual at the mercy of the market (Hook and Takeda 2007). A further pertinent, and perhaps more significant, fact is that the post-bubble economic recession, especially the rise of unemployment since the late 1990s, has increasingly pushed policy-makers and government research groups to look to western advanced nations for remedies and directions. For example, the Japan Institute for Labour Policy and Training in 2004 held an international symposium entitled 'European Employment Strategy: Suggestions to Policy in Japan' with the aim of incorporating European Union's approaches of 'social inclusion', as distinct from the OECD's focus on market mechanisms through deregulation policies (JILPT 2007).

To be sure, Japan is a remarkably reflexive country whose historical engagement with wider, outside systems makes compelling reading. To a great degree, the Japanese ruling elite are flexible in appropriating foreign ideas and adjusting them to domestic conditions. Such pragmatism is reflected in the production of deregulation policies, which draw on much of the neoliberal doctrine and, in turn, lead to the rapid expansion of *haken* and other non-regular workers in Japan.

Whilst taking into account global imperatives that bear on national policy-making processes, it is important to point out that Japan is also a country where internal dynamics often take the form of political debate that challenges the decisions of dominant groups. Significantly, as the following chapters will show, there is a need to examine how different interest groups with different agendas act as 'the social and cultural filters operating to select and or/reinterpret whatever may be coming in from outside' (Ortner 1984: 159). The corollary is that the wider implications of *haken*'s development rest largely on 'outcomes of struggles between contending social groups located in concrete social formations' (Edelman and Haugerud 2005: 14). This is all the more revealing in view of the widespread assumptions made about the inevitable 'convergence' of all industrial societies on a similar pattern characterised by market triumphalism.

Conclusion

In this chapter, *haken* is explored in macro-developmental contexts with the aim of showing how the changing state policy transforms *haken* from illegal labour supply that poses a threat to the Japanese employment system to a useful, flexible non-regular labour force that complements, if not replaces, the Japanese employment system.

The significance of accounting for *haken* in large-scale processes is three-fold. First, *haken*, despite its newly established legal form, is not really new in substance; there has been a historical continuity between today's *haken* and the customary use of internal job transfers (*shukkō*) and external dispatched workers (on-the-premises *ukeoi*). The historical entanglement with exploitative and illegal activities is also an important element that explains why *haken* employment and agencies in Japan today tend to engender controversy. Second, the examination of *haken*'s development highlights the glaring gap between ideologies and realities. Despite the much-touted Japanese style of management, the differential treatment between core and peripheral workers has always been a salient feature. This kind of labour dualism is renewed and intensified during the post-bubble era where the state deregulation policies not only grant *haken* a legal status but also expedite the expansion of non-regular workers as a whole. Third, the analysis of globalising processes shows that the emergence of *haken* is not a unique phenomenon in Japan; rather, it is closely intertwined with the rise of global neoliberalism, a new hegemonic model of ideology that promotes flexible forms of working as well as a new relationship of individuals to markets, employers, and the state.

5 *Haken* in the 'gap-widening' society

Introduction

In emphasising 'the rise of uncertainty, the fall of solidarity' in contemporary Japan, Tom Gill (2001: 196) explains:

> The Kobe earthquake, the collapse of the bubble economy, and the end of the Liberal Democratic Party's monopoly of political power are signs that forces of uncertainty are once more on the rise in Japan. The 1995 nerve gas attack on the Tokyo subway by the Aum Shinrikyō cult was followed in the late 1990s by a confidence-shattering series of bankruptcies among banks, stock brokerages, and even insurance companies. Then, in September 1999, the serious radiation leak at the Tōkaimura uranium-processing plant brought a terrifying reminder of the fallibility of the "authorities" who run Japan's infrastructure.

'Uncertainty' may be regarded as a highly subjective and immeasurable condition. Yet when people consistently speak of it as characterising their current lives and society, it should be treated as a social fact, as real to them as any measurable condition, such as increasing non-regular employment rates and deteriorating income levels. This growing sense of uncertainty in Japan continues well into the first decade of the millennium. With the increasing unpopularity of the Japanese tripartite establishment – party officials, ministry bureaucrats and business leaders – national solidarity has been conspicuously on the wane both at the macro-level of the society and at the micro-level of the individual.

The trend is most evident in the realm of work where recent popular discourse has divided the country into two contrasting groups: regular workers (*seiki shain*) and non-regular workers (*hiseiki shain*). Perhaps for the first time in the post-war era, class interests enter into the public arena in such compelling fashion that the Japanese term '*kakusa*' meaning disparity or divide is used as an all-embracing keyword in both the mass media and everyday conversation. The surge of interest in the widening gap between regular and non-regular workers and between haves and have-nots has led to a prevalent view that Japan is becoming 'a gap-widening society' (*kakusa shakai*). Drawing on a variety of materials presented in TV channels, magazines, newspapers and Internet forums, this chapter set outs to explore how *haken* and its associated phenomena has been involved in the media-generated '*kakusa* boom' which brings employment status differentials to the fore.

The Japanese mass media

From *haken*'s historical obscurity to its current prominence, the importance of the Japanese mass media cannot be over-emphasised. Indeed, much of social change can be ascribed to the intermediary role of the media, 'which explains how it is that a society can suddenly become fixated on a certain issue when that issue is in fact long-standing in nature and only one among many' (Goodman 2002: 7). Recent years have witnessed a similar pattern taking place in Japan: new problems or crises are first discovered, defined and measured by the mass media and then brought to the national policy agenda. This is particularly the case under the current political economy where deregulation policies and structural reforms are likely to heighten people's sensitivity to news. In emphasising the media's initiating effects, John Campbell (1996: 188) argues that most political science studies focus on the 'enactment' stage of the decision-making processes, thus failing to examine 'the more diffuse agenda-setting process by which social problems come to be seen as worthy of attention'. To be sure, the media, known as the 'fourth authority' in Japan ranked along with the ruling triumvirate, provides the most important link between public concern and state policy on a day-to-day basis; the decision-making elite frequently take from newspapers their own notions of what problems facing the nation deserve attention and what might be done about them (ibid. 1996: 187).

Like the majority of industrialised societies, media saturation is a salient feature in Japan; technology advancement has increased people's reliance on the mass media – especially the ever-sophisticated new media – for information and communication. What makes Japan somehow special, however, is a greater degree to which the media exert an influence on the general populace. For one thing, the country has perhaps one of the most educated populations in the world, who are known as voracious readers and TV watchers – here it may be argued that media consumption generally rises in tandem with the growing level of literacy. For another, the relatively centralised structure of newspapers and television networks means that the Japanese tend to take the media seriously, not least when it comes to what is written in the national 'Big Five' newspapers.[1] In her overview of the modern Japanese media, Susan Pharr (1996: 4–5) explains:

> The circulation of Japan's largest daily newspaper, *Yomiuri Shimbun*, is greater than that of the *New York Times*, *Washington Post*, *Wall Street Journal*, *Christian Science Monitor*, and *New York Daily News* combined. Over 72 million newspapers are published each day in a country where 90 percent of the public, according to one study, reads newspapers on a daily basis. Japan's per-capita newspaper circulation (581 copies per 1,000 persons) is the highest in the world, more than twice that for the United States

(250 copies per 1,000 persons). The penetration and influence of the print media are even greater than these figures suggest, since five newspapers (*Yomiuri, Asahi, Mainichi, Sankei* and *Nihon Keizai*) are national papers, each with a circulation of more than 2 million. In addition there are the local and regional newspapers, some of which have circulations exceeding those of many leading U.S. newspapers; daily mass-circulation party newspapers, such as the Japan Communist Party's *Akahata* (Red Flag); and magazines that range from book-length "comprehensive magazines" (*sōgō zasshi*) to the ubiquitous comic books (*manga*) read by young and old alike on the trains. NHK (Nihon Hōsō Kyōkai), Japan's public broadcasting organization, is the second largest broadcasting corporation in the world (after Great Britain's BBC) but increasingly it is losing audience to the "big five" commercial stations, each of which has organizational and financial links to Japan's major dailies. In Japan there are far more television sets than homes, and the average Japanese spends three hours and twenty-three minutes daily watching television. Radio and extensive mini-media published by various citizens' groups round out the picture.[2]

Media in Japan today emerges from a recent past that leaves a legacy of what Susan Pharr (1996) describes as 'dual traditions': the 'servant' for the state and the 'watchdog' against the state. Although the servant tradition was predominantly strong from the Meiji Restoration to the end of Second World War, 'the persistent efforts of the press to resist censorship measures, even in the face of possible fines and jail terms for writers and editors, also established a strong legacy for a "watchdog" role in the postwar era' (ibid. 1996: 12, also see Kasza 1988; Mitchell 1983). With constitutional guarantees of the freedom of the press, post-war Japan has witnessed a more complicated relationship between the media and the state in a diversity of areas including party fortunes, policy changes, political activism, social movements, consumption trends and foreign relations. More often than not, the media are inconsistent in the way they function. This is due largely to the fact that, in order to get 'scoops' and garner large audiences, the media must relate closely with a broad variety of groups, acting 'as a kind of social loudspeaker' amplifying, if not intentionally, the voices of both the strong and the weak (Kabashima and Broadbent 1986: 27). By giving prominence, often randomly, to different social strata, the media contribute to the creation of a 'pluralist referent' system (ibid.) in which ordinary people are exposed to a range of selected images and ideas with which they can choose to identify.

In his discussion of changing policy process regarding the Japanese elderly, John Campbell (1996) illustrates how press attention was manipulated by the state to either shift the public mood towards a new 'common knowledge' or quell disruptive and unpredictable effects. Significantly, the media can be viewed as a popular form of political strategies available for powerful actors to work to their own advantage, whether it be making proposals that purport to represent 'the people' or discovering problems aimed at galvanising citizens into political sympathy or repulsion. Thus, the media as a whole provides a dynamic discursive space where a number of politicians, business leaders, academics and pundits come together to compete for the legitimacy of their various claims about a certain subject. In what follows, I shall focus on this distinct aspect of the media by examining how *haken* has become involved in the recent political fray triggered off by the *kakusa* or gap-widening between regular and non-regular workers.

'Kakusa' and 'working poor'

Kakusa has become one of the most popular buzzwords in Japan since the former Prime Minister Junichirō Koizumi took office in 2001. The word literally means disparity or divide, which is different from, yet evokes euphemistically, the concept of 'class' for which the Japanese translation is '*kaikyū*' or '*kaisō*'. Although there has been a long and sophisticated Marxist tradition in the Japanese scholarship – Marxist and radical–liberal interpretations of Japanese society can be traced to the early 1950s (Sugimoto and Mouer 1989: 3) – post-war Japan has seen a recurring theme that Japan is a classless society. As Bernard Eccleston (1989: 162) explains:

> Perhaps the most immediate reason is that for over 25 years opinion surveys conducted annually by the EPA and the Prime Minister's Office show that between 80 and 90 per cent of respondents considered themselves to be middle class. These self-ascribed testimonials to the extent of social equality are then related to estimates of a more even distribution of incomes to produce a picture of an unusual capitalist society where class conflict is absent.

Such lack of class consciousness was in fact a modern phenomenon. There existed an officially specified stratification system in pre-Meiji Japan where the imperial family and prestige-holding court nobles had the highest position, followed by four classes called '*shi nō kō shō*': 'power-holding warriors' (*shi*) as rulers, below whom came 'peasants' (*nō*), then 'artisans' (*kō*) and finally 'merchants' (*shō*) (Befu 1981: 121). This caste structure prevalent during the feudal era was discarded when Japan embarked on the Meiji modernisation. With the establishment of a new nation state and the ensuing rapid industrialisation, the Japanese society gradually assumed a distinctive harmonious form, often portrayed as 'one-hundred-million middle-class' (*ichioku sōchūryu*). The emergence of the massive middle class, egalitarian society had much to do with the historically derived notion of a Japanese meritocracy, which presupposed occupational mobility through equality of opportunity in education. Such a powerful construction underlay much of the tendency among the Japanese not to affiliate themselves with the working class. As Rob Steven (1983: 290–291) puts it:

> One of the greatest accomplishments of Japanese education lies in how it makes the roles people play in society look like and be accepted as results of individual merits and failures. What people do at work and what they

receive in return seem to be shaped by what they are or have made themselves through their education. Upper-class life has been made to look like a reward for educational success and working-class life a punishment for laziness and a lack of ability.

The ideology of egalitarianism, however, became increasingly unsustainable in the aftermath of the bursting of the bubble economy. In many ways, sweeping structural reforms during the post-bubble era marks a new phase in the national awareness of class. Many of the reforms are direct imitations of western, or more specifically American, models, their ostensible purpose being to enhance national competitiveness in an increasingly globalised world. The transformation in the political economy plays an important role in shaping the perception of social reality. Perhaps nowhere is this more immediately felt than in the reorganisation of work where the state deregulation policies have led to a sharp rise in the ratio of non-regular to regular workers. The fact that one out of three workers in the national workforce is now working in non-regular employment has caused intense public concern. It is particularly worrying that younger generations of workers bear the main brunt of the structural changes and take up most of the insecure low-paid, non-regular jobs. Among them, signs of class reproduction and entrenchment are getting strong; as Ronald Dore (2007: 395) comments:

> After six generations of meritocracy – roughly three generations of social mobility limited by constricted educational opportunity, and three generations of much expanded educational opportunity and much less limited social mobility – class divisions in Japan are hardening and the intergenerational transmission of class status is increasing.

> As a consequence, whatever may be happening to latent working class consciousness the effectiveness of working class leadership is diminished. The talented union leaders of the 1950s and 1960s, forced on to the shop floor by family poverty have no successors. The Socialist Party has evaporated. The managerial middle class continues to drain talent from below, but is increasingly self-recruited. The growth of private secondary schooling is reflected in the increasing polarization of educational achievement. The top managers now retiring often came from large families of diverse occupational destinations and rubbed shoulders with their future subordinates in common, often rural, schools. The sense of empathetic cross-class rapport which was usual for their generation contributed a good deal to the quasi-community character of the Japanese firm. It is not being passed to younger generations.

Indeed, the social divide caused by employment status differentials has surfaced as a contentious issue. Newspapers, TV channels and popular literature have become fixated on *kakusa* or the widening gap between regular and non-regular workers, haves and have-nots or 'winners' (*kachigumi*) and 'losers' (*makegumi*). The corollary is that a proliferation of *kakusa* verbal compounds have been coined and popularised, for example, 'digital *kakusa*' (*jyōhō kakusa*), 'education *kakusa*' (*kyōiku kakusa*), 'health *kakusa*' (*kenkō kakusa*), 'love *kakusa*' (*renai kakusa*)[3] and 'marriage *kakusa*' (*kakusa kon*),[4] to name but a few. Suddenly, Japan has turned into a *kakusa*-infused society where *kakusa*, as an all-purpose concept, is widely used to refer to almost every aspect of social life.

Closely related to this '*kakusa* boom' is another hotly discussed phenomenon of 'working poor' (*wākingu pua* or *hataraku hinkonsō*). The neologism refers to a stratum of disadvantaged workers who live below the level of subsistence or 'livelihood protection' (*seikatsu hogo*) no matter how hard they work. It is common knowledge that the discovery of working poor is attributed to NHK's two special TV documentaries broadcasted in July and December 2006.[5] Based on year-long interviews across the country, the documentaries underline the spreading poverty and predicament facing non-regular workers including young people, women, the elderly and children, against the backdrop of Japan's changing employment and working conditions. A follow-up book edited by NHK (2007) describes working poor as 'the disease gnawing away at Japan' (*nihon wo mushibamu yamai*). The resulting impact is indeed profound; the issue of working poor has provoked a wave of heated debate in both the media and the national Diet sessions. After *kakusa*, working poor has entered the latest vocabulary for the popular portrayal of contemporary Japan – Figures 5.1, 5.2 and 5.3 show how the frequency of *kakusa* and working poor in *Asahi Shimbun* has increased dramatically since 2006, coinciding with that of '*haken* workers' (*haken shain*).

Central to the two TV documentaries produced by NHK is that an increasing number of Japanese are deprived of 'pride' (*hokori*) both in work and in 'being a human' (*ningen toshite no*) under the current working environment. A recurring theme is that younger generations of workers are getting mired in an employment predicament where they are unable to find a regular workplace even though they are desperate for a job (*hataraki takutemo hatarakuba ga nai*). Far from being indolent, remiss or self-absorbed – as such derogatory labels as '*freeter*' or '*nīto*' (see Chapter 2) would suggest – all the young people interviewed by NHK journalists are described as hardworking, earnest individuals who are simply rendered jobless by diminishing regular employment opportunities and thus forced to engage in insecure and low-paid non-regular arrangements such as *haken*, *ukeoi* and *pāto/arubaito*. The widespread problem faced by young workers, compared to shocking news about suicides committed by those of middle or advanced age,[6] remains 'in the shadow' (*me ni mienai tokoro*) (NHK 2007: 17). More and more young people fall into the desperate, hopeless situation of working poor, being engulfed by 'the ever-spreading darkness of poverty' (*todomarukotonaku hirogaru hinkon no yami*) which is besetting the morality and order of Japanese society (ibid.: 20).

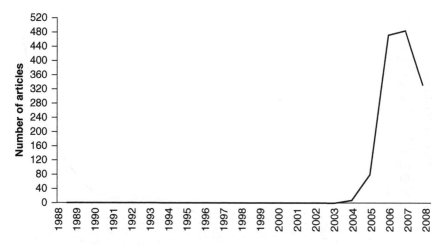

Figure 5.1 Kakusa shakai (gap-widening society) in *Asahi Shimbun.*

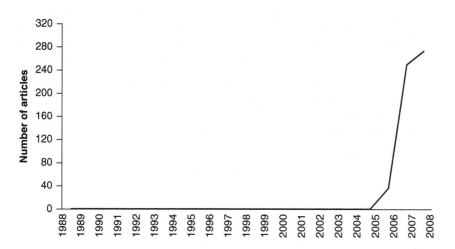

Figure 5.2 Wākingu pua (working poor) in *Asahi Shimbun.*

   The kind of poverty taking place in Japan is emphasised as 'new poverty' (*aratana hinkon*), in contrast to 'absolute poverty' (*zettaiteki hinkon*) broadly defined as the world starvation. A chief producer of the working poor documentaries provides a further explanation (NHK 2007: 7–8):

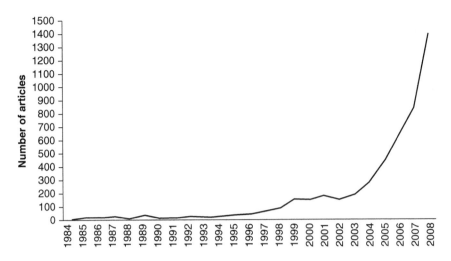

Figure 5.3 Haken shain (haken workers) in *Asahi Shimbun.*

According to the Constitution of Japan, Article 25 'the right to life, the state obligation to protect life', 'all people shall have the right to maintain the minimum standards of wholesome and cultured living'. Is this promise being delivered in today's Japan known as 'a big economic nation'?

The state should provide the safety net of livelihood protection so as to guarantee 'the minimum standards of wholesome and cultured living'. However, the reality is that a large quantity of working poor have emerged; many live below the standard of livelihood protection and are unable to achieve affluence no matter how seriously they take their work.

In every sense, the serious situation of 'new poverty' has arisen.

As a disturbing feature of this expanding 'new poverty', NHK turns the spot-light on 'a group of young people who are at the imminent risk of becoming homeless' (*hōmuresuka suru wakamono*). Such a concern is sparked off by a newly discovered phenomenon called 'net-cafe refugees' (*nettokafe nanmin*). Recent years have seen a rapid increase in the number of people who use 24-hour internet cafes as a home substitute to avoid the expenses of renting and living in apartments. Internet cafes in Japan are omnipresent, being originally designed for businessmen who want to rest for a few hours or for commuters who missed their last train home. In a typical Internet cafe, one can stay overnight for 1,000–2,000 yen in a small cubicle equipped with a reclining chair, a computer, a TV set, comic books and magazines. Many cafes offer free soft-drink refills and some even have showers and underwear for sale. Similar refuge can also be sought in round-the-clock manga cafes, fast food outlets and saunas, as well as cars.

According to *The Japan Times* (29 August, 2007), the government has been alarmed by growing reports of young working poor who expose themselves to both employment and health risks.

NHK blames the endemic problem of net-cafe refugees on the sharp rise in non-regular employment, maintaining that those young net-cafe inhabitants who take up non-regular jobs on a daily basis are 'the symbol of unstable employment' (*fuantei na koyō no shōchō*) (2007: 28). Many net-cafe refugees are 'day *haken* labourers' (*hiyatoi haken*); they rely on their mobile phones to receive calls/ emails from *haken* agencies which introduce jobs that last one day or a few days and do not require a fixed home address.[7] According to NHK (2007: 29), while they generally fall into the category of the homeless in the western world, in Japan only people who sleep in a bivouac or literally in the open, known as *nojyu-kusha* in Japanese, are officially counted as homeless. The government has, therefore, failed to grasp the real picture of the homeless in Japan, which could be much worse than expected.

Overall, NHK shows deep sympathy for the struggling younger generations of workers and sounds the alarm on the employment crisis that is detrimental to the Japanese society as a whole (also see Kadokura 2006; Yuasa 2007; Miyajima 2007). Michiko Miyamoto, a university professor who plays an important role in the production of the working poor documentaries, points out that (NHK 2007: 213):

> If 10% of the population is unable to climb up and thus becomes 'sedi-mented' (*chinden shita*), how does that affect the society? The terrible effect is that such sedimentation does not end in one generation. Family background, in which one was born and raised, becomes influential in one's future development. That is, not only those who are now pushed into 'the sedimentation layer' (*chinden sō*), but their children and grandchildren will be afflicted with the cross-generational poverty. This will eventually have adverse consequences for the society. For example, it is likely to result in an increase in crime.

In addition, Michiko Miyamoto contends that, in tackling young people's employment-related issues, Japan is far lagging behind western societies; the latter have taken measures to address such issues 20 years earlier. Given the long-existing nature of the matter, it is all the more important for Japan to deal with it promptly so as to prevent the reproduction of poverty across generations.

As to the reason for the expansion of working poor, experts' opinions sought by NHK, however, diverge considerably. Two contrasting views are juxtaposed in the documentaries. One is that the current problems regarding *kakusa* and working poor are caused by Japan's prolonged economic stagnation,[8] rather than the 'deregulation' (*kiseikanwa*) policies and 'structural reforms' (*kōzō kaikaku*) initiated by the former Koizumi government. This view is represented by Naohiro Yashiro, a university professor specialising in labour economy (NHK 2007: 214–215):

It has been fifteen years since the bursting of the bubble economy. During the period, the continuing deflation has stopped the rise of individual pay. It is this long-term economic stagnation that has decreased employment opportunities. To get out of the situation, it is imperative to facilitate a high level of economic growth that will increase employment opportunities, thereby providing the fundamental solution to working poor.

... Since we can't win the competition with the same products manufactured in China, high added value becomes necessary. This is why structural reforms are important. In particular, the delay in implementing structural reforms in the service sector is a major reason for the economic stagnation. There is an argument that the growth in the working poor is caused by structural reforms. Far from it. Until the Koizumi government, the previous governments had relied too much on the past successful experience during the high growth period and thus neglected the reforms in reaction to changing economic environment. This has brought about the current serious situation.

It should be noted that Naohiro Yashiro is also a member of the government's Council on Economic and Fiscal Policy (*Keizai Zaisei Shimon Kaigi*). He has been an active advocate for the government's sweeping labour reforms known as 'Labour Big Bang' (*Nikkei Business*, 6 February, 2007), which, in his view, are the key to ameliorate Japan's *kakusa* (NHK 2007: 216–217):

Unlike other societies, the *kakusa* between regular and non-regular workers in Japan is big. While regular workers are guaranteed employment security and seniority-based pay rise, non-regular workers generally have no pay rise. This is where the *kakusa* comes into existence. Thus, instead of simply turning non-regular workers into regular workers, it is essential to build up the labour market based on types of occupation, like that in western societies. It is too unrealistic to turn all 16 million non-regular workers into regular workers.

The labour market proposed above is occupation based, as distinct from the differential between regular and non-regular employment which has been a dominant feature of Japan's workforce during the post-war era. The shift has implications for both firms and workers. Firms are encouraged to use non-regular workers who have 'ready fighting power' (*sokusenryoku*) and thus reluctant to employ entry-level regular workers whom they have to invest both time and cost in training. For workers, those specialists or professionals whose skills are market-transferable are favoured over generalists whose firm-specific skills have limited application. While the employment *kakusa* is causing problems, occupational differences can be justified by the needs of the labour market. In view of the widespread concern over workers' safety net, this market-oriented approach is applied by Naohiro Yashihiro to Japan in the form of 'a sound market society' (*kenzen na shijyō shakai*) where market mechanisms are carried out in combination with efficient social security measures.

This stance, however, is diametrically opposed to that of Katsuto Uchihashi, one of Japan's famous 'economic commentators' (*keizai hyōronka*) who has made a strong impact by raising the public awareness of working poor. Katsuto Uchihashi appeared on both the NHK TV documentaries and was critical of the state and firms (NHK 2007: 218–219):

> The recent economic recovery has created the highest level of profit for companies. Yet the total sales haven't increased much. This is due to the restructuring of human resources that has led to the accumulation of profit. …

> Today's Japan, to a great degree, is propped up by the non-regular labour force. The social security cost has been reduced rapidly. Is there any pride befitting a company in those companies which resort to the workforce rationalisation so as to acquire 'strong international competitiveness'? Adding to that is the government which does nothing on the grounds that all will turn out well as long as the market takes care of everything. This is the reason why working poor have occurred. …

> As a result, workers whose efforts go unrewarded will lose the willingness to work. Japan, which has regarded industriousness as a virtue, will lose its previously held uniqueness. Whether the working population are rewarded or not reflects the country's real nature. …

> If the situation continues, 'the poverty majority' will emerge. 'Working poor' will cease to be limited to the minority. How could such a country be called a rich country? By neglecting the reality, the state fails to be a state. The state becomes estranged from its people. Such a country certainly will not achieve prosperity.

While describing Naohiro Yashihiro's view as 'practical' (*genjitsutekina*) in the sense that he observes Japan's situation in wider context, NHK echoes Katsuto Uchihashi's concern over 'the reproduction of poverty' (*hinkon no saiseisan*), concluding that despite the divergent opinions it is agreed that the problem of working poor does exist and needs to be grappled with. Throughout the TV documentaries, a strong message sent by NHK is that many working poor are 'making extraordinary efforts' (*kenmei ni doryokusuru*) and the state and companies should support the disadvantaged so that Japan will not become a country where 'human dignity' (*ningen no songen*), the meaning of work, and children's dreams and hopes towards the future are being taken away.

Haken: the main culprit of the 'gap-widening' society?

Amid the frenzy of speculation about *kakusa* and working poor, *haken* employment has increasingly become the target for criticism due largely to its rapid expansion enabled by the state deregulation policies. An argument has emerged that *haken* spawns working poor and is 'the main culprit of the gap-widening society' (*kakusa shakai no genkyō*). Speaking for the *haken* industry is JASSA,

Japan Staffing Services Association, the employer organisation of *haken* agencies. In an article entitled '*haken* and the gap-widening society', JASSA (2006b) defends the development of *haken* by drawing attention to the number and income levels of *haken* workers as well as the 'inevitability' of *kakusa*:

> Among the non-regular workforce, part-timers including *pāto* and *arubaito* are 11 million and contract workers around 3 million. By contract, *haken* workers are 1.2 million, only making up 8% of the non-regular workers (2% of the total employment). When it comes to the *kakusa* in employment status, measures to ameliorate the treatment and management of part-timers should be discussed first.

> Unlike other types of workers including regular, part-time and contract workers whose annual income distribution has one peak, *haken* workers are characterised by two peaks: one is 550–990 thousand yen and the other 2,000–2,490 thousand yen. While the first are short-term, short-hour workers, the second are full-time workers similar to regular workers. What is often emphasised, however, is the simplified average level that shows a gap between *haken* and regular workers. Regular workers' annual income includes bonus and housing and family allowances. So in terms of 'direct labour' (*chokusetsu no rōdō*), the gap should not be very big. … Income differentials are generally caused by the difference in skill, experience, and job content. …

> *Kakusa* is the product of a competitive society; the society's development cannot be achieved without competition. Our country must continue to strive for international competitiveness in globalising processes. Thus, a certain degree of *kakusa*, which results from the difference in 'effort' (*doryoku*), should be accepted ….

The point stressed by JASSA is that *haken* should not be blamed for Japan's widening gaps; on the contrary, it contributes to the prevention of unemployment by meeting the demands of both firms and individual workers. It follows that *kakusa* is necessitated by economic development and has much to do with individual difference in ability or effort. This line of reasoning reflects the argument of the pro-deregulation camp and is reinforced by *haken* agencies which interpret *kakusa* as an inevitable outcome of the increasing diversification of individual values. For example, Reiko Okutani, president of a personnel firm, receives special media attention for her view of Japan's *kakusa*. As she argues in an interview with *Nikkei* or *Nihon Keizai Shimbun* (22 May 2006):

> *Q: You have your own opinion about the issue of Japan's expanding social divide, do you not?*

> Everyone talks about whether the disparity between people has widened or not. Some people even say that although they see a yawning gap, it

is not a problem. These discussions are narrowly focused on a rich–poor disparity, or income gap. I do not accept the way people debate the issue of the social divide only from an economic viewpoint because I think there is more to life than economic values.

Q: In reality, however, there is a clear difference among the elderly in terms of wealth and a visible wage gap exists among the young. What is your take on that?

I do not think it is correct to label Japan as a divided society simply by citing the wealth gap among the elderly. And if the economy picks up further, the young people who are called "freeters" (due to their preference for part-time jobs) or "NEETs" (for their reluctance to be in education, employment or training) will gradually find regular jobs. In fact, we can already see such a tendency in line with the economic recovery. …

Q: From what perspective do you think we should view our society, other than an economic one?

The important thing is for everyone to develop values that form the foundations of the lifestyles we adopt. If we are more concerned about relative values, we will eventually put ourselves at the mercy of other people.

It is only natural that individual people differ from one another in their way of working and in their abilities, something that could unavoidably draw a line between those who earn high incomes and those who are paid more modestly. But it is a difference caused by a relative sense of value resulting from a comparison with other people.

In Japan's period of high economic growth from the 1960s through the 1970s, which was supported by a sense of uniformity among people, known disparagingly as the "all middle-class mentality", people in this country were not necessarily happy.

That fact gave impetus to Japan becoming a society characterized by diverse personalities and offering a range of alternatives for living. People with a strong sense of their own values will find it easier to live in present-day society, which prizes diversity.

Apparently, the Japanese 'relative values', along with the 'all middle-class mentality', are depreciated in favour of 'a strong sense of their own values'. In Reiko Okutani's argument, *kakusa* becomes something synonymous with 'diversity', as opposed to 'conformity', being portrayed as not only unavoidable but also desirable in terms of life pursuits. This new value construction is supported by many business practitioners; for example, the president of

Staff Service Co., a top player in the *haken* industry, is quoted as saying that 'in the old days, work came first, then life; today, life comes first, then work' (*Nikkei*, 25 September, 2006).

Despite the considerable publicity for the promotion of *haken* employment, there has been widespread criticism levelled against *haken* agencies. An Internet news forum at GIGAZINE (24 August, 2007) launches a stinging attack on JASSA, pointing out that the *haken* industry as a whole prioritises profit-making over workers' interests; it aims for 'exploiting systems' (*sakushu suru shikumi*), instead of establishing sound systems that ensure *haken*'s proper function in the society. In dissociating *haken* from, or even justifying, *kakusa*, the *haken* industry is condemned as abdicating its responsibility to narrow the gap between *haken* and regular workers. As the forum emphasises, the fundamental problem of *kakusa* lies in 'income disparity' (*chingin kakusa*), which is unjustifiable since *haken* workers do the same jobs as regular workers. Given the social problems caused by working poor and net-cafe refugees, *haken* employment contributes more to 'the stability of earnings' (*shūeki no antei*) for big firms than to the stability of employment and society. In commenting JASSA's recent campaign, '*haken*-working 2007', which collect examples of people who 'live a happy life by making the most of *haken*', the forum derides it as a patent strategy to protect the *haken* industry's own interests as well as a flagrant disregard for a variety of problems affecting *haken* workers such as dissatisfaction, insecurity, frustration, fear and the entrenchment of *kakusa* involved in the *haken* way of working.

The *haken*-bashing has gained momentum in recent years where corporate scandals in connection with illegal *haken* practices frequently hit the headlines. Among others, the problem of 'disguised' (*gisō*) *ukeoi* attracts special attention. As examined in Chapter 4, *ukeoi* has a long history in Japan; it is a common practice utilised by large companies to outsource tasks to their subcontractors. While 'off-the-premises' (*kōgai*) *ukeoi* is a standard type of outsourcing, 'on-the-premises' (*kōnai*) *ukeoi* is very similar to *haken*. The only difference is that *haken* workers are defined by the law to work under the direct instruction and supervision of their client firms whereas *ukeoi* workers are prohibited from taking orders from client firms. The difficulty in detecting violations of the superintendence rule means that on-the-premise *ukeoi* cannot be easily distinguished from *haken*, thus paving the way for the rampancy of disguised *ukeoi*. For client firms, the advantage of disguising *haken* as *ukeoi* is mostly concerned with cost reduction and convenience. Unlike *haken*, *ukeoi* doesn't require client firms to be responsible for workers' health and safety insurance; neither does it impose any restriction concerning the length of job assignments. As a result, *ukeoi* workers are vulnerable to work-related accidents and unlikely to be offered direct employment. Like the customary (illegal) use of on-the-premise *ukeoi* in the past, the current disguised *ukeoi* often takes place in Japanese manufacturing conglomerates which have an extensive network of group companies including various branches and subcontractors.

Despite its long-existing nature, disguised *ukeoi* until recently remained largely unnoticed. Like many well-hidden problems in Japan, it was first 'discovered' by the mass media. On a mission to dig deep into Japan's *kakusa* problems, *Asahi Shimbun*, one of the 'Big Five' newspapers, launched a press campaign over a year-long period between April 2006 and March 2007. A special team of reporters was set up to collect data concerning disguised *ukeoi* across the county. During the campaign, *Asahi* produced a series of feature articles disclosing a number of Japanese brand names, such as Canon, Matsushida, Hidachi, Toshiba and Toyota, which were implicated in disguised *ukeoi* and other problems affecting non-regular workers. The disclosure has not only raised public awareness of disguised *ukeoi* but also put the state and firms under considerable pressure. For example, *Asahi*'s first report published in 31 July, 2006 (morning edition) revealed that a local factory of Canon, despite being previously reprimanded for operating disguised *ukeoi*, continued to employ a large quantity of *ukeoi* workers who far outnumbered regular workers and were subject to harsh working conditions. The report had an immediate impact; according to the same day's newspaper (evening edition), Canon was forced to announce that it would address the disguised *ukeoi* problem seriously and solve it by turning *ukeoi* workers into *haken* or regular workers within the year – *Asahi Shimbun* (2007: 68) describes the reaction as 'Canon's public promise to the world' (*seken ni taisuru kyanon no kōyaku*) and a senior government official refers to it as '7.31 shock' (ibid.: 210). Because Canon's top executive, Fujio Mitarai, was also a member of the government's Council on Economic and Fiscal Policy, the *Asahi* report was used by a member of the Democratic Party at the House of Representatives to grill the labour minister and the prime minister about the issue of legal compliance.

Not only the lawbreaking client firms, the *Asahi*'s campaign against disguised *ukeoi* also sheds light on the wrongdoing of *haken* or personnel agencies. Amid concerns over the widening gap between regular and non-regular workers, the distinct employment relationship between workers and middleman agencies has come under close public scrutiny. In its feature article entitled 'the hidden side of *haken*' (*haken no uragawa*), *Diamond* (14 July, 2007: 28–51), a popular weekly business magazine, sets out to debunk the *haken* business by focusing on the mixed fortunes of Goodwill Group, the biggest agency in the *haken/ukeoi* industry whose gross violations of the law have received a huge amount of media coverage. In many ways, Goodwill is symbolic of *haken*'s dark side; it has been officially rebuked for committing almost all the typical illegal acts pertaining to *haken*, especially those regarding the mishandling of day *haken* labourers such as dishonest deduction of workers' wages and dispatching workers to prohibited jobsites. Along with Goodwill, another well-known agency called Fullcast is reported by *Diamond* as using exaggerated advertisements to attract young worker from various local areas. The reality awaiting them is, however, 'the factories that drive *haken* workers to despair' (*haken zetsubō kōjyō*); young people in the hope of pursuing a better career and life are treated as low-paid, uninsured, disposable workers. Similar exploitation is also reported among Japanese ethnic workers, as well as foreign trainees who are paid below the minimum wage level. The misconduct of Goodwill and Fullcast, both of which have substantial market share in *day* haken business, has caused widespread condemnation and prompted legal review of the day *haken* business (*The Japan Times*, 30 July, 2008, 5 November 2008; MHLW 2008).

Such high-profile illegal *haken* activities involving leading *haken* agencies have led to serious damage to the reputation of *haken* agencies as a whole, whose rapid business expansion is often said to be linked with working poor and gap-widening problems plaguing the Japanese society. The general public opinion is that the *haken* industry is making a quick profit at the expense of workers' well-being. In the face of growing animosity, JASSA (2008) pleads for 'a proper understanding of *haken*' (*rōdōsha haken wo tadashiku rikai shite kudasai*) by declaring, for example:

- Problems of day *haken* are problems of labour conditions.

The need to work short term among workers has been long-existing in *haken* employment. The recently raised problems including unfair deduction from workers' wages, unpaid work-related travel hours and enforced purchases of items required by job assignments are indeed violating the right of workers. They are, however, not the problem of *haken* as an institution, but rather that of Labour Standards Law. ...

- The association of short-term *haken* workers with net-cafe refugees and working poor is a mere imagination.

First, those who work only on short-term contracts occupy half of the entire short-term or day labourers. Second, those who spend their nights regularly at Internet cafes are in the minority, only making up 0.4 per cent. Most of the net-cafe users are interested in relaxation and thus have nothing to do with working poor.

In addition to this defensive position, JASSA pledges that it will regard 'labour protection' (*rōdōsha hogo*) as the first priority while striving to tackle the issue of legal compliance. Along similar lines, the president of Pasona, one of the most successful *haken* agencies in Japan, argues in an interview with *Diamond* (14 July, 2007: 51) that *haken* workers are the most important of all stakeholders:

The demand for *haken* is extremely high. The work is becoming wide-ranging. ... Most firms, due to the bitter experience during the bubble era, would not increase the number of regular workers in any dramatic fashion. At the same time, female *haken* workers are certainly on the rise. ... This is because women who once entered into the household have now begun to look for re-employment opportunities. ... Although my agency regards legal compliance as a matter of course, it is difficult to say that the overall personnel services industry has a high law-abiding awareness.

In my agency, female *haken* workers' hourly wages are by no means inferior to that of their regular counterparts at big firms. We have full application of social insurance, accident compensation, and health check systems. Some of our branch agencies have such a high level of welfare facilities that even big firms apply for membership of the facilities.

Among various stakeholders including shareholders, workers and client firms, I attach the greatest importance to *haken* workers. If *haken* workers can enjoy their work with us, then I believe client firms will surely be satisfied.

The view of the mass media as a dynamic, discursive space means that what is presented to the audience is not always consistent. Indeed, in many modern societies, the media, when acting collectively as an intermediary actor, often exhibit a 'tricksterlike' quality; 'they are as likely to tweak as to condemn, and crucially in the mosaic form they have adopted, they do both simultaneously' (Pharr 1996: 35). This is certainly true of the news production of *haken*. Along with the *haken*-bashing that sees the expansion of *haken* as a major contributor to Japan's widening gaps, there are reports that portray *haken* as meeting the demands of specific groups, which converge with *haken* agencies' public discourses. According to *Diamond* (14 July, 2007: 42–43), people are divided in their attitude towards *haken*; while clerical/secretarial *haken* generally wish to become regular employees, those who are driven by occupational interests or work–life balance consider *haken* as a better way of working than regular employment. The emerging picture is depicted as that where many are 'vacillating' (*yureugoiteiru*) between regular and *haken* employment; while the former provides better treatment, the latter confers more freedom.

Indeed, the contrast between *haken* and regular workers is a popular theme that has been widely seized upon by the media. Among others, a sensationalist report entitled 'below *haken*: the tragedy of salarymen/regular employees' published in a popular weekly magazine called *SPA!* (17 July, 2007: 36–43) provides a good example. Using interviews, surveys and questionnaires, the report illustrates how 'a reverse phenomenon' (*gyakuten genshō*) has come into existence where regular workers feel that they are falling behind their *haken* counterparts in almost every aspect. One reason underlined is that the media-generated *haken* phenomenon helps improve the labour conditions of *haken* workers whereas regular workers, despite the breakdown of life-time employment, are taken advantage of by firms under the name of 'regular workers'. It is also mentioned that although the average income level of regular workers is higher than that of non-regular workers, the difference has been steadily decreasing. According to a national survey conducted by *SPA!* on 'the psychology of regular workers' among those aged between 25 and 30, around 40 per cent of the respondents toyed with the idea of shifting to non-regular employment. The reasons why non-regular employment seems to be a better choice are cited as follows:

- Free from responsibility, relaxed
- Easy to take a break
- Easy to quit
- The amount of work is proportionate to the working hours
- No overtime, able to make use of personal time
- Need not have a put-on smile to superiors
- Need not deal with complicated jobs
- Able to take up part-time jobs from which regular workers are prohibited

Perhaps more provocative is that one in four regular workers, as suggested in the above survey, feels that they are 'completely beaten' (*kanpai*) by *haken* workers in terms of hourly pay because of the long unpaid working hours they have to put in. A salaryman aged 32 working in a hotel is quoted as saying that:

> My monthly salary after taxes is about 300,000 yen. The hourly wages of *haken* vary between 1,200 yen and 1,800 yen depending on the level of skills. If they work on the shift of early morning or late night, extra allow-ances will be paid. There is some student who earns 400,000 yen a month! Those *haken* workers who spend most of their income as pocket money and drive fancy cars are '*haken* parvenus' (*haken narikin*), as we regular employees call them.

> After work, those *haken* parvenus often make advances to cute female staff by suggesting, for example, 'where do you want to go for a drive tonight?', whereas we have to deal with various tasks including detailed check-up of the venues and document-making. It is hard to bear hearing those girls give a willing reply!

In particular, the fact that a minority of IT *haken* professionals earns an average of 550,000–600,000 yen per month arouses jealousy among the rank-and-file regular workers. According to another cited personal story, the frustration is more acutely felt by regular workers in restaurant and retail industries where non-regular workers are often in the majority and constitute the core workforce. In explaining the per-ceived reverse phenomenon, Hidetoshi Tokano, who provides his expert opinion on the *SPA!*'s report, comments that the emerging IT and service sectors do not have labour unions, which renders regular workers unprotected. This situation, com-bined with widespread illegal *service* or unpaid overtime, has pushed down the actual hourly pay – what *SPA!* suggests as 'the root of all evils' (*shoaku no kongen*).

Not only the hourly pay but also 'the social standing' (*tachiba*) of regular workers is portrayed as being threatened by *haken* workers. Since the legalisation of *haken*, a growing number of workplaces have more *haken* workers than regular workers. Instead of hiring and training new recruits themselves, firms are increasingly relying on *haken*, a new style of management described as 'aimed only at getting over the current situation' (*sonoba shinogi*). According to *SPA!*'s report, regular workers are instructed that they should treat *haken* workers 'with care' (*ki wo tsukau*), because their superiors are nervous about *haken* workers' complaints which via *haken* agencies could have adverse effect on their management assessment. Thus, regular workers are sometimes held accountable for mistakes made by *haken* workers. Even more compelling is a reported example where a young regular worker in his first career year claims that he has been bullied by his supervisor, 'a super or veteran female *haken*' (*otsubone haken*)[9] who has substantial influence with his direct superiors. Such intriguing depiction of regular workers as the underdogs suggests a decreasing level of employee satisfaction in the Japanese workplace, which is to some degree refracted by the discussion of *kakusa* and working poor among non-regular workers.

The 'bruised heart' (*kizutsuku kokoro*) of regular workers is also said to be caused by enforced routine duties, community voluntary work and after-work socialisation, from which *haken* workers are exempted. While *haken* workers have proper breaks and leave the office on the dot, regular workers toil long office hours, being kept busy with various tasks. A female regular worker aged 25, interviewed by *SPA!*, complains that her firm's frequent drinking sessions, described as another form of 'unpaid overtime', are more exhausting than daytime work. The reason why regular workers take those 'small matters' (*chiisai koto*) seriously is interpreted by Hidetoshi Tokano as that more and more young people wish to enrich private life because they are not interested in 'career success' (*shusse*) and because the seniority based promotion system is breaking down. Lacking career incentives to serve their firm, regular workers become attracted to *haken*'s freedom to pursue a balance between work and life, which leads to a sensitivity towards the 'trivial *kakusa*' (*samatsu na kakusa*), as opposed to the big *kakusa* concerning income and job quotas.

In general, the 'below *haken*' syndrome reported by *SPA!* reflects a heightened awareness of differences among the Japanese themselves. The well-discussed gap-widening or working poor problems not only throw into relief Japan's social divide between regular and non-regular workers, but also fire people's imagination with their work and life pursuits. With the post-war salaryman model under serious strain, what it means to be an ideal way of working is subject to considerable debate. The assumed 'tragedy' of regular workers is a good example of how *haken* and other non-regular workers, despite a host of difficulties facing them, are regarded as having certain attributes that disgruntled regular workers find attractive. Masaharu Shibata, another expert whose advice is sought by *SPA!*, points out that the personnel management of Japanese firms is problematic:

It is natural for firms to seek profits. However, if firms do not commit themselves to personnel training and instead focus on the rationalisation of work by hiring too many *haken* workers, they may achieve the present aim of reducing labour cost but fail to get hold of the whole picture. As a result, there will be an increase in the number of regular workers who do not know what kind of work they are currently doing. While firms may gain profits for the present, their manpower will certainly weaken in the long run, as well as their organisation. ...

If firms do not have an outlook on mutual development, regular workers might as well consider resignation. ...

I am interested in the reform of 'corporate climate' (*kigyō fūdo*), which requires workers to have 'the ability to make proposals' (*teianryoku*). The problems in a firm usually do not come out easily and there are superiors/bosses who lack sensitivity. If you joined that kind of firm, you should first identify the firm's nature and then make proposals that will improve the working environment.

What is proposed by *SPA!* is a relationship of 'mutual consideration and love' (*sōshisōai*) between workers and their firm. That is, the solution to relieve the frustrations of both *haken* and non-regular workers lies in the creation of a new workplace where both parties can work together in harmony.

Conclusion

Haken in the gap-widening society is primarily a media-generated phenomenon, which raises important issues, arouses anxiety and fear, and stirs excitement and various anticipations. Such high-profile media activities as NHK's special TV documentaries about working poor and *Asahi Shimbun*'s year-long campaign against disguised *ukeoi* play an important role in drawing attention to Japan's *kakusa* or the widening gap between regular and non-regular workers, as well as the fast-growing, and yet scandal-laden, *haken* industry. Significantly, the media sympathy for those struggling young people who are forced to take up insecure, low-paid *haken* and other non-regular jobs has provoked intense public concern. There has been widespread condemnation of misconduct on the part of client firms and *haken* agencies which disregard legal rules and put profit-making before workers' interests.

The media agenda-setting process is, however, by no means straightforward. Along with the speculation over *haken*'s adverse effects, the media also turn their attention to the sensationalist contrast between *haken* and regular workers, as illustrated by the reported 'below *haken*' phenomenon, which contributes to the promotion of *haken* as a fashionable and desirable way of working, albeit in often contradictory ways.

6 The search for meaningful work

Introduction

In the previous chapters, I have introduced the contemporary and historical background of *haken* including its distinct triangular employment system and how *haken* becomes involved in media speculation over Japan's widening gap between regular and non-regular workers. This chapter turns to an examination of individual workers, which takes an intimate look at how *haken* work is consumed by real people in real situations based on my own interactions with them in the fieldwork. The purpose is to flesh out the impersonalised skeleton of much-represented *haken* and to draw heuristic comparisons between forces of ideological discourse and individual choices and decision-making in everyday life.

Such an exercise focuses on more mundane forms of *everyday experience* – around which clusters a bundle of interrelated concepts, for example, *agency*, *practice* and *action*, which have interested scholars in anthropology and other fields (see Ortner 1984). Individual thinking and activity provide a close-up lens into the unfolding of the *haken* phenomenon and the processes involved in the reproduction and transformation of core values such as personhood, thus forming an indispensable part of the understanding of contemporary Japan. Indeed, the more empathy we develop with ordinary people's life, the easier it is to think explicitly about the taken-for-granted assumptions that link their narratives, actions and silences in day-to-day interactions. Herein lies the importance of long-term, immersed ethnographic research where participant observation allows the researcher to unravel the intricacies of what the studied people say they know, say they should do and actually do. It is in this combined sense of absorbing and analysing, that is, the mutual engagement of practice and theories, that fieldwork contributes to a deep understanding and 'thick description' (Geertz 1973) of a particular context in which to investigate any research subjects.

Throughout my fieldwork working as a *haken* in two client firms, Miracle and Vision, I had been following, and constantly inspired by, a multiplicity of small details arising from socialisation with fellow *haken* and regular workers. Both Miracle and Vision are well known in Japan, especially Vision, a long-established traditional Japanese conglomerate which sells its brand products across the world. Due to the difference in job requirements, the two groups of white-collar, office *haken* workers I met in Miracle and Vision differed considerably. While almost every *haken* worker in Miracle had what the current labour market considered as highly in demand job skills such as English proficiency and IT or financial knowledge, those in Vision generally fit into the mainstream of *haken* workers, who carried out relatively unskilled, clerical or secretarial tasks. Their narratives and realities are by no means representative of all the *haken* population in Japan, but they collectively serve the purpose of offering an actor-centred, micro-level perspective, as distinct from the perceived problems and values of *haken* discussed in the public arena.

'To work is to live'

> All people shall have the right and the obligation to work.

Thus stipulates *The Constitution of Japan* (Article 27, 1947). One strong message sent by the popular drama of *Haken's Dignity* is 'to work is to live' (*hataraku koto wa ikiru koto da*). In Japan, as elsewhere, work is a prominent theme that infuses many areas of life. The search for meaningful work is a perpetual subject; any changes in work are bound to have an impact on the Japanese worldview. While the expectation of financial compensation might be no less strong in Japan than in other societies, it is often said that Japanese people, especially men, tend to seek the meaning of existence more from work and the workplace than from other spheres of life such as family and leisure. The Japanese conception of work, in its broadest sense, has connotations of 'making yourself useful to others' and 'improving one's own body and mind' – whether it be household chores, community voluntary services or paid employment. Idling life away incurs disapproval and disdain. Thus, rather than a treadmill from which one dreams of escaping, work is widely regarded as one of the important life stages where the Japanese are taught to achieve adulthood or a sense of becoming 'a person of society' (*shakaijin*) as opposed to children and adolescents. Important here is the general acceptance of work as an essential social role that an individual learns to play in order to develop a full personhood.

In his account of how Japanese and Americans make sense of their worlds, Gordon Mathews (1996) adopts an approach using a Japanese term called '*ikigai*', which can be glossed as 'that which makes one's life seem worth living'. He distinguishes two conceptions of *ikigai*: one as 'sense of belonging to, sense of oneness with' (*ittaikan*) and the other as 'self-realisation' (*jikojitsugen*). While the former 'carries with it the premise that selves are most essentially their roles', the latter 'carries with it the premise that there is an underlying self more essential than social role' (ibid.: 18). Despite often contradictory expressions, the majority of Japanese people are committed to neither conception of *ikigai* but rest uncertainly between them (ibid.: 25). This argument is actually concerned with the anthropological notion of personhood, which sees a particular, actual person in any human societies as being composed of both self and social roles. The relationship between the two is at the heart of what is conceived as meaningful work and life, although such ideological constructions as 'socialism' or 'individualism' tend to emphasise either social roles or self. By contrast, the Japanese construction of personhood is more pragmatic in the sense that it allows for both self and social roles, with the emphasis on the fulfilling of the latter in a proper manner without the intrusion on the former. This distinct relationship is predicated upon *kejime* or 'distinction', which refers to a complex of values that separate self and roles in accordance with varied contexts and stages in life (see Chapter 1).

Given the predominance of organisation-oriented social life in Japan, perhaps nowhere is *kejime* more significant than in the workplace. In the case of *haken*, the triangular employment relationship represents a new way of working where corporate belongingness is less valued than professional ability and personal needs. This emphasis on professionalism and freedom makes a marked contrast to the so-called 'company person' (*kaisha ningen*), which defines the post-war salaryman model and presupposes the subordination of individuality and private life to corporate values and norms such as superior-subordinate hierarchy and ritualised bonding with colleagues. While 'the observance of *kejime*' (*kejime wo tsukeru*) as a general rule remains important, *haken* and its associated phenomena signal the changing meaning of *kejime*, that is, the reconfiguration of self and roles. What it means to be the ideal Japanese person thus hangs in the balance, being subject to the redrawing of the boundary between self-pursuits and social expectations. To explore this dynamics in the workplace, I shall first examine ethnographic data concerning regular workers before focusing on the narratives and realities of individual *haken* workers.

Between corporate belongingness and self-development: regular workers

Post-bubble Japan is characterised by the declining importance of belonging to a firm. The much-touted 'company-as-family' model that used to be cited as the key to explaining Japan's post-war economic miracle has fallen out of popularity; indeed, today's Japan is often described as ushering in a new era where 'the demise of familism in the workplace' (*kaisha kazokushugi no shūen*) is an undeniable fact (*Yomiuri Weekly*, 21 January, 2007). Despite the state's continued rhetorical support for the life-time employment – which never applied to the inner periphery of insecure regular workers within the firm nor to the outer periphery employed as non-regular workers (Gill 2001: 93; Chalmers 1989, also see Chapter 4) – the idea of being loyal to a single firm throughout one's lifetime is replaced by 'long-term' (*chōki*) or 'regular' (*seiki*) employment. More and more people are now changing firms in pursuit of a better career and the trend is particularly striking among the younger generations of workers, as evidenced by a newly discovered phenomenon where around 30 per cent of newly hired university graduates resign within three years of taking their jobs (see Jyō 2006).

At the same time, the Japanese firm has undergone a transformation in organisational forms and hiring practices; in the words of Ronald Dore (2007: 395), Japanese firms appear 'more solicitous of and deferential to the owners of their capital and more inclined to treat their employees as means rather than ends'. A substantial body of popular and academic literature has emerged arguing about the new face of the Japanese firm as well as the new relationship between firms and workers (*Nikkei Shimbun* 2006; Iwai *et al.* 2005; Ohta 2006; Mitarai and Niwa 2006). Along with the increased use of *haken* and other non-regular workers, the state deregulation policies have had a noticeable effect on regular workers, who are often reported as suffering from 'malicious laws' (*akuhō*) and 'bullies' (*ijime*) inflicted by the state and firms (*Yomiuri Weekly*, 21 January, 2007). When I was conducting my fieldwork, a new labour policy called 'white-collar exemption', as a major step towards the government's sweeping labour reforms known as 'Labour Big Bang', provoked considerable controversy. The proposed policy would make dismissals easier and exclude regular workers earning more than a certain threshold from overtime premiums and restrictions on working hours.[1] While business leaders strongly lobbied for the exemption, saying that it would contribute to the flexibility of work, the policy met with fierce opposition from the wider public, as well as labour unions which feared the change would simply lead to a 'zero-overtime pay system', causing white-collar workers to work even longer unpaid hours (*Nikkei Weekly*, 12 February, 2007).

The growing animosity towards firms was evinced by three of my informants who belonged to 'the group of people who have escaped from the salaryman life' (*datsusaragumi*). All of them were articulate, ambitious young men aged between late 20s and early 30s, who gave up their enviable membership of a large corporation for similar reasons. One was a journalist of a major Japanese newspaper, who fell foul of his bosses by expressing his critical view of the corporate management on his personal homepage. After refusing to shut down the homepage, he was suspended from his usual duties. The infuriated young man then filed a lawsuit against the newspaper firm for what he described as 'a flagrant breach of freedom of speech'. Lacking sufficient funds for hiring good lawyers, he eventually lost the case but found a new purpose for himself:

> The Japanese firm is corrupt from within. I felt so suffocated by a number of 'unreasonable' (*rifujin na*) rules and regulations imposed by it. There is virtually very limited room for individual freedom and development. In my view, the way in which the Japanese firm and the Japanese society operate is essentially communist, albeit under a cloak of democracy. ...
>
> I am now a freelance writer, spending most of my time talking to young people and voicing their concerns on their behalf. The younger generations of workers are most vulnerable to corporate abuse and exploitation. Through my work, I wish to make an impact by revealing the wrongdoing of the Japanese firm. This is, I believe, what a proper journalist should do.

The other two former salarymen had less dramatic stories. But like the journalist, they felt betrayed by the Japanese firm whose management favoured senior workers at the expense of the needs of young workers. Both of them subsequently set up their own enterprises which provided work-related consultation for young people. By the time I was about to end my fieldwork, they had achieved considerable success. Their books were among the bestsellers at bookshops and one of them became a well-known advocate for young people, being frequently interviewed by magazines and TV programmes.

Unlike those vociferous opponents of the Japanese firm, the majority of salaried workers lead an ordinary organisational life, depending much on their firm for financial as well as emotional well-being. Yet, even among them, there has been a growing sense of detachment from the firm. The term 'salaryman' (*sararīman*) is now often used in a pejorative sense, referring to a man of one's father's generation, or the so-called *oyaji* type, who toils long hours for his firm, only socialises with his fellow workers or clients through after-work drinking or golf-playing on weekends, rarely spends time with his wife and children, much less does anything about household chores. Tadashi, a 26-year-old young man of a major Japanese trading house with whom I regularly socialised after work during my fieldwork, denied 'being a normal salaryman' (*futsū no sararīman*). As he said:

I am proud to be a member of the current trading firm which is, in my view, perhaps the most successful one of the same kind in Japan. But I am not going to 'bury my bones' (*hone wo umeru*) or stay until retirement in the firm. I will resign definitely within 10 years, maybe as early as 5 years from now. Actually I am already doing some research through the Internet for my next job – a job that will stretch my ability and offer me more management responsibilities. Meanwhile, I'd like to take advantage of what a big firm can provide. I am soon being sent by the firm to Italy to learn Italian language for a couple of months. ...

I love what I am doing now, even though I have to put in long hours. I frequently go on business trips to the US and some European countries to bring the latest overseas fashion trends back into Japan. In a sense, I feel that I contribute, through my work, to the diversity of beauty and art in Japan. ... Most important is that I am not playing a role of 'doing simple things at the bottom of the hierarchy to support superiors' (*sokozumi*). Although it is only my third year with the firm, I am already responsible for what used to be assigned to a 'section manager' (*kachō*). ... For me, it is a demonstration of 'my own ability' (*jibun no nōryoku*) and a great boost to my confidence.

I am not workaholic; I do have dreams such as 'wandering around' (*hōrō suru*) the world. I may go to graduate school at some stage of life. But, at the moment, work is a top priority; I aspire to a successful career. ... I do not want to follow in my father's footstep, having a typical but boring salaryman life – 'absolutely not' (*zettai shi nai*). I always try to make friends out of my work network so as to broaden my horizons and enrich my life. … My father was rarely at home when I was little; I was brought up by a strong mother figure. When I get married, family will be as important as my career. I want to be a good father who cares for his children, spending as much time as possible playing with them.

It was evident that Tadashi wanted to distance himself from his father's generation in his search for meaningful work and life. Indeed, Tadashi was not alone; many young regular workers showed the same tendency in one way or another. Even the old generation of workers was not always happy about the 'traditional' values it was proud of. A senior director in his 50s once went to some lengths to explain to me why he was not a salaryman:

> The normal salaryman does things as he is told. I have always been trying to use my own initiative since I was young. Besides, I am paid according to an 'annual salary system' (*nenpōsei*), whereas a salaryman is paid monthly. … Much of my current success can be ascribed to the 'courage' or 'guts' (*dokyō*) needed to pioneer something new. It is a pity that my generation didn't have much 'room' (*yoyū*) to explore various opportunities in life other than work. Times have changed now. I think it is fine for today's young people to have different styles of life, as long as they make themselves useful for others. I am open to new ideas although it is too late for me to put them into practice. Perhaps it is sensible to think about how to make the most of my present situation …

During my interactions with regular workers, what struck me as most interesting was that although belonging to a firm, especially a large, famous one, remained important in boosting one's social standing, more and more young people began to stress their occupational role or professional ability, that is, what they were actually doing and excelled at in the firm. For example, I met an IT engineer in his early 30s who worked for a large foreign-affiliated firm. Like Tadashi, he pulled a wry face when I implied that he was a salaryman, arguing that:

> Technically I am not the kind of salaryman you are talking about. I am an IT engineer. I used to work for an ordinary Japanese firm where I studied engineering from scratch. I changed my job twice before working for the current foreign-affiliated firm. … The occupation of IT engineering is challenging and requires a substantial amount of self-study. I am planning in the near future to set up a private association of engineers across different firms so that we can exchange information and enhance our professional quality, as well as building up a network of friendship.

While the Japanese salarymen under the 'firm-as-family' architecture identify themselves with the firm and derive much self-worth from their commitment and loyalty to the firm, the occupation-conscious, new generation of workers take pride in self-motivated career progression, which is as much, if not more, important as securing a membership in a famed, large firm. Such a shift reflects an increasing emphasis on self-development and individuality, a long-existing trend that has become prominent since the end of the post-war high growth. Ronald Dore and Mari Sako (1998: 172) point out that *jikokeihatsu*, a buzzword literally meaning self-enlightenment or self-study emerged after the 1984 legislative reforms where the old word 'vocational training' (*shokugyō kunren*), which had overtones of disciplined slog, was changed to 'vocational skills development' (*shokugyō nōryoku kaihatsu*), which had learner-participative overtones. Much had since been made of the trend in autodidactic efforts and a new expression of 'the cultivation of human talents' (*jinzai ikusei*) began to appear in the 1996 Ministry of Labour White paper (ibid.). Such tropes as 'creativity', 'innovation', 'diversity' and 'uniqueness' have consequently assumed great importance in the Japanese business world.[2]

During the post-bubble era, this emphasis on self-development has acquired novel features that are different from what has been sought in the past. Compared to the traditional 'incremental innovation', Japanese firms are now aiming for new models of innovation that will support radical breakthrough in business through more rapid entry and exit from business areas and stronger external labour markets based on portable professional qualifications (Jackson and Miyajima 2007: 14). As demonstrated by the increased use of *haken* and other non-regular workers, the current language of self-development is geared towards the need for a more flexible and professional workforce characterised by 'ready fighting power' (*sokusenryoku*). As a result, suitably qualified, diverse individuals with specialised skills become increasingly popular. With *haken* workers being increasingly professionalised, regular workers are urged to catch up with 'the unprecedented boom' (*kūzen no būmu*) by studying career-focused skills and qualifications (*Yomiuri Weekly*, 2 December, 2007).

In addition to the popularity of professionalism in career development, personal attributes in other areas such as human relations and leisure have begun to be valued more favourably than before. That is, the degree to which the role of individuality (*kosei*) in the social evaluation of a person is changing in relation to the importance of collective concerns and hierarchical relations in the Japanese workplace. When I was working as a *haken* at Vision, Makoto, a young regular worker in his early 30s sitting opposite me, often intrigued me with his various small 'idiosyncrasies'. In contrast to the ambitious young men whom I mentioned earlier, Makoto was not enthusiastic about his career promotion and seemed content with his current rank-and-file position, as he put it:

> I am not interested in 'climbing up the ladder of career success' (*risshin shusse*). Nowadays those who are in managerial positions are not earning as much as you might expect. They risk losing a big portion of income, if they fail to obtain good results. They are not protected by the corporate union and have to rely on themselves. ... If I were married and had a family to feed, I probably would like to take the risks. I will get married someday but

it is not a matter of concern now. ... Yes, my parents whom I live with often complain and want me to get married soon, but I simply ignore it.

It is important to 'cherish your own time' (*jibun no jikan wo taisetsu ni suru*). Frankly, I do not have much ambition about work. As you see, I just get on with it. Unless necessary, I'd avoid working overtime. I tend to balance out the overtime hours on some days by working less on other days. So, on average I put in normal hours and thus never claim overtime pay...

If there were something that I would like to do with my career, I hope I could be transferred to a Vision's foreign branch soon, preferably in America, Australia or Germany, for a couple of years. As a matter of fact, I am currently waiting for my turn as there is a long queue for such transfers. ... The way Americans work is much more relaxed and efficient. It would be a great experience indeed, although I do not envisage myself living abroad for too long. In many ways, Japan is still the best place to live.

Like many young regular workers, Makoto was keen to separate himself from the old generation of salarymen. In his spare time, he often spent hours browsing the latest fashion magazines at bookshops so that he could make a difference by dressing not like a boring salaryman. Perhaps more interesting was that Makoto was a very popular figure at Vision because of his friendly personality and broad leisure interests. He was famous for being 'the man who knows everything' (*nandemo shiteiru otoko*) and was willing to share useful tips for buying tickets from reliable airlines, having a healthy diet or choosing hot tourist spots. Many colleagues including *haken* workers liked to talk to him or ask him for help. His popularity was also related to the fact that he made the least effort to curry favour with superiors and bosses, often making an only token gesture towards hierarchical rules. In some cases, his air of nonchalance bordered on the rude, but neither his direct superiors nor other high-ranking bosses seemed to be much bothered. Makoto frequently declined to attend drinking sessions organised by his own section and instead preferred to socialise with his own 'drinking friends' (*nomi nakama*) who were not work-related but based on mutual interests. The enforced after-work socialisation aimed at smoothing human relations in the workplace didn't happen very often at Vision; indeed, it became something of a rarity for some sections.

   Makoto's case indicates that personal attributes are making inroads into firm-centred values and obligations; there is growing tolerance and sympathy towards elements of individuality provided that one performs his or her job professionally. The lessening of the degree of loyalty and commitment to the firm is also reflected by the changing role of Japanese men from work to family. Many married men are inclined or encouraged to take more domestic responsibility and help reduce working women's burden at home. In describing *Ikujiren*, a Tokyo-based association which promotes the idea of child-caring salarymen, Masako Ishii-Kuntz points out that the changing nexus of company–family is influenced by both individual autonomy and the state policy on work-life balance aimed at tackling Japan's falling fertility rate, 'the product both of social interaction and everyday practice and of governmental schemes, ideologies and institutions' (2003: 213). Thus, what it means to be a hegemonic male Japanese person is a dynamic 'crafting' and 're-crafting' process (Dasgupta 2004),[3] as evidenced by the declining importance of corporate belongingness and the increasing emphasis on self-development in both professional and private areas.

Such a shift, however, doesn't occur without complications; forces of change and continuity are inherent in any societies. A new term called 'Me-Fetishism' (*mīfechi*) has recently been coined to refer to 'the new generation of workers who have strong narcissistic tendencies' (*jikoai no tsuyoi sedai*). As *Yomiuri Weekly* (2 March, 2008) describes, those 'childish employees' (*okosama shain*) are self-centred, having a big attitude and yet easily being cast down; they show an aversion to cumbersome hierarchical relations and frequently evade obligatory drinking sessions; they enjoy their leisure only with a small group of four or five people with whom they share mutual interests and can easily get along. The criticism points to the delicate balance of *kejime*, as well as the importance of maintaining it. Although self-development or individuality is encouraged in the areas of freedom and choice, it could easily come into conflict with socially endorsed values and slip into the individualistic sense of autonomy informed by 'individualism'. Hence, to avoid being stigmatised as 'selfish', 'immature' or 'narcissistic', one has to keep a wary eye on *kejime*, giving due consideration to the social while continuing to explore the self.

To recapitulate, the current Japanese workplace is characterised by the changing perception of *kejime*, which results from the declining importance of corporate belongingness and the increasing emphasis on self-development. As my ethnographic examples suggest, a growing number of young regular male workers are creating a new relationship with the firm; they either relinquish corporate affiliation altogether or, more likely, shift from the firm to other areas of life, such as occupation-focused career development, leisure pursuits and parental involvement. What does this general trend in contemporary Japan mean to *haken*, a new category of non-regular workers who face a different set of issues and problems? Based on my own experience of working as a *haken* in two client firms, Miracle and Vision, I now focus on the narratives and relatives of *haken* workers with whom I was fortunate in having opportunities of sharing frustrations and joys.

The individual consumption of *haken* work

It is one thing to talk about a new style of work and life; it is quite another to actually live by it. In contrast to the glut of official discourses that purport to offer transparent windows into social reality, the voices of those targeted are often silenced, or rendered insignificant, or reduced to the neatly arranged categories that serve the purpose of political argument. In the case of *haken* workers, certainly many do not relish the prospect of being a flexible (and disposable) *haken* at the expense of employment security and corporate benefits; nor does everyone subscribe to the view that non-regular workers are merely the victims of the shifting political economy. Everyday experience is both more and less than ideology; the typical picture that emerges is an intricate pattern of practice that combines, in subtly shifting and complex ways, the reproduction and the transformation of imposed social values. It would be erroneous to assume that individuals can only either conform to or contest the existing social order, acting in what is often described as 'rational' fashion.

Gender

The consumption of *haken* work is, therefore, immensely varied, depending on a number of intersecting factors that affect different individuals in different ways. Among others, gender is the most salient feature of *haken*. Although there has been a steady increase in the number of men, *haken* is still a predominantly female phenomenon in contemporary Japan (see Chapter 2). Certain general themes concerning the nature of men and women appear across a wide array of societies, but the degree to which gender is formalised and elaborated is greater in Japan than in many other industrialised societies, as illustrated by the ideology of 'good wife, wise mother' (*ryōsai kenbo*)[4] encapsulating women's familial roles. Despite their long-existing participation in the labour market, Japanese women until recently were not recognised as pertinent to the discussion of important issues taking place in the male-dominated workplace. The popular assumption was that women's involvement in regular or non-regular employment paled in comparison with their roles as mother and wife in the household; the former was often considered as 'not an alternative to home-making' but rather 'an extension of the domestic role' (Smith 1987: 16). Louella Matsunaga (2000: 147) also points out how women's balancing family duties with outside work is constructed as 'an appropriate, even laudable, alternative to being a full-time housewife', 'the badge of the mature woman' who possesses a quality of '*gaman*' – the ability to endure and persevere – much prized in Japan. Even though the state recently introduced policies aimed at making family needs and work demands compatible for women, such policies were mainly driven by concerns over Japan's population crisis caused by an unfortunate combination of a rapidly ageing population and dropping fertility rates.[5] In addition, the existing tax and benefit systems play an important role in deterring women from seeking ambitious career opportunities.[6] The idea that a labour division by gender is 'natural' remains relatively intact in Japan, although the popular culture which captures imaginary and leisurely spheres of life often suggests otherwise.[7]

It is, therefore, interesting to investigate how the construction of gender roles mediates the way in which individuals search for meaningful work through their engagement in *haken* work. As described in previous chapters, the majority of female *haken* workers are concentrated on white-collar, clerical jobs – the so-called *jimukei*. This phenomenon has much to do with the Japanese gendered employment convention which preserves the 'auxiliary' employment track (*ippanshoku*) for female workers, as opposed to the 'comprehensive' career track (*sōgōshoku*) which leads to positions in management for male workers. The arrangement is based on the postulation that Japanese women are shifting, if not transient, workers who have a distinctive pattern of labour participation.[8] Since the legalisation of *haken*, many Japanese firms have now replaced (female) regular workers allocated to the auxiliary employment track with *haken* workers (Keizer 2007: 7–8). Hence, it could be argued that there is certain continuity between the current clerical *haken* workers and the previous auxiliary female regular workers, who are popularly referred to as 'office ladies' (see Ogasawara 1998; Lo 1990).

Megumi

The continuity of 'good wife, wise mother' is manifested in the experience of *haken* work among some women I met in the fieldwork. For example, Megumi, a single woman in her middle 40s, perceived *haken* as, among other things, a means of finding a life partner. Megumi and I were both working at Miracle and we often spent time together over drinks and meals. Megumi was born into a middle-class family background where her father was an editor of a well-known Japanese newspaper and her mother was a professional housewife. All her child-hood and early youth had been perfectly normal and happy until one day her father ran into serious financial trouble. Due to the sudden change of circum-stances, her parents chose to support only her elder brother to university. Megumi was very upset by the decision but didn't hold any grudges against her parents:

> I am a girl, 'a fact that you cannot argue about' (*shikata ga nai koto da*). But I was determined to make a future for myself. After graduation from secondary school, I spent two years doing various part-time jobs so as to save tuition fees and went to a two-year vocational college afterwards. I did it all on my own. Thanks to the then booming economy, it was easy to secure a full-time office job after I finished the vocational college. I worked at a mid-size trading firm for about five years and gradually became bored. When a new job opportunity came out, I moved to an audit firm where I worked for another five years as a regular worker. During the second job, I attended an evening school for English Translation. …
>
> I thought a certificate of English proficiency would allow me to choose more interesting workplaces and meet more interesting people. Upon attainment of the certificate, I gave up my regular job and joined the *haken* world, which was then popular and seemed worth trying. That was seven years ago. In total, I have worked as a *haken* for five years, hopping from one job to another. There was a two-year interval where I was sick and underwent a major operation.

In spite of all those life ordeals, Megumi remained optimistic. There were several failed, bitter relationships in her past, but that didn't stop her from longing for a happy marriage. When I asked why she had stayed in *haken* employment for such a long time, Megumi said:

> *Haken* offers a wide range of job opportunities and makes it easy to shift from one workplace to another. I usually choose jobs with hourly pay no less than 2,000 yen and in large or famed firms. What is most important for me is 'exciting encounters' (*deai*) where I can meet my future life partner. If the working environment didn't look promising, I would simply refuse to renew the *haken* contract, even the highly paid one, and move on. So far I haven't had any luck with finding a suitable man, but I will keep searching. Besides, I depend on *haken* to make a living.

Megumi was not always certain about her choice. All too often, she was caught up on the horns of a dilemma; on the one hand, *haken* had the advantage of enabling her to look for her ideal husband from a larger pool of candidates in various firms, but, on the other, the prospect of working permanently as a *haken* filled her with anxiety and fear:

> I 'should provide for my old age' (*rōgo ni sonaerubeki desu*), especially considering my age and weak physical condition. After all, moving from one job to another is not that easy; registration sessions and interviews are often time-consuming and frustrating. Sometimes I have to endure a long time of unemployment between job assignments. ... Well, I do not deny the benefits of regular employment, but isn't it important to follow your heart, to pursue what you really desire in life? The times have changed; many of the Japanese traditions are out of date. Whether it be marriage or work, I think it is important 'not to make compromises' (*dakyō shimasen*).

Megumi's case indicates that although the Japanese gender ideology bore importantly on her decision-making, as evidenced by her strong desire for married bliss over career development, Megumi didn't accept the socially sanctioned women's roles without demur. By being uncompromising, she was challenging them in her own small ways.

Tomiko and Atsuko

There were another two female *haken* at Miracle, Tomiko and Atsuko, who were close to Megumi's age and used *haken* as a better substitute for traditional part-time jobs. Both of them were motivated by short-term financial gains and therefore showed little interest in their roles in the workplace. Tomiko was a mother of two children, who wished to supplement her husband's main income, as she mentioned:

> My children's education expenses are getting higher and higher, so I have to earn more to contribute to family income. I chose the job at Miracle not just because of the high hourly pay but also the proximity of the workplace

to my house so that I can best deal with any emergencies concerning my children. The only problem that worries me is that the job requires regular working hours and sometimes overtime. But the manager seems very nice; perhaps I will try to negotiate when I need to go home early.

Tomiko was frequently the first one to leave the office. Based on my conversation with her, I had an impression that because of her duty as a mother she would not make any extra effort to improve her job performance or help other co-workers. However, like Megumi, Tomiko was very amiable, often behaving in a way that reminded me of the soft 'office lady' in the Japanese workplace.

By contrast, Atsuko was a 'bold' figure; while she knew how to maintain a feminine demeanour in accordance with general expectations, she would not hesitate to confront adverse situations. Atsuko divorced twice and was keen to save as much money as possible before embarking on a new life in Australia in the near future. She was working right across from my desk so I could have a good observation of how she got on with her job every day. She often spent long time chatting with others or frequently taking breaks during the working hours and made excuses to work overtime, which could increase her overall income because of a premium of 25 per cent on overtime hours. The situation took a dramatic turn after Atsuko ignored several mild warnings from a male Japanese manager. One day, the manager finally lost his temper and berated Atsuko in front of all workers at the open, large office. Atsuko didn't easily give in and went on to defend herself against his accusations. The quarrel went on and on and that was indeed a long awkward time for everyone at the office. Atsuko called in sick the following day but resumed her work as normal after that. Surprisingly, she stayed and renewed another fixed-term contract. One thing was clear to me when I left Miracle: the firm was short of manpower and the management was desperate to recruit and secure those *haken* who could speak English.

Natsumi

Compared to the above examples, the ideology of 'good wife, wise mother' seemed to be more willingly embraced by Natsumi, whom I met when working on my second *haken* assignment at Vision. Different from those at Miracle who were bilingual and had IT skills, most *haken* workers at Vision were responsible for clerical or secretarial jobs. Natsumi, a single woman in her middle 30s, spent most of her work life filing documents, answering phones and dealing with miscellaneous office back-up tasks. Like many others, she used to be a regular office worker, albeit at a mid-size firm. Despite the change of employment status, she still referred to herself, along with other female workers, as *ōeru* or 'OL' (short for Office Lady). From the first day, she introduced me into her OL lunch-time group, which included both regular and non-regular workers of different ages.

In many ways, Natsumi was the epitome of a Japanese office lady. She smiled sweetly, used Japanese honorific words perfectly, and had impeccable business manners. When she spoke on the phone, her soft voice was always brimming with femininity and courtesy – although not everyone at the office found it very comfortable since I was told by a young girl that some were apparently mocking Natsumi's 'affected girly' voice behind her back. To be sure, Natsumi aspired to regular membership of Vision, which could offer her a fuller and bigger package of remuneration and benefits. Yet, given her undistinguished educational background and general secretarial skills, it struck me that she contented herself with the *haken* status in a big firm which she otherwise would not be qualified to enter as a regular candidate in the first place. As she put it:

> I have worked as a *haken* in different workplaces of Vision for eight years. I was dispatched to the current workplace two years ago when the previous one was suddenly dissolved due to a corporate restructuring. I do not know where I will be after three-year employment on the current job assignment, perhaps another different office within the Vision group firms.[9] ...

> Vision is a big firm and I like the working environment here. ... Rarely will such a big firm turn non-regular workers into regular ones. Nowadays the firm has its own difficulties; it is faced with more challenges than ever before. Just see the number of annual regular recruits, which has decreased dramatically.

Natsumi's 'understanding' of the management could be partly explained by her special relationship with two powerful male superiors. She was not subtle at all in currying favour with them, whether it be preparing snacks or offering sympathetic words when they were under pressure. Such services, however, were quite unusual; other female workers, especially those in *haken* employment, were more interested in getting their work done than nurturing human relations. In return, Natsumi obtained some power that was usually impossible for a non-regular worker. For example, Natsumi was present at my interview with Vision, along with two senior managers. Naturally, I thought Natsumi was a regular worker who perhaps had an important role in personnel management. I was quite surprised when later it turned out that she was a *haken*. Rumour also had it that Natsumi was the 'boss' of her section behind the scenes and that she once gave a hard time to a new recruit who was openly antagonistic to her.

For Natsumi, women's central focus lay elsewhere other than work; in her words, work was after all 'the men's world' (*otoko no sekai*). During lunch breaks, she often talked a great deal about her wish to marry the right man.

> I want to get married and to be a professional housewife who takes good care of her children and husband. But it is really difficult to find a good match. I have asked some superiors to introduce someone from their circle of friends or acquaintances. But they didn't seem to take it seriously; they probably thought I was only joking.

In her spare time, Natsumi took lessons for 'cultural accomplishments' (*naraigoto*), such as the tea ceremony, flower arranging and kimono-dressing – which are traditionally designed to train women to become 'the truly sophisticated Japanese woman' known as '*yamato nadeshiko*' in preparation for a good marriage.

Takeshi and Hayato

Takeshi and Hayato were the only two male *haken* at Vision with whom I had interacted during my fieldwork. Compared to their female counterparts, male *haken* were relatively underrepresented in the public arena. In the Vision's giant office where I worked, there were approximately 10 female *haken* and 2 male *haken* among a total of 90-strong workers. Takeshi and Hayato, aged between 30 and 35, were working in my neighbouring sections. Both of them were friendly and hardworking, but they usually kept a low profile at the office.

Apparently, it was less easy for male, white-collar *haken* to integrate into Vision's male-dominated workplace. As opposed to 'good wife, wise mother', the gender-specific expectation for Japanese men is embodied in the notion of *dai-kokubashira*, a term literally meaning 'the main pillar which supports a traditional Japanese household'. To a great degree, a man's social standing depends on the size of the firm he belongs to as well as the hierarchical order of his role in the firm. As Louella Matsunaga (2000: 151) remarks, 'an employee of a large company is a more desirable husband and son-in-law than an employee of a small company, and certainly more desirable than a casual labourer, and hence there is a good deal of pressure on young men to find such employment at least by the time they enter their mid- to late-twenties and are approaching marriageable age'. Despite the declining profile of the Japanese salaryman and the increasing emphasis on diversification of identity and life styles, the position of work in the ideological make-up of hegemonic masculinity in Japan has not altered significantly (Dasgupta 2004). This was reflected in the experience of *haken* work by Takeshi and Hayato, whose non-regular employment often meant that they had to make extra efforts and endure some kind of emotional pain that often went unnoticed.[10]

Takeshi was single and lived with his parents. Despite a long commute from his home to Vision, he always came to the office earlier than other regular workers in his section and was often the last one to leave. He wore a shirt and tie everyday, which was actually unnecessary as Vision didn't have a strict dress code and many workers dressed casually. Like female clerical *haken* workers, his work was of an auxiliary nature, involving copy-making and information-circulating. Most of the time he was working quietly at his desk, rarely interacting with others – a young girl in his section once described him as an 'invisible' (*medatanai*) figure who had an 'unusual personality' (*kawatta seikaku*).

Takeshi was always polite and humble when asking others for help regarding business matters. Sometimes, he was sent by his section to consult with my boss, a senior manager, in order to collect certain information – cross-section communication at Vision was surprisingly bad; many workers in different sections rarely talked to each other despite the fact that they sat in close proximity to each other. Unfortunately, my boss was notorious for being mean to subordinates. There were a couple of times when he deliberately ignored Takeshi's small request, leaving the latter standing there, awkward and embarrassed. I surmised that Takeshi as a male clerical *haken* might be suffering from other cold eyes as office bullying could take various subtle forms.

Compared to Takeshi, Hayato fared much better at Vision partly because of his specialist role. Not only did he provide senior managers with his expert opinions on Vision's products but also was responsible for supervising and training new recruits. He was extremely popular with young workers who genuinely admired and respected him for his excellent technical skills and charming personality. Hayato had worked in different sections of Vision for more than 5 years. He frequently went on business trips alone to foreign countries on behalf of Vision, which was extremely unusual for a non-regular worker. When I asked if he had tried to apply for a regular position at Vision, he said:

> I wish I could become a regular worker at Vision. But the personnel system of a big firm is not flexible. Neither the current boss at Vision nor the dispatch firm, which is my main employer, has the power to push the idea even if they were willing to help me. Now that *haken* is the norm, mid-career direct hiring could become more difficult. ...
>
> Looking on the bright side, I can take advantage of what a big firm can provide: learning new things, trying out technical skills, and building up experience. At least, work at Vision is never boring and I am grateful to have the current job opportunity. ...
>
> Surely I'd have much better pay, promotion opportunities, and a career ladder to move up if I were a regular worker. It is indeed unfair to have such differentials based solely on employment status. Many of my frustrations come from the fact that no matter how much I contribute to the firm, the part I am allowed to play in the big picture is always limited. Because of my non-regular employment status, the management keeps certain corporate information secret from me.

Beneath his successful exterior, Hayato was faced with a situation where he struggled to reconcile the benefits of staying in a big firm with the desire to have his skills and hard work properly recognised and rewarded.

Young women's career ambitions and life pursuits

In addition to gender, generation is another key element which mediates the way individuals consume *haken* work. Growing up with Japan's post-war affluence, young people today have a propensity not to reinvent the wheel, as Gordon Mathews and Bruce White (2004: 199) point out:

> Today, however, more than in previous generations, a pivotal moment of historical generational change may have arrived. In the ways the young people ... perceive society as offering them a variety of options, in the ways they form generational identities and interactions enabling them to

live out these alternatives, and in the ways they begin to displace ideas fundamental to old institutional orders, we see considerable change in Japanese society,

The change we envision will probably not come about through organized protest or even conscious generational solidarity, but rather though a vast array of individual choices and micro-interactions. That this accumulation of change is occurring in the intimate and individual settings of people's lives points to the importance of ethnographic and anthropological approaches in understanding change in a complex society like Japan.

The challenge posed by young people in Japan, as elsewhere, has always been accompanied by social panics brought about by 'youth problems' (see Yoder 2004; Ambaras 2005). Despite an endless list of labels such as 'parasite singles' and '*freeters*' (see Chapter 2), younger generations of workers, compared to their parent generation, are resilient in their envisagement and exercise of alternative life paths. They tend to rail against conservatism and pioneer new meanings of work and identities by appropriating popular discourses that foreground professionalism and individuality. In their eyes, firms have increasingly become consumer products to suit what they need, namely 'not only employment, but also, ideally, a fashionable image and lifestyle' (Matsunaga 2000: 40). That is, for an increasing number of young people, work is 'another means of self-fashioning performed through consumption of goods and styles' (Smith 2006: 175).

An intimate look at many of the young *haken* women I got to know in the fieldwork indicates tangible changes along the same lines. Even though marriage continues to dominate a Japanese woman's life course, many try to reinterpret and replace themselves in a wider world of challenges. The picture that emerges is, therefore, a new synthesis of marriage, work and other areas of life, as well as a growing diversity of individuals. Compared to their male counterparts, Japanese women might be 'the primary bearers of generational change in Japan today, since they, more than men, can escape the pressure of having to fulfil narrow adult social roles' (Mathews and White 2004: 194). Such a liberating view should be balanced by a consideration of the individual difference in, for example, education attainment and family background, so as to avoid the danger of slipping into 'a tendency to romanticise resistance' (Abu-Lughod 1990). Although most of my informants in this study fit more or less in the category of middle-class background, class is clearly an important element in the study of individual experience; parents' class standing or financial input plays an important role in the preparation of young people for the future. The point to note here is that actors are affected by the existing social order, noticeably unequal political and economic relationship, even while simultaneously undertaking the reimaging and challenging of that order. In the following ethnographic examples, I shall explore the complex ways in which young *haken* women challenge, ignore, or accept their sex-segregated roles in their search for meaningful work and life.

Chika and Chie

Although many either drift into or are forced into the *haken* world, there is a minority of skilled, career-oriented individuals who consciously use *haken* employment to their own advantage. Chika and Chie were among those highly motivated young women, who regarded *haken* as a stepping stone towards better prospects of employment. Both of them were keen to accumulate a wide range of market-demanding skills and qualifications through *haken* work. In marked contrast to those *haken* women motioned earlier who prioritised women's roles in the household, Chika and Chie committed themselves to the world of work where they endeavoured to seek an ambitious career by constantly improving themselves.

Chika, in her mid-20s, was one of the female *haken* workers at Miracle. She was the most talented *haken* I met during my fieldwork. In addition to a high level of English language skills, she was familiar with various areas of specialised knowledge, ranging from accounting, banking, to IT engineering, which she acquired through different *haken* jobs. She was enthusiastic about her job and eager to learn from the IT project at Miracle. She also showed strong leadership on some occasions where her team run into difficulties. Many co-workers were impressed by her professional ability and commitment. For me, she was a perfect example of a confident, accomplished and determined modern career woman. Speaking of *haken*, Chika had her own viewpoint:

> The reason why I was drawn to Miracle's job is that I want to gain further knowledge about IT software, something I dabbled in during other *haken* jobs. …
>
> I do not get along well with the current boss in my team; the Indian young guy is stubborn and unresponsive. Well, I do not see myself staying in this job for a long time, maybe just another three months. … Of course, my ultimate goal is a regular job. But I do not want to settle in a mediocre one. That is why I think *haken* is a useful means of trying out different work-places and lines of work. I am not sure now which exact profession I would eventually choose in the future, but I will keep looking for my calling while soaking up whatever interests me. …
>
> Last year, I nearly joined a foreign-affiliated big firm which offered me a regular position after screening me during a *haken* assignment. I initially said yes but changed my mind after I found out that the future middle-aged male boss was someone I disliked. I have passion for work and my career is most important, but I just couldn't bear the thought of working under such an unpleasant boss every day!

Like Chika, Chie put her career before anything else and consequently accorded great importance to work. I first met Chie at a Japanese 'year-end party' (*bōnenkai*) shortly after I arrived in Tokyo. She worked as a *haken* for a major Japanese trading firm after graduation from university. Chie was a vivacious young woman and tended to be outspoken in her remarks. She talked a lot about work-related topics and often gave a good analysis of how things had gone wrong in the Japanese workplace. Once at a party in front of her close friends, Chie pulled a serious face and announced that her future dream was to be an entrepreneur or a 'female president' (*onna shachō*).

Chie grew up in the country of a remote prefecture and now led an independent life in Tokyo. At the weekend, she often took part in volunteer activities – I was once invited by her to take care of disabled children in a non-profit organisation. She also frequented a cosy Japanese-style bar (*izakaya*) in her neighbourhood, where she unwound and chatted with older salarymen. In her view, there were still many things one could learn from the older generation about the Japanese business world. For her, the current *haken* job provided a much-needed process of learning about herself, as she said:

> When I was in school, I didn't really know what it was like to work at a firm; nor was I sure where my career path would tend. Given the lack of experience, I thought *haken* might be a good start to figure out what exactly I would like to do. Besides, it was very tempting that *haken* could enable me to work in famous, large firms – I didn't graduate from a high-ranking university so, you know, I was not a strong candidate for permanent positions in such firms.
>
> To be honest, I have now become utterly disappointed by the Japanese work culture after two years working as a *haken* at the most famous trading firm in Japan. My job is to assist the section manager so I can get a pretty clear picture of the workings of the trading business, which is very inefficient because of complex and unreasonable human relations. I start to wonder why so many people are only driven by the name or size, not the substance, of firms. … I now have a better idea about my future career. As a matter of fact, I am in the middle of job searching and I will terminate the current *haken* job soon. I think it would be better to work for middle-size or even smaller firms where it is easier and quicker to get hands-on experience and management skills.

Towards the end of my fieldwork, I got an email from Chie, telling me that she had been given an informal offer of permanent employment by a mid-size firm and that she was so happy because the firm assigned her to the sales and marketing department just as she wished. It was clear that she was full of life and looking forward to her new career as a regular worker, a step closer to her dream of starting her own enterprise.

Sayuri and Mayumi

Not everyone was as intent on career-building as Chika and Chie. To be sure, many young *haken* women thought of *haken* either as a path to mature womanhood through adopting adult roles in the organisation or as a way of earning money for consumption of goods and styles. Sayuri and Mayumi were both working as clerical *haken* at Vision. While their major interest might lie elsewhere other than career success, their perceptions and decisions about the relationship between work and marriage suggested a departure from their mother's generation.

In contrast to the majority of *haken* workers who were employed as 'general registered *haken*' (*ippan haken*), Sayuri was a 'special *haken*' (*tokutei haken*), that is, a regular worker of her *haken* agency (see Chapter 2). Put another way, Sayuri had the same employment status as salaried workers; the difference is that her employer was an in-house agency which operated under the umbrella of the Vision conglomerate. Except for certain corporate benefits such as pay increases and bonuses pertaining to regular employment, the way Sayuri was required to work was similar to other general *haken* at Vision, as she described:

> Although I was a full-time worker, there is a huge difference between employers. Compared with Vision, what my agency provides for me is really nothing, 'too meagre to be compared' (*kurabe ni naranai*). I am not paid on an hourly pay system but a monthly salary. The agency is really 'stingy' (*kechi*); my salary was increased by only 1,000 yen last year! …
>
> Well, I still get paid during the in-between period when I shift from one job assignment to another, which is different from general *haken*. But I have to come to the agency's office like ordinary work, sitting there and 'standing by' (*taiki*). And my agency is 'absolutely useless' (*zenzen yakudatanai*), when it comes to dealing with problems at the client firm. I heard that some agencies take *haken* workers' complaints seriously and are willing to negotiate with the client firms on their behalf, but it is certainly not the case for my agency.

Being a full-time *haken* of an intermediary employer was not Sayuri's own choice. She was desperate to find a regular job after graduation from college. Having tried in vain to find a normal employer, Sayuri was forced to accept an offer of regular employment from a *haken* agency – in her words, it was a decision to 'resign herself to fate' (*unmei ni makaseru*) driven by a sense of crisis facing a young graduate.

Sayuri considered work as an adult duty that was no less meaningful than women's roles in the household. She worked hard and showed a professional attitude towards her job. But she was not happy about her current situation at Vision and often suffered from work-related stress, which she ascribed to the difficulty in understanding the psyche of the salarymen who lost the basic ability to communicate with people:

There is a middle-aged man who sits right next to me. He would write a rambling email over something urgent instead of explaining to me in person. And I am often the one who is to blame for misunderstanding things. That really puts me off. …

Since they are so boring and bizarre, I am not interested in cultivating a good working relationship here. Unless necessary, I would rather not interact with them. I just want to do my job properly and professionally so that those arrogant men won't assume that my work is sloppy simply because I am a woman and a *haken* worker! …

I usually work like crazy at some points of every month. I remember that once I stayed very late to meet some deadline and was the last one out of Vision's high-rise building. That was really something.

Sayuri was living with her parents and was the only daughter. Her two brothers moved out long ago. Her mother, a professional housewife, seemed to be a very domineering figure at home, which became more evident after her father retired and turned into the so-called 'bulky garbage' (*sodai gomi*). Sayuri often made derogatory comments about her father, saying how he frequently caused disaster when dealing with very simple household tasks and got an earful from her mother as a result. Because of her close relationship with her mother, Sayuri was thinking of having her future husband marrying into her family.[11] Her parent's home, in a sense, provided a haven, or a back-up plan in her words, in case she would never find an ideal partner. As she put it:

I do not have financial worries. I have free accommodation and food at home, although I did have to pay for the new furniture I recently bought for my room. My mother often says, half in jest, that if a good husband eludes me, I can make myself useful by staying at home and taking care of them when they are too old to get around. Well, there is no doubt that one's own daughter is more reliable than daughters-in-law or even sons.

I do want to get married and have children one day, but I will not stop working. I do not see the two as contradictory. … I know very well that marriage does not necessarily leads to ultimate happiness. I just do not like to die alone; it is too sad. …

I have given up hope of finding a possible match within Vision. Now I am trying to establish my circle of friends elsewhere. I recently joined an internet friends-making network introduced by my old schoolmates, which I enjoy very much.

Like Sayuri, Mayumi had her own thought about work and marriage. Mayumi was an exceptionally beautiful young woman, who worked at Vision's most popular section which had a relaxed atmosphere. Prior to her first *haken* experience at Vision, Mayumi was a regular worker of a middle-size travel firm. She loved the job very much because it involved a wide range of tourist information across the globe and frequent contact with foreigners, which made her feel that she was in some sense connected with the wider world. But the heavy workload involved, as well as long unpaid overtime hours, took a heavy toll on her health and she had to quit after ending up in hospital twice. She left her first job with what she described as 'damaged heart and body' (*shinshin boroboro*).

Mayumi was determined to find a humane firm which could treat workers with respect. So she was attracted to a *haken* job in Vision, a large firm which she thought wouldn't flout the law by exploiting employees' unpaid overtime work. Having worked on the *haken* job about a year, she decided not to renew the contract. As she explained:

> I think I've got a good idea of what it is like working at a big firm. There is nothing more I can learn from the current job; I have had enough. I like the co-workers in my section very much; they are young, smart, and easy-going. Some of them have become my friends. What really bothers me is the routine job I am doing. I need a stimulating, challenging job that fits in with my interests and enables me to learn new things.

> Anyway, the *haken* experience at Vision is not a waste of time. At least, it can make my CV look more attractive. I am going to find another *haken* job preferably at a foreign-affiliated firm which can help improve my English skills. I am yearning to study or live abroad some day. Things in Japan are becoming boring and I am curious about the unknown world.

For Mayumi, work was not only an important adult role, but also had to be something enjoyable and contributing to self-development, although she was not as career focused as Chika and Chie and didn't envision herself competing with male workers on an equal footing.

As with work, marriage was granted new meanings. Mayumi recently broke up with her boyfriend whom she had known since college. In her view, relationship or marriage was about mutual respect and true love:

> It was not easy to end such a long-term relationship but I am glad I did it. He was a self-centred man who always put his career before my needs. He didn't even discuss with me first before making an important decision that would transfer him to one of his firm's foreign branches. I can't put up with men who think women are only secondary to their life.

> At least, a woman deserves to be treated as an equal partner with due respect. Ideally, I want my life partner to regard me as more important than anything else. Is that the essence of a true relationship or marriage?

Except for the above examples, there were young girls who saw *haken*, like part-time work, as a solution to filling a void or as a period of relative freedom where they could follow their own aspirations in various pursuits before a transition to the more constricted world that marriage and family would normally enforce. I knew two girls who reached what their parents referred to as 'the marriageable age' (*kekkon tekireiki*) but refused to simply follow the traditional path of woman-hood. Benefiting from free food and accommodation at home, they enjoyed themselves in leisure consumption such as shopping and travelling. They were not hesitant to deride their parents' views as anachronistic and to criticise the conventions of the Japanese firm and salarymen. Many of them might eventually reproduce a middle-class life that their parents had expected them to lead. Yet, the decision to delay such a life itself has consequences on both individual and societal levels.[12]

Conclusion

This chapter examines how *haken* work is consumed by real people in real situations. The micro-level analysis provides a contrast with the oft-simplistic official representations. What is immediately striking is that the great majority of *haken* workers are far from being the beneficiary of the neoliberal flexibilisation of work. For some, life indeed turns out to be nothing short of dismal. It is safe to say that the purported 'individualised labour relations' (*rōdō kankei kobetsuka*) based on diversified individual choices endorsed by the state (Chapter 4) is a luxury that only the cream of the non-regular legion who successfully negotiate the labour market can afford. The newly constructed individual liberty and responsibility underpinning increased flexibility and employment differentials are flying in the face of forced social conditions which many *haken* and non-regular workers are unable to unshackle.

The above generalisation, however, should be qualified by taking into careful consideration the diversity and complexity of individual experience. All the *haken* and regular workers, with whom I worked together or interacted in other various ways, are not Weberian 'ideal' types of individuals, even though they at times exhibit some of the 'idealised' attributes.[13] Their different perceptions and practices reveal the oft-subtle negotiations facing individuals in everyday life between self-driven goals and dreams and socially imposed roles and expectations, as well as the ever-changing meaning of workplace, work and personhood. The emergence of *haken* and its associated phenomena is accompanied by a growing trend towards self-development as opposed to the declining importance of corporate belonging-ness in the Japanese workplace. This trend is evident in some of my ethnographic examples where a group of young *haken* women engaged in the creation of new relationships between work and other important areas of life such as marriage; their career ambitions or self pursuits were challenging and changing, in myriad small ways and to varying degrees, the important Japanese gender roles.

7 Conclusion

Haken's 'symbolic' values

> Individuals enter the labour market as persons of character, as individuals embedded in networks of social relations and socialised in various ways, as physical beings identifiable by certain characteristics (such as phenotype and gender), as individuals who have accumulated various skills (sometimes referred to as 'human capital') and tastes (sometimes referred to as 'cultural capital') and as living beings endowed with dreams, desires, ambitions, hopes, doubts and fears.

In the ideology of neoliberalism often subsumed under the rubric of 'globalisation', such individuals, as described above by David Harvey (2005: 168), are reduced to an exhilarating version of persons acting mainly in conformity with market exchange. According to so-called 'free-market' principles seen as an ethic itself and a guide for all human action, individuals are entitled to free trade and private property but also morally obliged to be employable and entrepreneurial (Treanor 2005). This market-oriented person designed to be moving away from the regulations of the state apparatus is at the heart of the flexibilisation of work, a popular discourse on political economy which prefers short-term contractual relations such as temporary agency work or *haken* employment in the Japanese context.

The emergence of *haken* during the past two decades corresponds with the rise of the neoliberal regime across many parts of the world. Tom Gill (2001: 198) points out that a transformation in the pattern of casual labour in Japan is accompanied by a change in nomenclature; non-regular workers who are given appealing new names such as *pāto* (part-timer) and *furītā* (free *arbeiter*) turn into 'solitary casuals, driven by metaphors of freelance entrepreneurship' and as a consequence, 'the visible casual workforce, with its potential for solidarity or even rebellion, and its susceptibility to stigma, is evaporating'. Quite similarly, with the rapid expansion of *haken* in the Japanese workplace, '*haken*' has become a key word referring to a fashionable mode of non-regular employment and a new category of self-confident individuals who are invested with a veneer of individuality and professionalism.

If key words, as Anna Wierzbicka (1997: 16, 31) puts it, provide a condensed introduction to *how* basic patterns of everyday life and cultural scripts are organised around them, then they are also a useful vehicle for studying *why* a specific society becomes fixated on certain cultural patterns or scripts at a specific point of time. The need to investigate both these *how* and *why* aspects of key words lies in the view that society is in a state of flux, constantly being constructed and reconstructed. Thus, the study of *haken* and its associated phenomena is essentially to explore the internal dynamics of Japan. Along with *haken*, the concept of 'dignity' has risen to prominence, often manifesting itself in the form of verbal compounds popularised by Japanese best-sellers such as 'women's dignity' (Sakahigashi 2006), 'men's dignity' (Kawakita 2006), 'parents' dignity' (Sakahigashi 2007), 'the company's dignity' (Ozasa 2007) and 'the nation's dignity' (Fujiwara 2005). The dignity of *haken*, as portrayed in the popular TV drama of *Haken's Dignity*, consists in *haken* workers' professional attitude and ability, which questions the sharp division of treatment between regular and non-regular workers in the Japanese workplace. The implication is that what it means to be meaningful work and the ideal Japanese person is in transition; the pendulum of emphasis has increasingly swung to the self and correspondingly away from the social. A new relationship between workers and firms and between work and other areas of life is in the making. Such a transformation has much to do with the Japanese mass media, which plays an important role in the initiation of high-profile agendas spotlighting a number of problems and issues surrounding *haken* and other non-regular workers. Those agendas, in turn, have provoked a series of fierce debates among a plurality of powerful actors and groups, resulting in a 'social phenomenon' (*shakai genshō*) which continues to reverberate throughout Japanese society.

The *haken* debate

The development of *haken* is closely linked with the prolonged recession in the aftermath of the bursting of the bubble economy in the early 1990s, from which Japan only recently began to slowly recover.[1] Under the new slogan 'deregulation' (*kiseikanwa*), the state has introduced sweeping labour market reforms with the aim of bringing the nation's economy in tune with global trends. In the state wide-ranging deregulation efforts, *haken* has received most attention, being first legalised in 1985 and drastically liberalised since 1999. However, the subsequent rapid growth of *haken*, combined with the increasing ratio of non-regular to regular workers, has engendered considerable controversy. As explained in Chapter 5, *haken* has become an important element of the media-generated 'gap-widening boom' (*kakusa būmu*) where the widening socio-economic gaps between non-regular and regular workers, along with the emerging new poverty known as 'working poor' (*wākingu pua*), have attracted a great deal of public attention.

In the face of widespread concern over Japan's *kakusa* and working poor, the policy-making elite have come up with a new set of rhetorical devices and epithets in an attempt to deflect criticism. For instance, in opposing a suggestion that the post-bubble deregulation or structural reforms were to blame for Japan's yawning gaps between regular and non-regular workers, between haves and have-nots and between winners and losers, former Prime Minister Koizumi was famously quoted in the press as saying that 'there is nothing wrong with *kakusa*'; 'it is important to provide all with chances that will improve ability'; 'there are both successful and unsuccessful individuals in any historical periods'; 'the equality talked about in the past was false' (*Mainichi Shimbun*; *Nikkei Net*, 1 February, 2006).

In a similar vein, the chairman of *Nihon Keidanren*, the Japanese business federation of large firms, argues that the failure of individuals in market-centred competition is caused either by the lack of competence or by personal preferences and it is important to take the defeat stoically in accordance with the principle of 'self-responsibility' (*jikosekinin*) (*Keidanren* 18 January, 2006). Hence, for the pro-deregulation and pro-growth camp who are empowered by neoliberalism and its tenet on the flexibilisation of work, *kakusa* is a natural result of competition in Japan's shifting national and internal circumstances. It follows that *haken* employment, as the vanguard of the reorganisation of work, is a boon to both firms and individuals; while it helps improve firms' competitiveness in an increasingly globalising economy, *haken* caters to the needs of individual workers, contributing to the so-called 'individualisation of labour relations' (*rōdō kankei kobetsuka*) (see Chapter 4). In marked contrast to the prevailing national consciousness in the past characterised by the massive middle class, social division or the difference among individuals in the labour market becomes a social fact, which, if not avoidable, should be embraced and granted new meanings – an approach popularly described in Japanese as *hirakinaotta*.

However, such a stance has met with various forms of protest. Former Democratic Party of Japan leader Naoto Kan accused Prime Minister Koizumi of accelerating the polarisation trend towards 'liberalism for the strong', which he said is turning more people into either '*Horiemon* (referring to the young Internet mogul Takafumi Horie) or homeless' (*The Japan Times* 4 January, 2006). Drawing attention to the abject poor among non-regular workers, a number of academics, opinion leaders and civil activists express concern over the widening gaps and cast doubt on the state's deregulation policies. Kazumichi Goka (1999), for example, criticises the liberalisation of labour markets, suggesting that the rapid expansion of *haken* employment is detrimental to the interests of workers who are susceptible to unfair treatment. The government discourse of 'self-responsibility' has come under attack as well. As Glenn Hook and Hiroko Takeda rightly point out, 'self-responsibility', is a useful tool for the state to shape and legitimise its relationship with citizens; 'being self-responsible' is essentially to promote 'a self-sufficient life, that is, a life in which each "productive self" shoulders the responsibility to deal with his or her own economic and social risks' (2007: 109). In his criticism of the state-endorsed 'self-responsibility' theory, Makoto Yuasa (2007), an activist who argues for wide social support for the disadvantaged, states that individual effort and ability alone cannot explain away *kakusa*; there are a number of inadequate social elements such as family background, educational attainment, corporate benefits and state welfare systems, which are responsible for the widening social disparity in Japan.

In the discussion of Japan's gap-widening trend, perhaps most influential is Masahiro Yamada, a sociologist at Tokyo Gakugei University, who has written a best seller called 'Society of Expectation Gaps' (*Kibō Kakusa Shakai*) (2004). According to Yamada, *kakusa* is most acutely felt by Japan's younger generation among whom two groups have emerged: regular workers and permanent non-regular workers. The latter are regarded as 'losers' (*makegumi*) who not only lack financial security but also lose 'hope' or 'expectation' (*kibō*) because they are stuck in a predicament where their efforts cannot be rewarded. The increase in the number of such youngsters will exacerbate the low-fertility problem, threaten the family system, and increase crime rates, thereby undermining the social order in Japan, as Yamada argues in his proposal for a 'New Equal Society' (*Shin Byōdō Shakai*) (2006: 114–115, 137–138):

> The widening gap in individual income obstructs and deconstructs the for-mation of family. The percentage of unmarried people is increasingly high. Compared to 1990 when unmarried people were 32.6% for males and 13.9% for females, they rose to 47.7% for males and 32.6% for females in 2005, according to the latest national survey. ... This is because the income of males, who continue to be considered as the main breadwinners, is becoming polarised and unstabilised. In Japan, the general view remains strong that men are responsible for supporting the family, so few women will marry a man with a small and unstable income. ... Recent years have seen a decrease in the number of children among married couples, which attests to a growing anxiety towards their future income. The income gap among women is widening, so it is difficult to succeed in achieving stable double income by both husband and wife. The reality is that the number of couples who both work on non-regular employment is on the rise. In addi-tion, the past decade has seen a substantial increase in the number of divorces. Many cases are concerned with couples married within 5 years, where it is believed that the collapse of family finance caused by the hus-band's unemployment or falling income was the main reason.
>
> ...
>
> If the number of people who lose hope keeps increasing, this will cease to be individual problems and is likely to do harm to the society as a whole. More and more people take up unproductive jobs which make their efforts go unrewarded. As a result, they lose hope and incentive for work. If the situation continues, it will result not only in the loss of opportunity to make the most of their potential abilities but also a decline in labour quality for standardised, unskilled or auxiliary jobs. ... For firms, although the increasing use of non-regular workers may lead to a rise in profit for a short period, the deterioration of unskilled jobs will cause a fall in profit in the long run. Since no matter how much effort they put into their work their life standard cannot improve, those who lose hope in life will become a key element in social instability, an impediment to social integrity. As explained in detail in *Society of Expectation Gaps*, increased crimes can arise from 'the unfortunate cohort' (*fukō no michizure*), who tend to delay entry into

the society that doesn't offer hope (i.e. escape from risk), or to turn their eyes away from the hopeless reality and instead indulge in a life of pleasure, or to abandon oneself to despair. In other words, if more people think their efforts cannot be rewarded, this will pose a threat to not only the individual concerned but also the social order. If being neglected, *kakusa* will come back, like dioxin pollution, to undermine social stability.

More troubling to many critics are the inequalities in education. Takehiko Kariya, a well-known critic of government educational reforms, coins the phrase 'incentive divide' (2001) to describe how a series of education policies focusing on more respect for diversity and individuality will only result in a widening gap in educational attainment between children from different social strata. In Kariya's view, such inequality is caused by differences in incentive that are related to difference in social background; children who are born into the lower strata of society under the current policies tend to feel good about themselves even without educational ambitions, thus contributing to the reproduction of class in Japan. Arguing from an economic point of view, Atsushi Miura, a marketing analyst and the author of a best seller entitled 'Lower-class Society' (*Karyū Shakai*) (2005), suggests that the increasing percentage of Japanese people who think of themselves as lower middle class or lower class will bring about lower levels of consumption and thus lead to the stagnation of national economy. In other words, social division, whether it is actually widening or widely imagined among the general populace, has an adverse effect on many important areas of Japanese life.

The controversy over *kakusa* means that the emergence of *haken*, as a rapidly expanding new category of non-regular employment resulting from the state deregulation policies, is a highly contentious issue. Compared to other various non-regular arrangements, *haken* embodies many of the newly discovered worrying problems in the gap-widening society, which include the expanding new poverty or working poor reported by NHK and corporate scandals in connection with illegal labour dispatch, as, for example, revealed in *Asahi Shimbun*'s campaign against 'disguised *ukeo*i' (see Chapter 5). In particular, the penetration of white-collar, office *haken* workers across a variety of firms and industries calls into question the sharp division between non-regular and regular employment in the Japanese workplace. An argument has emerged: how can it be justifiable for *haken* workers to work alongside regular workers with more or less the same skills, working hours and task performances and yet to be worth less in terms of remuneration and benefits? Two contrasting views are prevalent as to whether the development of *haken* contributes to the inequality of employment status in the Japanese workplace: one lays emphasis on individual needs and motivations and the other believes the strategies of employers worsen the unequal treatment facing *haken* and non-regular workers as a whole – what Heidi Gottfried (2002b: 245) summarises as 'the usual divide between supply-side and demand-side approaches to explaining labour market phenomena'.

'The Authors Debate' on non-regular labour in contemporary Japan in *Social Science Japan Journal* reflects the above different views and foregrounds either 'flexible ways of working' voluntarily chosen by individuals or 'unstable employment' inflicted by the state and firms (Suehiro 2001). Hiroki Satō presents a benign view of Japan's changing employment practices, which are not only a necessity of economic development but also an outcome of individual choices. Drawing exclusively on government surveys and questionnaires as evidence of levels of satisfaction among individual workers, Satō *et al.* (2001:179, my brackets) argues that:

> This exercise made it clear that, compared with regular employees, part-timers and dispatch personnel (i.e. *haken*) – especially females in the latter case – tended to attach greater importance to lifestyle as opposed to their jobs. Hence we may conclude that, when workers in atypical employment selected their mode of employment, they did so with an emphasis on finding work that would be easy to fit in with their personal lifestyles. This tendency seems particularly striking in the case of female dispatch personnel and part-timers of both genders. Indeed, atypical employment does provide the worker with greater control over his or her working hours than does regular employment, enabling it to meet the needs of people who select one of these ways of working.

It is difficult to speculate whether Satō identifies himself with the political and economic circles by proposing the correlation between personal lifestyles and choices and non-regular employment. Yet, his methodology clearly begs the question as to whether the cited official statistics reveal the actual opinions of the respondents or the preconceptions of those who collect and publish such statistics.

By contrast, Mari Osawa (2001) and Charles Weathers (2001) contest the alleged individual autonomy by focusing on the consequences of government deregulation reforms and corporate strategies for individual workers. For both of them, the much-touted flexibilisation of work is primarily designed to benefit employers whose aim is to curb labour costs, rather than workers who often suffer from discrimination based on their non-regular employment status. Osawa's article also shows how a number of renowned Japanese academics are involved in the reinforcement of the state policy on the use of differentiated employment systems, thus serving to justify the exclusion of non-regular workers from the same array of benefits as are available to regular workers. The poor working conditions among non-regular workers feature importantly in Weathers's analysis of female *haken* workers, who are described as being surrounded by 'a web of gender, age and status discrimination, coupled with constant worries about job security and income' (2001: 202).[2] In Weathers' view, neither *Haken* Law nor Equal Employment Opportunity Law has proved to be effective in ameliorating, or indeed being relevant to, compensation disparity between regular and non-regular employment; wages for non-regular workers have not risen proportionally despite their increased skills and productivity in recent years. In short, the future of non-regular labour in Japan looks rather gloomy against the current backdrop where a mix of factors including 'fairly high satisfaction levels, strong efforts to legitimize differentiation and weak union impact – combined with a sagging economy – suggest that the status and pay of non-regular employees will not be rising any time soon' (Satō *et al.* 2001: 223).

Heidi Gottfried (2002b) comments that the 'supply-side considerations' and the 'demand-side considerations' are not mutually exclusive; they reflect both features of the expanded space for increasing diversification and individualisation of employment practice in Japan. Perhaps more importantly, the above debate shows different views of the individual on the part of scholars. Rather than seeing the individual as simultaneously being affected by and effecting structural changes in society, the theoretical significance of this dialectical relationship is largely overlooked in favour of a one-sided approach. The corollary is that, while individual workers, for some, are empowered by the current flexibilisation of work, they are seen by the others as the victims of shifting labour policies and corporate strategies. The divergence is echoed in the popular representation of *haken* as either benefiting or besetting the Japanese way of life – a feature often accentuated and amplified by the Japanese mass media, which confers on *haken* a blend of positive and negative values in their tendency to sensationalise the contrast between *haken* and regular workers in various contradictory ways (see Chapter 5).

In the case of *haken*, there is a need to investigate a relatively undiscussed aspect, namely *haken* agencies, the middlemen between the supply side and the demand side. In their paper on the nature and experience of TAW in the United Kingdom, Chris Forde and Gary Slater (2003: 8) point out that:

> A historical analysis also points to the centrality of the agency industry itself in shaping developments, facilitating the use of temporary labour and legitimising the role of the employment intermediaries within individual economies. This has, for examples, taken the form of sustained lobbying by individual agencies over the legal definition of agency employment, and opposition over the proposed tightening of regulations pertaining to agency employment at given points in time. In recent years, the interests of agencies have been increasingly mobilised at a national or super-national level through industry bodies, keen to promote agency employment as meeting the needs of a diverse range of individual firms and workers, in the light of both a rising interest in human resource management policies and impending regulatory reform of the industry.

In many ways, the development of *haken* agencies in Japan follows a more or less similar pattern. Since the legalisation, *haken* agencies have grown exponentially; the industry was already worth more than 50 billion US$ in fiscal 2006 (see Chapter 2). With the rapid industrial expansion, *haken* agencies have gained considerable political and economic leverage over the past decade; they have diversified their services in a number of new fields and regions, although office auxiliary or *jimukei* jobs remain the major part of their sales. In collaboration with the state, they have earned a reputation as a helper to integrate those who are pushed outside mainstream into the national workforce. By taking it upon themselves to mobilise and train women, the elderly and inexperienced or 'problematic' young people, they present themselves as contributing to employment stability and economic development. In particular, the intermediary personnel industry has made a great impact on the transformation of meaningful work by purporting to connect firms and workers in mutually beneficial ways. To be sure, much of the popularity of *haken* work can be ascribed to the increasingly powerful role of *haken* agencies in defining concepts, managing discourse and creating impression, to which I now turn.

The discourse of *haken* agencies

Applying Irving Goffman's concept 'impression management' (1959), Brian Moeran (2006: 77) in his study on a Japanese advertising agency describes how 'the management of a credible impression is ultimately a businessman's and business organisation's trick of the trade'. Such credibility management depends largely on the strategic use of performative language, which concerns not only linguistic metaphors and tropes, but also knowledge control, or the creation, negotiation, and distribution of power in political discourse (Parkin 1984). Just as an advertising agency must ensure that it manages different kinds of impression on both supply and demand sides of its business, the success of *haken* agencies lies in how to foster a credible impression by making the most of their claimed professional understanding of both firms and individual workers.

If state policy serves as an immediate instigator of *haken* employment, *haken* agencies are the linchpin, a key actor transforming official guidelines into strategic practices. In order to achieve their ambition to become the so-called 'comprehensive personnel services business' (*sōgōteki na jinzai bijinesu gyō*), *haken* agencies are flexible and imaginative in the implementation of labour policies. Amid widespread demographic concerns in contemporary Japan, the main focus of their marketing strategies has increasingly shifted from client firms to individual workers.[3] The discourse of *haken* agencies has been centred on the cultivation of fashionable identities and lifestyles so as to attract and secure as many workers as possible from a seemingly dwindling labour pool. As a new flexible way of working, *haken* is often portrayed as meeting the needs of specific individual groups, for example, as JASSA (2008) claims:

- The important point is whether the work style suits the individual.

  It is wrong to assume that only regular employment is a desirable way of working. Despite the difference in employment status, workers' satisfaction level is similar, which can be ascribed to the importance of whether the work style and content suits individual desires. ... Both the demand and the supply sides of labour have their respective views. A mature, good society should acknowledge the diversification of work that responds to the diverse needs of individual workers.

- The *haken* way of working is favoured by people of middle and advanced age and women after child care.

  While *haken* is typical of those in their 20s and 30s, it also provides opportunities for people aged above 45 and women after child care. Since the work population of regular employment remains more or less unchanged, the number of *haken* workers especially women will keep growing. Thus, it is expected that *haken* will play an important role in a rapidly aging and low-fertility society.

- It is possible to develop abilities and career through *haken* work.

  Haken means *shūshoku* or 'entrance into an occupation', rather than *shūsha* or 'entrance into a firm'. In contrast to the firm-specific training of job rotation for regular employees, *haken* makes it possible for individuals to increase the chance of taking up favourite jobs, thereby contributing to the building-up of work experience and the improvement of career prospects.

The emphasis on the individual, as described above, is concerned with not only a diversity of needs and desires among different individuals, but also an individual-tailored career focusing on occupations rather than firms. The meaning of work is being shifted from a firm-based activity where corporate belongingness is fundamental to one's social status and career success, to a self-oriented process where occupational specialisation assumes great importance and the way people work is a matter of free choice. Accordingly, in the world of *haken*, individuals become self-activating, free agents who can make their own decisions. Far from being insecure, low-paid and peripheral workers, individuals are endowed with a host of new possibilities where they can relate themselves to work, firm and the wider world in different ways, as well as developing career-focused professional skills. Such a liberating portrayal is characteristic of many of *haken* agencies' political and commercial discourses, as exemplified by the following advertising slogans constructed and promulgated by leading *haken* agencies between 2007 and 2008:

- Adecco
  Better work, Better life
  Adecco supports your ideal work and lifestyle.
  (*Adeko wa anata no risō no shigoto to raifusutairu wo sapōto shimasu.*)

- Pasona
  Make the most of people. That is Pasona's job.
  (*Hito wo ikasu. Sore ga pasona no shigoto desu.*)
  Pasona supports you who value your own self.
  (*Pasona wa jibunrashisa wo taisetsuni suru anata wo ōen shimasu.*)

- Staff Service
  Be ready to succeed.
  (*Koete ikō.*)

Attain the goal you have decided for yourself.
(*Jibun ga kimeta mokuhyō wo* kuriā *suru.*)
Have the feeling of improvement.
(*Seichō shite iru to iu jikkan ga aru.*)
Strongly support you who enjoy daily work with a forward-looking attitude.
(*Mainichi no shigoto wo maemukini tanoshinde iku anata wo kyōryokuni sapōto shimasu.*)

- Recruit Staffing
  Help create a world where anyone can work happily and both people and firms are radiant with success.
  (*Dare mo ga ikiikito shigoto wo shite iru, hito mo kigyō mo kagayaite iru, sonna yononaka tsukuri no otetsudai wo shi tai.*)
  Contribute to the society and the creation of new employment opportunities for people and firms.
  (*Hito to kigyō no aratana shūgyō kikai wo tsukuridashi, shakai ni kōkenshite ikitai.*)

- Manpower Japan
  Carefully develop the only career in the world that is tailored to you.
  (*Sekai ni hitotsu shika nai, anata dake no kyaria wo taisetsuni sodatte ikitai.*)
  So that you can smile after one year, and five years …
  (*Ichinengo mo, soshite gonengo mo, anata ga waratte irareru yōni.*)

It is easy to see that the discourse of *haken* agencies and the stance of the state converge on the promotion of the market-oriented person informed by the neoliberal doctrine. Both invoke such fashionable concepts as 'self-development' (*jikokeihatsu*), 'individuality' (*kosei*) and 'diversity' (*tayōsei*) to stress the need to develop a more flexible and occupation-based labour market in Japan where an increased use of non-regular workers is the single most important aspect. Moreover, in the face of the negative interpretations of *kakusa*, they are frequently forced to defend themselves on the same ground; the scandal-laden *haken* industry is particularly subject to criticism. Nevertheless, it might be difficult to suggest that there is concerted action; while the state and business leaders, as shown in Chapter 4, continue to endorse a core-peripheral labour duality with non-regular employment complementing the Japanese long-term employment conventions, *haken* agencies commit themselves mainly to the creation of enticing images of work and life where it is up to the individual who makes choices in accordance with his or her own dreams and ambitions; such an endeavour often presents *haken* workers as the very antithesis of the post-war salaryman and office lady model.

Haken's 'symbolic' values

Significantly, what emerges from the *haken* debate and the discourse of *haken* agencies is 'symbolic values', the assumed positive or negative elements that are described as either beneficial or detrimental to the Japanese society. The Japanese mass media provides a discursive space where a number of powerful groups and actors vie to claim expert knowledge and where different images and ideas are juxtaposed, clashed and negotiated. In this dynamic symbolic competition, *haken* and its associated phenomena serve as 'the captured event', which 'does not start out by regarding differences of status as necessarily causal'; that is, the image of capture tends to deflect attention from the question of asymmetry and inequality in discursive power and the relationships among those who have 'semantic creativity' to name, define or objectify and thereby impose meaning of malleable symbols (Parkin 1982: xlvi–xlvii).

The anthropological study of political discourse addresses both symbolic statement and action (Cohen 1969). On the one hand, symbols, whether they are languages, objects, values or rituals, offer important analytical windows onto culturally and historically specific ways of thinking and doing. On the other, however, they are 'multi-vocal' (Turner 1967) and malleable in meaning construction, as evidenced by the debate where there are different interpretations of *kakusa* and *haken*. The debate throws into relief the hegemonic aspect of symbols; the metaphorical play of political language among the ruling elite and the intelligentsia impinges importantly on the way in which people perceive, experience and act upon the ever-changing social life. Thus, the link of *haken* employment with individual freedom or autonomy has much to do with, for example, the role of *haken* agencies in 'crafting', 'aestheticising' and 'professionalising' the images of non-regular work (Smith 2006: 187). Suffice it to say that the much vaunted flexibilisation and individualisation of work is to a great extent foisted upon the general populace. Such discursive power inherent in asymmetrical and unequal social relations is well illustrated by David Parkin (1982: xlvi):

> Power, then, returns to our centre in social anthropology. But it is not simply the power which rest on the acquisition of land, myth, and material objects, but rather that which comes from unequal access to semantic creativity, including the capacity to nominate others as equal or unequal, animate or inanimate, memorable or abject, discussor or discussed. The struggle to objectify others (i.e. to remain principal or sole agent) is paralleled by the struggle to make acceptable new modes by which this may be done: systems of naming and entitlement; the innovative use of metaphor and other tropes; redefining an existing epistemology and/or privileging another; providing "definitive" or "authentic" cultural translations; and widening, narrowing, and ranking the available range of communicative codes.

The content analysis of political language *in action* provides important clues to the understanding of the unfolding *haken* phenomenon, as well as the shifting meaning of work and personhood in Japan. Together, those factors shed light on the internal dynamics within the Japanese establishment. The intense interactions between and among a number of power groups attest to the complex process of political discourse where complications frequently arise – which questions, as Angela Cheater (1999: 4) points out, Foucault's over-straight link between discourse and (dis)empowerment. In the *haken* discourse, there are forces of both change and continuity at work. As mentioned earlier, in challenging the market-oriented neoliberal person advocated by the pro-deregulation camp, many opinion leaders sound the alarm over the worrying problems of *kakusa* such as working poor among non-regular workers, which are likely to undermine Japan's harmony-focused traditional values that have sustained important areas of life like family, education, and work. In addition, there is also a faction within the demand side, which has reservations about the growing reliance on non-regular workers. Some firms are concerned that recent personnel changes could jeopardise Japan's worldwide reputation for producing high-quality goods. For example, the president of Matsushita Plasma Display Panel Co. was quoted as saying that 'unless we secure experienced workers on the factory floor permanently, we won't be able to maintain high product quality' (*Nikkei*, 15 November, 2006). Others, like Sumitomo Mitsui Banking Corp., maintain that hiring regular employees will not significantly increase labour cost because billings from *haken* agencies have been rising rapidly (*Nikkei Weekly*, 3 March, 2008). The point is that although *haken* workers are flexible or 'just-in-time', they are not necessarily cheap, especially compared with other non-regular arrangements.[4]

The divergent opinions provide an important perspective on 'the self-conception of powerful groups' in shifting political relationships (Carrier 1996), which is revealed by the different ways in which they draw on discursive material, 'traditional' or 'global', depending on their political agendas, for example, whether they aim to protect or change the status quo. The acknowledgement of this political pluralism is crucial to grasping the changing ideological discourse in Japan, which in turn has profound implications for ordinary people in everyday life. In contrast to the perceived oft-simplistic symbolic values which either enfeeble or empower the individual, the consumption of *haken* by real people in concrete situations is extremely complex and varied. This is particularly the case among those who constitute the subject of the *haken* debate but are rarely given the political space to articulate their feelings. As examined in Chapter 6, there is a yawning gap between public representation and everyday practice, not least when it comes to the harsh reality faced by many *haken* workers whose non-regular employment status puts them in a much more vulnerable position than their regular counterparts. The newly sanctified individual freedom on the part of the political and economic elite certainly eludes the bulk of the non-regular population. Yet, this observation should not lead to the reductionist view that all *haken* and other no-regular workers are the victim of structural reforms in contemporary Japan. To be sure, individuals do not simply conform to or contest imposed policies and discourses in what is often referred to as 'rational' fashion; their experience being embedded in the nitty-gritty of daily life and struggle is both more and less than officially represented symbolic values, often depending on a nexus of intersecting variables such as gender, generation and class. The typical picture that emerges is an intricate pattern of everyday practice where individuals constantly negotiate between self-driven goals and dreams and socially imposed roles and expectations in subtly complex and shifting ways. In this connection, what Anthony Giddens (1979) and others (e.g. Ortner 1984) variously describe as the heterogeneous and dynamic relationship between 'structure and agency' or 'system and practice' bears repeating.

Despite the fragmentations and limitations at both macro and micro levels, *haken*'s symbolic values have a reality of their own; they are powerful in mobilising motivations, transforming commitments and reorganising experiences. The discursive impact is two-fold. First, the dark side of *haken* employment, as highlighted by media revelations of the mishandling of workers on the part of client firms and *haken* agencies, has exposed a number of pressing issues regarding the legal protection of non-regular workers, with which the state has to contend. As a result, several legislative revisions have been enforced to tackle problems such as working poor affecting non-regular workers and to improve non-regular workers' working conditions. For example, new principles with respect to 'livelihood protection' (*seikatsu hogo*), 'the minimum standards of wholesome and cultured living' (*kenkō de bunkatekina saiteigendo no seikatsu*) and 'the real situation of employment' (*shūgyō no jittai*) were added to Minimum Age Law (*Saitei Chingin Hō*) and Labour Contract Law (*Rōdō Keiyaku Hō*) (*Asahi Shimbun*, 28 November, 2007).

Moreover, the various speculations over Japan's widening gaps have laid bare the limitation of the existing social safety net and welfare systems, which are devised mainly to protect regular workers. The problem is further underlined by soaring rates of dismissal of non-regular workers at the end of 2008 when a global economic downturn hit Japan hard; the nation's economy, the second-largest in the world after that of the United States, was reported to suffer from the biggest contraction since the 1974 oil crisis in the last three months of 2008. The massive layoffs have provoked a new wave of concern over non-regular workers' poor treatment and inequality in the Japanese workplace (Weathers 2009). Pressure has piled upon the state to take non-regular workers' vulnerable situations seriously; in addition to proposals to reform the existing unemployment benefits system and to introduce new supporting measures, there is criticism of the recent revisions of *Haken* Law, which are said to only result in the deterioration of unemployment among non-regular workers under the current economic recession (*Nikkei*, 22 December, 2008).

At the same time, the perceived positive values of *haken*, that is, the emphasis on individual needs and choices promoted most enthusiastically by *haken* agencies, have provided fresh discursive material through which Japanese people reinterpret and reposition themselves in the wider world of challenge. Recent years have seen a growing trend towards individuality and self-development coupled with the declining importance of corporate belongingness in the Japanese workplace. As explained in Chapter 1, this trend is germane to the anthropological understanding of Japanese personhood, which is centred on the changing relationship between self and roles. With the collapse of the 'firm-as-family' ideology, the idea of being loyal to a single firm throughout one's lifetime is not as popular as before; the term 'lifetime employment' (*shūshin koyō*) has been replaced by 'long-term employment' (*chōki koyō*) or 'regular employment' (*seiki koyō*). No longer is it taken for granted that personal achievements and interests should be subjugated to group-oriented corporate values and obligations. The notion of *kejime*, which defines the ideal Japanese person by separating self from social roles in a proper manner, is thus under reconstruction.

The changing perception of personhood has consequences for the image production of new types of workers. The media increasingly favour suitably qualified, diverse individuals with marketable, specialised skills over well-educated, middle-level individuals with firm-specific, generalised skills, as evidenced by the portrayal of the 'super *haken*' Haruko in *Haken's Dignity*. While the previous interpretations stress the pursuit of individual ambitions and needs within largely firm-centred contexts, the current language of self-development or individuality is geared towards the need for 'ready fighting power' (*sokusen-ryoku*), that is, stronger external labour markets based on portable professional qualifications, as well as for increasing use of non-regular workers. The argument that it is important for workers to 'enter into an occupation' (*shūshoku*) rather than to 'enter into a firm' (*shūsha*), as proposed by *haken* agencies (JASSA 2008), has gradually gained in popularity.

In addition, with the adoption of new 'hybrid' forms of corporate governance involving 'a mix of elements from the "old" Japanese model and "new" more Anglo-American practices' (Jackson and Miyajima 2007: 39), Japanese firms have undergone significant changes in labour management, which have an important bearing on the welfare of employees. As Gregory Jackson (2007) points out, although Japanese firms continue to support lifetime employment in principle, the introduction of 'merit-based remuneration principles' (*seikashugi*)[5] with certain considerations of individual performance and ability, together with other shareholder-oriented adjustments,[6] has resulted in a shrinking core of lifetime employment and potential for growing social closure to these jobs for young Japanese.

Indeed, the impact of the above changes under a welter of confusing arguments is particularly striking among the younger generations of workers, who are more willing than their parent's generation to envision and exercise new ideas of identity, work and life (Gordon and White 2004; Lunsing 2006). As my ethnographic examples (Chapter 6) show, a growing number of young regular and *haken* workers actively engage in the creation of new relationships in myriad small ways between themselves and firms and between work and other areas of life, which contrast sharply with implicit and explicit norms established by the post-war salaryman and office lady model.

The emergence of a new category of non-regular workers

This study of *haken* is prompted by a research puzzle: why has *haken* become such a powerful symbol in both political discourse and everyday life, given the fact that it only accounts for a relatively small proportion of the non-regular workforce especially compared to part-timers, by far the largest and most long-standing non-regular group in Japan? In solving the puzzle, I have examined *haken* from a number of interconnected perspectives including historical, political, economic and socio-cultural, which take into consideration both macro-level and micro-level analyses.

What immediately distinguishes *haken* from other non-regular labour arrangements is the triangular employment structure where *haken* workers have a dual relationship with both the *haken* agency and the client firm to which they are assigned. This recently developed institution is a barometer of fast-moving national and international conditions in Japan; it has pertinence to the shifting relationship of labour to the state, to firms, to entrepreneurial opportunities and to the wider world. To a great degree, the emergence of *haken* as a new category of non-regular workers is brought about by the internal dynamic political debate where a number of contending powerful groups and actors come together with different agendas to compete for the legitimacy of their divergent discourses. It is the resulting 'symbolic values', combined with forces from outside, that have made *haken* a powerful symbol of contemporary Japanese society.

Glossary of terms

Japanese terms

agura wo kaku   rest on one's laurels

akuhō   bad or malicious law

aratana hinkon   new poverty. Also see *zettaiteki hinkon.*

arubaito   a type of part-time jobs in Japan particularly popular with students. The term is originated from the German word *arbeiter.* Also see *pâto.*

bara no michi   thorny path

benri   convenient

bônenkai   year-end party

chiisai koto   small matter

chingin kakusa   income disparity. Also see *kakusa.*

chōki koyō   long-term employment. Also see *seiki koyō.*

chōki koyō kanrei   long-term employment convention

chōkakuteki na rōdōsha   core labour

daikokubashira   the main pillar which supports a traditional Japanese household. The term is used to emphasise the role of Japanese men as the main breadwinner in a household.

dakyô shimasen   not to make compromises

deai   encounter

dokutokusei   uniqueness

dokyô   courage or guts

datsusaragumi   former salaried (male) workers who have escaped from the salaryman life. The term suggests a relatively free life independently of corporate restraints imposed by the Japanese firm.

deshabari   obtrusive

donichi ranchi kai   Saturday-or-Sunday lunch gathering

doryoku   effort

eikyū fumetsu   immortal

ekimu   service

enpuroiabiriti   employability

fuantei   unstable

fuantei na koyō no shōchō   the symbol of unstable employment

fukō no michizure   the unfortunate cohort

furītā freeter.   The term is a combination of the English 'free' and the German '*arbeiter*'. It was created in the late 1980s to capture the phenomenon of young people postponing their entry into the regular labour market and instead engaging in temporary jobs after leaving school. It now generally refers to young people who hop from one temporary job to another. Aslo see nīto.

futsû **no sararîman**   normal salaryman

gaman   endure or persevere

gamigami onna   battleaxe

Gekkan Jinzai Bijinesu   Monthly Personnel Business. The first nationwide B2B *haken* magazine mainly subscribed to by *haken* agencies (70 per cent) and corporate and government personnel departments (20 per cent).

genryō keiei   the rationalisation or downsizing of management. The term is originated from a government campaign in the aftermath of the oil crisis in the 1970s, which urged firms to step up their efforts to whittle down the core workforce.

gisō ukeoi   disguised *ukeoi*. The term refers to a widespread illegal practice of disguising *haken* workers as *ukeoi* workers. It is difficult to distinguish between the two as both workers are dispatched to work in the facilities of client firms. The only difference is that *haken* workers are legally defined to work under the direct instruction and supervision of their client firms, whereas ukeoi workers are prohibited from taking orders from client firms and are only subject to the authority of their own employers, i.e. dispatch firms. For client firms, the use of *ukeoi* workers costs less and is free from certain regulations such as restrictions on contract length. Also see *haken shain* and *ukeoi*.

gyaku tama no koshi   a man married to a woman of wealth. The idiom means the gender reverse of *tama no koshi* or 'a woman married to a man of wealth'. Also see *kakusa kon*.

gyakuten genshō   reverse phenomenon

haken   dispatch. The term is commonly used as an abbreviation to describe 'dispatched workers', 'dispatch firms' or 'dispatch employment/service'. Also see *haken* shain and *haken gaisha*.

haken **gaisha**   haken agencies. A newly developed type of intermediary employ-ment agencies which employ and dispatch workers to client firms. Also see *haken shain*.

Haken **Jinrui**   *Haken* people. Also see *haken*.

haken **narikin**   *haken* parvenu. A derogatory term used by some to refer to a minority of high-earning *haken* workers.

haken **shain**   dispatched workers. A newly developed category of non-regular workers, who are involved in a triangular employment system where they work at the facilities of and under the authority of client firms whilst being typically employed and dispatched by employment agencies. Until the first enforcement of *Haken* Law in 1986, such labour leasing in the private sector was legally banned during post-war Japan.

hatarakigai wo kanjiru   feel the meaning of work or feel fulfilled in one's job

hataraku hinkonsō   working poor. Also see *wākingu pua*.

hataraku hitobito no ishiki   working people's way of thinking or point of view

hataraku koto wa ikiru koto da   to work is to live

hidoi   awful or terrible

hinkon no saiseisan   the reproduction of poverty

hirakinaotta   taking a defiant attitude or being prepared to confront adverse situations. The term often means a sudden shift in stance from defending to attacking.

hirôdôryoku   non-functioning or dormant labour force

hiseiki   non-regular. Also see *seiki*.

hiseiki koyō   non-regular employment. Also see *seki koyō*.

hiseiki shain   non-regular workers. Also see *seiki shain*.

hiyatoi *haken*   day haken labourers/business. The term refers to a type of *haken* employment where workers are dispatched to client firms on a daily basis, usually via their agencies' mobile phone networks. Also known as on *kōru wākā* and *wan kōru wākā*.

hiyatoi rôdôsha   day labourers

hokori   pride

hōmuresuka suru wakamono   young people who are becoming homeless

hone wo umeru   bury one's bones. The idiom means making a place one's last home, often being used as a figurative expression for staying in a firm until retirement.

honne-tatemae   real intention and professed intention. Also see *ninjyo-giri* and *uchi-soto*.

Horiemon   a recent neologism referring to the young Internet mogul Takafumi Horie, who is often portrayed as a symbol of Japan's widening socio-economic gaps. Also see *kakusa*.

hōrō suru   wandering around

ichioku sōchōryu   one-hundred-million middle class

ie   the Japanese traditional family system

ijime   bully

ikigai   that which makes one's life seem worth living

Ikujiren   the Tokyo-based association which promotes the idea of child-caring salarymen

ippan *haken*   general *haken*. The term refers to *tōroku* gata or 'the registered type' of *haken* workers who are registered with *haken* agencies. Also see *tokutei haken* and *jyōyō koyō gata*.

ippan *haken* gaisha   general *haken* agencies. One of the two major types of *haken* agencies, which are allowed to hire both 'the registered type' (*tōroku gata*) and 'the employed type' (*jyōyō koyō gata*) of *haken* workers. Their business start-up requires the sanction of MLHW. Also see *tokutei haken gaisha*.

ippanshoku   auxiliary employment track. One of the two common regular employment tracks in the Japanese workplace, which involves clerical or secretarial jobs and is typically reserved for female workers. Also see *sōgōshoku*.

ittaikan   sense of belonging to or sense of oneness with

izakaya   the Japanese-style bar

jibun no jikan wo taisetsu ni suru   cherish or make the most of your private time

jibun no nōryoku   my own ability

jikojitsugen   self-realisation

jikokeihatsu   self-development, self-enlightenment or self-study. Also see *kosei*.

jikosekinin   self-responsibility

jimukei   clerical or secretarial work, which usually involves office jobs of an auxiliary nature

jimushori saabisu   clerical service

jinzai ikusei   the cultivation of human talents

jittai   reality

jizen mensetsu   ex-ante interviews

jiyō   freedom

jyōhō kakusa   digital divide. Also see *kakusa*.

jyōyō koyō gata   the employed type, also known as *tokutei haken*. One of the two major groups of *haken* workers, who are employed as full-time workers by *haken* agencies. Also see *tōroku* gata and *ippan haken*.

kachigumi   winners. Also see *makegumi*.

kachō   section manager

kaigai *haken*   overseas *haken*. A type of *haken* employment where *haken* workers are dispatched to client firms operating abroad.

kaikyū   class. Also see *kaisō*.

kaisha kengaku   a tour around the workplace

kaisha ningen   company person

kaishashugi   company-centred principles

kaisha kazokushgi no shūen   the demise of familism in the workplace

kaisū   class. Also see *kaikyū*.

kakusa   disparity or divide. The term is closely associated with a surge of interest in Japan's widening socio-economic gaps between regular and non-regular workers in a number of areas of life including education, health, marriage and work.

kakusa būmu   the gap-widening boom

kakusa kon   marriage divide. The term's popularity has much to do with a high-profile celebrity marriage in 2007 between Noriko Fujiwara, a superstar actress, and Tomonori Jinnai, a celebrity comedian. The couple are well-known for their 'divide' in income, fame and appearance. Also see *kakusa* and *gyaku tama no koshi*.

kakusa shakai   the gap-widening society

kakusa shakai no genkyō   the main culprit of the gap-widening society

kakushin   innovation

kanpai   completely beaten

kao awase   face-to-face meeting

Karyû Shakai   Lower-class Society. The term is coined and popularised by Atsushi Miura's bestseller (2005).

kawatta seikaku   unusual or strange personality

kechi   stingy or narrow-minded

Keidanren   the abbreviation for *Nihon Keizai Dantai Renmei* or the Japanese Federation of Economic Organisation, which is the most powerful employers' organisation in Japan. Also see *Nikkeiren*.

keiken   competence or experience

kekkon tekireiki   the marriageable age

keiretsu gaisha   group of companies, which usually operate under the umbrella of a Japanese conglomerate and include its subsidiaries and subcontractors.

keiyaku   contract

keizai hyōronka   economic commentators

Keizai Zaisei Shimon Kaigi   the Japanese government's Council on Economic and Fiscal Policy

kejime   differentiation. The term refers to the knowledge and ability needed to separate self and social roles properly in various contexts and stages of Japanese life

kejime wo tsukeru   the observance of *kejime* or differentiation. Also see *kejime*.

kenkô kakusa   health divide. Also see *kakusa*.

kenzen na shijyō shakai   sound market society

kibishī   harsh or severe

kibō   hope or expectation

Kibō Kakusa Shakai   Society of Expectation Gaps. The term is coined and popularised by Masahiro Yamada's bestseller (2004).

kigyō fōdo   corporate climate

kigyô kumiai   company unionism

kindaika   modernisation

kikokushijyo   returnee children

kiseikanwa   deregulation. Also see *kōzō kaikaku*.

kisetsukō   seasonal workers. The term refers to a former category of male-dominated temporary workers. Also see *rinjkō* and *pāto*.

ki wo tsukau   care about or be sensitive to

kizutsuku kokoro   bruised or injured heart

kodawari jyôken   individualised preferences

kōgai ukeoi   off-the-premises outsourcing workers. Also see *ukeoi*.

kokoro no yutakasa   the richness of mind or heart

kokusaika   internationalisation

kōnai ukeoi   on-the-premises outsourcing workers. Also see *ukeoi*.

konpuraiansu   compliance

kojinshugi   individualism. The term is distinguished from individuality (*kosei*) and has connotations of selfishness and immaturity. Also see *kosei*.

kosei   individuality

kōreika shakai   aging society

kōzō kaikaku   structural reforms, which were initiated by the former Koizumi government. Also see *kiseikanwa*.

kurabe ni naranai   cannot be compared

kōzen no bōmu   the unprecedented boom

kyōiku kakusa   education divide. Also see *kakusa*.

kyokasei   license system

makegumi   losers. Also see *kachigumi*.

mattô na   serious

mēkā   manufacturers

mensetsu   interview

medatanai   invisible or not easily noticed

mīfechi   Me-Fetishism. The neologism is coined to criticise a new generation of young workers who are described as having strong narcissistic tendencies, known as *jikoai no tsuyoi sedai*.

mikeiken kangei   welcome the inexperienced

nandemo shiteiru otoko   the man who knows everything

naraigoto   cultural accomplishments, which are traditionally designed to train women to become 'the truly sophisticated Japanese woman' (*yamato nadeshiko*) in preparation for a good marriage. They usually include tea ceremony, flower arranging and kimono-dressing.

nenkôjyoretsu   seniority-based promotion and remuneration systems. Also see *seikashugi*

nenpôsei   the annual pay system, which is distinct from the monthly pay system of the Japanese salaryman

nettokafe nanmin   net-cafe refugees. The neologism is created to describe a recently discovered phenomenon where an increasing number of people use 24-h internet cafes as a home substitute to avoid the expenses of renting and living in apartments.

nihon wo mushibamu yamai   disease gnawing away at Japan

Nikkei   the abbreviation for *Nihon Keizai Shimbun*, one of the major Japanese newspapers

Nikkeiren   the abbreviation for *Nihon Keieisha Dantai Renmei* or the Japanese Federation of Managers' Organisation, which was formulated in 1948 and merged into *Keidanren* in 2002. Also see *Keidanren*.

nijyū *haken*   double *haken*, an illegal labour supply practice where *haken* workers are redispatched to a third party. Also see *haken*.

ningen no songen   human dignity

ninjyo-giri   human feelings and obligation. Also see *honne-tatemae* and *uchi-soto*.

ninpukashi   the leasing of labour. The term is often used in a pejorative sense, indicating the exploitative nature of labour-supply business.

niito NEET, which is originally coined by the Social Exclusion Unit of the British cabinet in 1999, referring to young people who are Not in Employment, Education or Training

nojyukusha (homeless) people who sleep in a bivouac or in the open

nomikai drinking sessions

nomi nakama drinking friends

nukegara dead skins or slough

ōeru OL, short for Office Lady

okosama shain childish workers

on kōru wākā on-call workers, also known as *wan kōru wākā* or *hiyatoi haken*

onna shachô female president

otoko no sekai men's world

otsubone *haken* powerful, veteran female *haken*, who have substantial influence in the workplace. The word *otsubone* originally means a dignified lady who has her own private chamber or office at court or in the shogun's castle. It is now commonly used as a derogatory term, referring to ill-natured or ill-tempered women, as evidenced by *otsubone ijime*, or the bullying inflicted by powerful, usually unmarried, female office workers.

oyabun-kobun kankei quasi-parent–children relationship

oyakata masters or bosses. In the context of labour development, the term refers to the senior member of Meiji working-class society, who, like today's *haken* agencies, organised and dispatched workers to Japanese firms.

pāto part-time work/workers, a major category of non-regular work/workers dominated by females. The term *pāto* became common in the late 1960s when a female-dominated group of temporary workers gradually replaced former categories of male-dominated temporary workers known as *kisetsukō* (seasonal workers) and *rinjikō* (emergency workers).

pawā hara short for power harassment

pinhane rake-off

renai kakusa love divide. Also see *kakusa*.

Rengo the abbreviation for *Nihon Rōdō Kumiai Sōrengōkai* or Japanese Trade Union Confederation. *Rengo* is the largest national trade union in Japan.

rifujin na unreasonable or unjust

Riku Nabi short for Recruitment Navigation

rinjikō emergency workers, a former category of male-dominated temporary workers. Also see *kisetsukō* and *pāto*.

risshinshussei climbing up the ladder of career success or advancement in life/career, also called *shussei*

rōdō kankei kobetsuka individualisation of labour relations

Rōdō Keiyaku Hō Labour Contract Law

Rôdô Kijyun Hô Labour Standards Law

rōdōryoku labour force

Rōdōryoku Chōsa Labour Force Survey

Rôdôsha *Haken* Hô *Haken* Law, short for Law for Ensuring the Proper Operation of *Haken* Business and Improved Working Conditions for *Haken*

Workers *(Rôdôsha Haken Jigyō no Tekisei na Unei no Kakuho oyobi Haken Rōdōsha no Shūgyō Jyōken no Seibi nado ni kansuru Hōritsu)*

rōdōsha hogo   labour protection

Rôdôsha *Haken* Jigyô Hôkoku   *Haken Business Report*, which is summarised and published by MHLW based on the annual report submitted by all types of *haken* agencies

rōgō ni sonaerubeki desu   should provide for the old age

ryôsai kenbo   good wife, wise mother

sōbisu zangyō   unpaid overtime work

Saitei Chingin Hō   Minimum Wage Law

sakushu suru shikumi   the exploiting system

samatsu na kakusa   trivial disparity or divide

sararīman   salaryman or salaried workers

seikashugi   merit-based or individualised pay and promotion systems. Also see *nenkôjyoretsu*.

seikatsu hogo   livelihood protection

seiki   regular. Also see *hiseiki*.

seiki koyō   regular employment. Also see *choki koyō* and *hiseiki koyō*.

seiki shain   regular workers. Also see *hiseiki shain*.

seirei 26 gyômu   26 designated occupations, which are perceived as more professional and specialised than newly liberalised *haken* occupations known as '*jiyûka gyômu*'.

seku hara   short for sexual harassment

shagaikō   outsiders or outside workers. The term was used in the past to refer to non-regular, especially *ukeoi*, workers, as opposed to insiders or regular workers.

shakai genshō   social phenomenon

shakaijin   a person of society. The term has connotations of maturity and respectableness.

shikata ga nai koto da   a matter that you cannot avoid or argue about

shitauke geisha   subcontractors or subcontracting firms

shi nō kō shō   the officially specified four-class system in pre-Maiji Japan: 'warriors' (*shi*), 'peasants' (*nō*), 'artisans' (*kō*) and 'merchants' (*shō*).

Shin Byōdō Shakai   New Equal Society (Yamada 2006)

shinshin boroboro   damaged or broken heart and body

shoaku no kongen   the root of all evils

shōkai yotei *haken*   the temp-to-perm *haken*, which provides a screening period for both *haken* workers and the client firm as a step towards permanent employment

Shokuan   the abbreviation for *Shokugyō Antei Jyo*

Shokugyō Antei Hō   Employment Security Law

Shokugyō Antei Jo   the former government employment institution, which has been replaced by 'Hello Work'

shokugyō kunren   vocational training

shokugyō nōryoku kaihatsu   vocational skills development

shokutaku   entrusted workers. The term refers to a specific type of contract workers in Japan who are rehired after mandatory retirement.

shōshika shakai   low-birth rate society

shōeki no antei   the stability of earnings

Shōgyō Kōzō Kihon Chōsa   Employment Structure Survey. The survey is conducted by the Japanese government every 5 years.

shukkō   one of the two common internal labour adjustments utilised by Japanese firms to transfer excess regular workers to their subsidiaries or subcontractors. *Shukkō* workers remain a nominal regular member of the original parent firm while working at the transferred firm. Also see *tenseki*.

shōsha   trading firms

shozoku   belonging

shussei   career success. Also see *risshin shussei*.

shūsha   entrance/entering into a firm. Also see *shūshoku*.

shūshin koyō   lifetime employment

shōshoku   entrance/entering into an occupation. Also see *shūsha*.

sodai gomi   bulky garbage

sōgōshoku   comprehensive employment track. One of the two common regular employment tracks in the Japanese workplace, which leads to positions in management and is dominated by male workers. Also see *ippanshoku*.

sōgôteki na jinzai bijinesu gyô   comprehensive personnel services business

sonoba shinogi   a short-term solution that only helps get out of the current difficult situation

sokozumi   in the bottom. The term typically means a role at the bottom of hierarchy in the Japanese workplace which involves doing simple or unskilled jobs to assist superiors.

sokusenryoku   ready fighting power

sōshisōai   mutual consideration and love

sōzōsei   creativity

tachiba   social standing/position

taiki   standing by

tayôsei   diversity

tehaishi   unscrupulous labour brokers. The term is often used to condemn intermediary employment agencies for mishandling or exploiting workers.

teianryoku   the ability to make proposals

tenseki   one of the two common internal labour adjustments utilised by Japanese companies to transfer excess regular workers to their subsidiaries or subcontractors. *Tenseki* requires workers to permanently change their corporate membership to the transferred firm. Also see *shukkō*.

todokesei   report system

tokutei *haken*   special *haken*, also known as *jyôyô koyô* gata or 'the employed type' of *haken* workers who are employed as full-time workers by *haken* agencies. Also see *ippan haken* and *tôroku gata*.

tokutei *haken* gaisha   special haken agencies. One of the two major types of *haken* agencies which are restricted to the management of only 'the employed type' (*jyōyō koyō gata*) of *haken* workers and can be easily established provided that a notification is submitted to MHLW. Also see ippan *haken gaisha*.

tōroku gata   the registered type, also known as *ippan haken*. One of the two major groups of *haken* workers who are their *haken* agencies' contingent registrants. They are only considered as *haken* workers when actually working on a job assignment. Also see *jyōyō koyō* gata and *tokutei haken*.

tsūkai na inshō   thrilling impression

tsukiai   after-work (enforced) socialisation

uchi-soto   inside and outside. Also see *giri-ninjyo* and *honne-tatemae*.

ukeoi   subcontracting or outsourcing. The term refers to an external labour arrangement often adopted by large firms to outsource tasks to their subcontractors. There are two types of *ukeoi*: 'off-the-premises' (*kōgai*) *ukeoi* and 'on-the-premises' (*kōnai*) *ukeoi*. While the former means subcontractors carry out the contract outside the client firm's premises, the latter means subcontractors send their workers to work inside the client firm's premises. Also see *gisō ukeoi*.

unmei ni makaseru   resign oneself to fate

wagamama   selfish, immature or egoistic

wake no wakaranai   unreasonable or preposterous

wākingu pua   working poor. The neologism is popularised by NHK's two special TV documentaries broadcast in July and December 2006. It typically refers to a stratum of disadvantaged non-regular workers who live below the basic level of subsistence or 'livelihood protection' (*seikatsu hogo*) no matter how hard they work. Also see *hataraku hinkonsō*.

wan kōru wākā   one-call workers. Also known as *on kōru wākā* and *hiyotoi haken*.

wazurawashî ningenkankei   cumbersome human relations

yamato nadeshiko   the truly sophisticated traditional Japanese woman

yoyû   room

yureugoiteiru   vacillating or wavering

yuruyaka na henka   gradual change

zenzen yakutadanai   absolutely useless

Zesei Shidō Hyō   Rectifying Advice Sheet, the official form issued by MHLW to law-breaking firms

zettai shi nai   absolutely not

zettaiteki hinkon   absolute poverty. Also see *aratana hinkon*.

zokusei   attribute

Notes

1 Introduction

1 [ ] indicates screen subtitles as TV narration goes.
2 According to *Nikkei Woman* (January 2008), Miho Nakazono, the female freelance screenwriter of *Haken's Dignity*, was inspired by her interviews and informal interactions with *haken* workers to whom she felt deeply sympathetic.
3 Unlike regular workers, *haken* workers are not prohibited from engaging in part-time work outside the workplace.
4 As Louis Dumont (1985, 1986) points out, although the view of man as the autonomous being is all-powerful in the modern ideology of individualism, it is 'perpetually and irremediably haunted by its opposite', that is, collectivism or the social. Also see a volume by Steven Lukes (1973) which explains how individualism is imbued with a range of unit-ideas that incorporate religious, political and economic doctrines in the Anglo-Saxon world.
5 During Mao's period, especially such social convulsions as the Cultural Revolution and the Great Leap Forward, the only permitted individual expression in China was 'self-sacrifice' (see Dore 1976; Evans 1997).
6 The role and influence of Japanese firms in the wider social life has interested many scholars, especially with respect to their distinct relationship with the state and the family (see, e.g. Wolferen 1989; Okimoto and Rohlen 1988; Eccleston 1989; Clark 1979; Fruin 1980).
7 In addition, as Abner Cohen (1969: 222) comments, many often 'alternate in their analysis between these two variables, though some do so more consciously, explicitly and systematically than others'.
8 Inspired by the social saliency of those paired expressions, scholars have devoted enormous work to the understanding of the Japanese person, for example, in early socialisation (Hendry 1986; Ben-Ari 1997), family/household-based workplace (Kondo 1990; Hamabata 1990), health and illness (Ohnuki-Tierney 1984), and sexuality (White 1993).

2 *Haken*

1 Non-regular employment, as opposed to regular employment, is variously described by scholars as 'atypical', 'non-standard' or 'irregular' employment. Regular or salaried workers are typically defined as working full-time for a firm with which they are expected to be loyal and identify themselves with for potentially the duration of a lifetime. It should be pointed out here that the much-touted post-war Japanese salaryman paradigm is represented by the cream of the regular legion, that is, workers at large firms who only account for a small minority of the working population in Japan. In this study, *haken* and other non-regular workers are also distinguished from those salaried workers who are subject to corporate internal transfer arrangements such as *tenseki* and *shukkō*, thus falling into the so-called 'grey zone' of life-time employment (see Chapter 4).

2 Day labourers have a long history in Japan (Gill 2001; Leupp 1992). Since the legislation of *haken* employment, many former day labourers have turned into 'day *haken* labourers' (*hiyatoi haken*), popularly called 'one-call workers' or 'on-call workers', who are listed with *haken* agencies and respond to their work calls via mobile phone networks (Kadokura 2007).

3 As Heidi Gottfried (2002a) comments, there is little disagreement that many non-regular workers do not enjoy the same array of benefits as available to regular workers. Yet, it seems that workers fare better in *haken* employment than in other non-regular working arrangements. Around 66 per cent of *haken* workers have universal health and pension insurance coverage while only 33 per cent of part-timers receive the benefit. Within the *haken* category, a small percentage of workers have access to private enterprise annuities, bonus payments, lump sum retirement payments and transportation and vacation allowances (ibid.: 32).

4 Among the four volumes (Genda and Maganuma 2004; Kosugi 2005; Genda and Kosugi 2005; Futagami 2005) reviewed by Wim Lunsing, only Nōki Futagami's work has a specific focus on the young people concerned based on the author's own interaction with them.

5 There is a divide within the Japanese government as to who should be identified as *freeters*. The Cabinet Office defines *freeters* as those who are not in regular employment including *haken*, contract workers and part-timers except for students and professional housewives, whereas the Ministry of Health, Labour, and Welfare (MHLW) only counts those who voluntarily choose to be *freeters*. Accordingly, the statistical number of *freeters* differs greatly; there are more than 4 million in 2001 for the Cabinet Office, compared to 2 million in 2001 and 1.8 million in 2007 for MHLW.

6 As David Harvey (2005: 19) argues, the 'theoretical utopianism' of neoliberal argument which seeks to bring all human action into the domain of market leads to 'a creative tension between the power of neoliberal ideas and the actual practices of neoliberalisation that have transformed how global capitalism has been working over the last three decades'.

7 The growth in non-regular employment has also coincided with the decline in family- and self-employment in which many married Japanese women take part. This has led to an increase in the supply of women seeking non-regular jobs outside, which in turn helps to accommodate the increase in demand for non-regular workers (Nagase 2003; Houseman and Osawa 2003; Rebick 2005).

8 *Haken Business Report* (*Rōdōsha Haken Jigyō Hōkoku*) is summarised and published by MHLW, based on the annual report submitted by all general and special *haken* agencies.

9 Much of the information about *haken* agencies in this study comes from *Nikkei News* and *The Nikkei Weekly* by *Nihon Keizai Shimbun* between November 2006 and October 2008.

10 *Monthly Personnel Business* (*Gekkan Jinzai Bijinesu*), the first nationwide B2B *haken* magazine, is mainly subscribed to by *haken* agencies (70 per cent) and corporate and government personnel departments.

11 The Japanese government has recently put certain public employment services up for competitive bidding in the private sector, with the aim of using private firms' personnel expertise to improve efficiency and reduce administrative costs. As a vital part of the government's nationwide employment administration, Hello Work operations provide a wide range of services ranging from job placement services and employment training to the handling of inquiries and paperwork for the 2 trillion yen ($16.7 billion) unemployment insurance programme (*Nikkei* 14 May, 2007).

12 Under *Haken* Law, client firms are obligated to 'make efforts' to directly employ *haken* who work on the same job for more than 1 year and must offer direct employment to those who work on the same job for more than three consecutive years.

3 Working as a *haken* in a triangular employment relationship

1 Apparently, the personality test can provide some scope for registrants to work to their own advantage. According to Colin Smith's account (2006: 189), although the

personality test does not constitute the most important proof of registrants' competence, staffing agencies often take it into consideration when matching *haken* workers
with suitable jobs.
2 Unlike retail/service and other emerging industries where the core and periphery
boundaries tend to be blurred, in many of the Japanese long-established manufacturers
such as Vision the distinction between regular and non-regular workers coincides more
or less with the so-called core/male and peripheral/female labour dualism. Female
workers seem to be particularly affected by social divide based on employment status;
as some scholars emphasise (e.g. Kadokura 2007; Yamada 2004), the gap in annual
earnings between regular and non-regular employment status is wider for the female
population than for the male population.
3 Because of frequent placement and replacement of *haken* workers, the induction ritual
took place once or twice every month at Vision.
4 *Haken* workers' pay level is subject to the discretion of both the client firm and the
haken agency, which often results in the pay discrepancy in the same category of work.
For *haken* workers, there are two ways of improving their hourly wages. One is to ask
the *haken* agency to negotiate with the client firm on their behalf. The other is to associate with a different agency which has business with the client firm and pays higher
than the current agency – described as 'ultra C', or a difficult, trouble-inviting tech-
nique (*Diamond*, 14 July, 2007).
5 At the time of writing up this book, Japan was hit hard by a new global economic
downturn caused by the collapse of financial systems which had spread joblessness
and distress across the world. Amid widespread layoffs and hiring freezes, non-regular
workers such as *haken* made up the overwhelming majority who were taking the brunt
of cuts in employment. Undoubtedly, losing jobs is most financially devastating for
non-regular workers since they can expect little in the way of unemployment benefits.
The Japanese government has a relatively small amount of budget for unemployment
benefits, which accounts for about 0.3 per cent of its GDP, far below Western
European countries. More importantly, the limited job-loss benefits are designed to
help those lifetime employees; for instance, to receive unemployment benefits, workers must have held the same job for at least 1 year, which effectively excludes the
majority of *haken* and other non-regular workers whose contracts are often as short as
2 or 3 months. According to government officials, at least half of Japan's 17.8 million
non-regular workers are ineligible for unemployment aid (*The New York Times*, 8
February, 2009).
6 JCUF, known as *Zenkoku Yunion*, was founded in March 1988 with the aim of protecting those who have been excluded from *Rengo* or Japanese Trade Union Confederation
(*Nihon Rōdō Kumiai Sōrengōkai*), the largest national trade union centre in Japan,
which is said to be mainly committed to the protection of core regular workers at large
corporations. There are branches of JCUF such as *Haken* Union and *Haken* Network
based in Tokyo, which deal with a variety of issues concerning *haken* workers. JCUF
received most public attention in October 2005 when its female committee chairman
challenged the leader of a powerful employer federation, which has more than 200
times members than JCUF, in a run for chairman at the *Rengo*'s annual convention.
Despite the expected defeat, the high-profile election played an important role in drawing attention to a number of problems faced by non-regular workers.

4 *Haken* in historical perspective

1 Under certain conditions, labour unions and schools were allowed to engage in private
job placement, although the former were not active in the area. Only a few occupations
were permitted, such as medical and pharmaceutical processions, lawyers, interpreters
and house helpers, which were regulated by occupational associations (Imai 2004: 3).
2 *Shokuan*, the abbreviation for *Shokugyō antei jo*, is now popularly called Hello Work
(see Chapter 2, note 12).

3 Legal issues in Japan are a fascinating area to explore the difference between the so-called western-derived universal laws and informal customary practices. Although the Japanese legal system on the surface is typical of a democratic nation with all the necessary apparatus including a written constitution, legal codes and recognisable institutions of parliament democracy, it is 'a cornucopia of contradiction derived from the synthesis of indigenous and extraneous influences', which entails careful contextualised analysis of the concept of law, the historical development and sources of legal practices, the legal profession and alternative forms of dispute resolution in Japan (Dean 2002).

4 Temporary workers here referred to male-dominated 'seasonal workers' (*kisetsukō*) or 'emergency workers' (*rinjikō*), a former category of underpaid, insecure employment widespread in manufacturing firms. Their number diminished considerably between the 1950s and 1970s but was replaced by a female-dominated group of non-regular workers called 'part-timers' (*pāto*). Despite the change in gender and nomenclature, part-time workers played the same role as seasonal or emergency workers in the Japanese employment system. The new vocabulary 'part-time' only became common in the late 1960s when the Labour Ministry in its 1967 White Paper described 'part-time' as a major phenomenon, just 2 years after the last discussion of 'temporary workers' as a major problem (Gordon 1985: 406–407).

5 In addition to hiring freezes and internal transfers of regular workers, unions' focus on job security enabled managers to gain great leverage over job definitions – what is described by Andrew Gordon (1985: 400) as 'a tremendous gain for business in an era of continuous technological innovation'. Historically, Japanese unions have never been craft or trade organisations; they were not committed to protecting particular occupations under attack but to defending jobs at a firm' (ibid.: 390; also see Gordon 1993).

6 After the legal revision in 1999, the system of *haken* has become very complex. The law divides 'the designated 26 occupations' (*seirei 26 gyōmu*), which is extended originally from the 1986's positive list, from other newly liberalised occupations (*jiyūka gyōmu*). The former is generally more skilled and specialised than the latter, although the division is criticised by *haken* agencies as incorrect and unnecessary (JASSA 2006a). Regulations regarding contract length differ depending on the occupational type, but the difference has been significantly reduced since the positive list was replaced by a negative or prohibited list in the 1999 and the 2003 revisions.

7 Japan's real incidence of joblessness during the decade of stagnation is a contentious issue. Some argue that unemployment rates remain low by international standards (Genda and Rebick 2000). Others, however, point to a higher level of unemployment than reported figures would suggest by drawing attention to a number of problems inherent in official statistics including the quantitative method, the definition of 'completely employed' and the 'non-participation' group including many women, young people and older workers unregistered on the unemployment statistics (Crump 2003: 145).

8 MOL, the Ministry of Labour, was replaced by MHLW, the Ministry of Health, Labour, and Welfare in 2001.

9 *Nikkeiren*, the Japanese Federation of Managers' Organisation (*Nihon Keieisha Dantai Renmei*), which was formulated in 1948, was merged into *Keidanren*, the Japanese Federation of Economic Organisation (*Nihon Keizai Dantai Renmei*) in 2002.

10 Since the late 1990s when foreign direct investment emerged as a vital means of revitalising economy, corporate governance reform in Japan was intended to promote international investment by facilitating M&A, privatising government business or liberalising the use of stock options (Aoki *et al.* 2007: 10). The shift was accompanied by a new emphasis on compliance with the law with the aim of improving internal transparency and social responsibility. To achieve this goal, some large companies began to introduce external or independent executives or directors – an element that had been conspicuously absent in the Japanese style of management. In addition, the shareholders' interests were, to some extent, stressed and re-evaluated within a context

of obligations towards a wider set of stakeholders) – although this has proved to be a highly contentious issue (see Dore 2007; *Nikkei Shimbun* 2006; JCGF 1998, 2007).

11 From an economic point of view, the increasing ratio of non-regular to regular workers has much to do with inherent strains in the Japanese employment system which is predicated upon continued rapid economic growth. In addition, a decline in family- and self-employment, which causes an increase in the supply of women seeking non-regular jobs, also contributes to the trend (see Houseman and Osawa 2003; Nagase 2003; Rebick 2005).

12 Anthropology was born of an enlarged frame of time and spent a difficult adolescent time wrestling with a grand thought-structure of historical depth and geographic scale characterised by twentieth-century diffusionism and evolutionism – two obvious and least fashionable frameworks that today's globalisation studies tend to evoke (see Evans-Pritchard 1961; Lewis 1968; Trautmann 1992; Thomas 1989; Eriksen 2003). Such an 'embarrassment' in the discipline's formative past has made anthropology of mature years not only retreat from blatant generalisations but wary of speculating about macro-level theories of any sort.

13 In this connection, it is probably useful to recall economic historian Karl Polanyi's critique in his classic *The Great Transformation* (1944) which emerged out of classical liberalism but remains germane to the discussion of neoliberalism.

14 At the time of writing up this thesis, the neoliberal regime of 'finance everything' was on the brink of collapse, suffering from a devastating blow to its worldwide financial system caused by the so-called 'credit crunch' starting from July 2007. As the capital freeze was taking its toll, major nations actively 'resumed' state power in an attempt to pull their country out of the current global economic recession.

15 Embedded liberalism, as opposed to neoliberalism, was widely accepted during the 1950s and the 1960s which saw the rise of the welfare state in many advanced countries. It is a different theory of political economic practices which promotes an interventionist state, that is economic dynamics should be embedded in politics or controlled through the application of Keynesian fiscal and monetary policies (see Harvey 2005)

5 *Haken* in the 'gap-widening' society

1 Leading newspapers in Japan adopt a quite similar format and generally follow each other's themes closely. As Ikuo Kabashima and Jeffrey Broadbent (1986: 31) put it, '(t) he reader is likely to be bombarded with the same message wherever he or she turns, reinforcing the "reality" of the message'. Moreover, press club systems, as well as media industry networks and associations, have an influence on the interrelationship between journalists and news sources, thereby limiting the way in which news is reported in Japan (Freeman 2000; Feldman 1993).

2 It should be noted that newspaper circulation and revenue in Japan as elsewhere are declining amid competition from the Internet and other new electronic media. Nonetheless, newspaper, together with television, remains influential in the Japanese perception of broader life. According to J-READ (2006), a Japanese national newspaper survey database, the percentage of household delivery subscriptions in Japan was 91.7 per cent and newspapers were ranked as by far the most reliable source of information, with television coming second. World Press Trends 2007 also shows that the number of copies per 1,000 adults in Japan was 630.9, compared to 335.4 in United Kingdom and 241.2 in United States.

3 See Masayuki Ishii and Kaori Ishii (2005), Toshiaki Tachibanaki (2008) and Shin Watanabe (2007).

4 The emergency of '*kakusa kon*' has much to do with a high-profile celebrity marriage in 2007 between Noriko Fujiwara, a superstar actress, and Tomonori Jinnai, a celebrity comedian. Their wedding ceremony was broadcasted live and received a high viewing

rate. The couple are well known for their apparent '*kakusa*' in income, fame and appearance – what is known as 'the gender reverse of a woman married to a man of wealth' (*gyaku tama no koshi*). As an interesting refraction of the gap-widening society, they attracted a huge amount of media attention.

5 According to NHK (2007: 19–20), the use of working poor as the title of the documentaries was inspired by Michiko Miyamoto, professor of the Open University of Japan (Hōsō Daigaku), who frequently invoked working poor when acting as a commentator in NHK's programme, 'Close-up Today: Please Offer Me a Job' (*kurōzuappu Gendai: Shigoto wo Kudasai*). It is also possible that the language is originally derived from David Shipler's *The Working Poor: Invisible in America* (2004).

6 Japan has one of the highest reported suicide rates in the industrialised world. In past years, the suicide rate peaked each time the country's economy fell into recession. There are fears of further increases in the number of people taking their own lives under the current global economic downturn. In early 2008, the Japanese government released the results of a survey which suggested that one in five men and women in the country had seriously thought of taking their own life (*BBC News*, 6 October, 2008).

7 Day *haken* labourers are now popularly called 'one-call workers' (*wan kōru wākā*) (Kadokura 2007) or 'on-call workers' (*on kōru wākā*) (NHK 2007: 227). They have a long and complex socio-economic history in Japan. Prior to the liberalisation of *haken*, day labourers generally referred to those working-class men who looked for casual work at early-morning street labour markets called *yoseba*, and tended to live in cheap lodging houses called *doya*, often concentrated in areas called *doyagai* (Gill 2001, 2003).

8 Opinions leaders tend to use various quantitative data to argue for or against the existence of Japan's *kakusa* or working poor. For example, Toshiaki Tachibanaki (2006), points out that the level of income distribution and poverty in Japan is conspicuously high among OECD countries; in 2006, the poverty percentage in Japan rose to15.3 per cent, ranked second only behind 17.1 per cent in America. There is, however, a faction of commentators who flatly deny Japan's widening gaps by using 'Gini coefficient', a macro-economic indicator for gauging the inequality of income distribution (*Nikkei Business*, 7 August, 2007 and 25 October, 2007).

9 In ancient times, *otsubone* means a dignified lady who has her own private chamber or office at court or in the shogun's castle. In current usage, it refers to veteran, often unmarried, female employees who are powerful in the workplace. Different from its original meaning, it is now commonly used in a pejorative sense, carrying connotations of ill nature, ill temper and fault-finding. The bullying inflicted by *otsubone*, or '*otusbone ijime*', has become established as one of varied forms of bullying in Japan.

6 The search for meaningful work

1 The current Labour Standards Law limits work to 8 hours a day and requires employers to pay a 25 per cent premium for overtime.

2 Education reforms since the mid-1990s have been closely linked with the national policies on the labour market; the prolonged post-bubble economy recession has hardened the belief that the existing education system, especially the university sector, needs to be adjusted in order to meet the market demands of new types of workers (Okano and Tsuchiya 1999; Eades *et al.* 2005). This market-oriented approach has provoked an overhaul of the Japanese system of educational qualifications designed to be conferred upon students of 'general ability' (Dore 1976). The focus on general ability contributes greatly to the production of high-quality, middle-level workers via firm-specific vocational training programmes – this explains why employers used to be reluctant to hire the employees already qualified including those postgraduates for fear that they might be difficult to train in their own way of doing things.

3 Also see a volume edited by James Roberson and Nobue Suzuki (2003) which shows how the salaryman as a metonym for all Japanese men and what it stands for contradict the diversity of identities and experiences found among Japanese men including those marginalised and subversive versions of masculinity.

4 The 'good wife, wise mother' model is informed by Confucian teaching and a key concept in the modernisation of Japanese society (Ishii and Jarkey 2002; Uno 1993; Smith 1987). Intriguingly, the similar ideology is expressed in China as 'wise wife, good mother' (*kensai ryōbo*). This may result from greater importance of the mother–child relationship, that is, the continuity and maintenance of the Japanese household, than the wife–husband relationship (see Dore 1958; Hendry 1981; Yanagisako 1979).

5 The Japanese government came up with a series of family friendly policies in the 1990s including 'the Angel Plan' and 'the Sam campaign' for fathers' involvement in childrearing, in an attempt to create an environment that would encourage women of reproductive age to have children while continuing to work (Roberts 2002).

6 The tax and insurance systems in Japan are premised on the assumption that men are the prime wage earner with women as dependents or temporary workers. Accordingly, certain tax exemptions and insurance benefits are designed to be received on condition that the spouse's annual income and work hours meet specific standards, which are effective in keeping women in part-time jobs or in positions that have low wages (Rebick 2005: 120–121; Houseman and Osawa 2003: 199). Moreover, such gendered systems mean that those who do not fit the prescribed typology such as single working mothers are at high risk of slipping into poverty (Sato *et al.* 2001: 223).

7 The perceived irreducibly joined union of sex, marriage and childbirth is often challenged by theatrical and commercial themes, noticeably the fusion of masculine and feminine attributes in the all-girls theatre Takarazuka Revue (Robertson1992, 1998) and the emerging 'host club' where charming young men serve their female clients (Takeyama 2005). It should be noted that the social organisation of such popular fantasies simultaneously reflects and destabilises prevailing gender and heterosexual norms in Japan.

8 Compared with major industrialised countries, labour force patterns for Japanese women are characteristic of a so-called 'M curve' which has a distinctive fall in participation rates between the ages of 25 and 34, women's main child-bearing years, followed by a gradual rise again from the age of 35–50 (Matsunaga 2000: 121, also see Eccleston 1989; Brinton 1993; Rebick 2005).

9 According to *Haken* Law, employers are obligated to directly employ *haken* workers in certain occupations including clerical or secretarial office jobs, who have worked in the same position for three consecutive years. In order to evade such obligation, many employers simply modify the job's description or move *haken* workers to different departments or branches (also see Chapters 2 and 3).

10 A recent survey by MHLW suggests that single males in non-regular employment have a much lower marriage rate than that of regular employees. According to the survey, only 12 per cent of single males who worked as non-regular workers got married over the 5-year period from October 2002, compared to 24 per cent of regular workers. The survey also shows that by annual income range, only 8 per cent of men who earned less than 1 million yen got married, while 21 per cent of those who made 4–5 million yen got married (*The Mainichi Daily News*, 13 March, 2009).

11 Such an arrangement has become increasingly popular in Japan due to changing generational interactions, which influence young women's thoughts and decisions over their marriage partners, educational development and career choices. For example, Lynne Nakano and Moeko Wagatsuma (2004) present interesting case studies in which public discussion of a new generation of women provide the discursive material through which mothers and daughters formulate a new relationship and negotiate with each other about a wealth of choices and opportunities that are hitherto unavailable to the older generation (also see Rebick and Takenaka: 2006).

12 The Japanese government confirms that the increasing number of young people who delay their marriage or remain single has resulted in the country's falling fertility rates. In relation to this, Hiroko Takeda (2005: 199) argues that the post-war New Life Movement which constructs family life with a limited number of children as rational and happy contributes to the current situation in which the state's favourite daughters delay their marriage and autonomously organise their actions, just as they have been taught.

13 Compared to an explicit approach to Marx, Weber and Durkheim in sociology, anthropological theories are implicitly built upon, or developed in opposition to, the seminal work of those three founding figures in modern social sciences. Weber's work offers much inspiration in the working out of agency, that is, how individuals define their reality in ways that potentially contest the analyst's constructs, although his representation of ideal types of individuals in terms of mechanical models invites criticism (see Gellner 2001: 7–8).

7 Conclusion

1 When I was conducting my fieldwork between 2006 and 2007, the economic trend in Japan was widely portrayed by the mass media as 'outlasting the Izanagi Boom' (*izanagigoe*), which means an upswing from February 2002, lasting even longer than the 1965–1970 economic expansion known as 'Izanagi Boom'. Although the general growth rate (2 per cent) was far less than that of the Izanagi Boom (10 per cent), the stock market and major Japanese firms had been gaining great profits over the past 5 years. The general view was that Japan had finally emerged from the shadow of the post-bubble recession often referred to as 'the lost decade'.

2 In a follow-up of 'The Authors Debate', Marcus Rebick (2002) addresses gender issues in the disparate treatment of regular and non-regular employees, explaining that while in the United States or in Europe, gender-based segmentation primarily takes place along occupational lines, in Japan it is located within occupations along the lines of employment regular/non-regular status.

3 It is widely estimated that the number of *haken* registrants will fall considerably over the medium and long terms in the face of Japan's rapidly ageing population and declining fertility rates. In addition, after years of exceptional growth, competition between *haken* agencies has become increasingly fierce and the industry has begun to show some signs of reshuffling. As Colin Smith (2006: 184–185) comments, it is a fast-growing and yet highly competitive business and the *haken* market in Japan is dominated by bigger, more established players such as Pasona, Adecco, Recruit staffing, Manpower and Staff Service. For mid-size and small agencies, the situation is often described as fighting over a shrinking pie.

4 There are other reasons why firms are not always happy about the use of *haken* workers. For example, because *Haken* Law places a restriction on contract termination, the layoff of *haken* workers is less easy than other non-regular workers such as part-timers.

5 Merit-based pay systems are developed as opposed to 'seniority based pay and promotion systems' (*nenkōjyoretsu*), which reward workers based on age and years of service. The linking of salary to organisational rank or age, rather than ability based grades or particular occupational requirements, encourages long-term commitment and provides a high degree of functional flexibility within firm-internal labour markets required by the Japanese lifetime employment (Jackson 2007).

6 The recent corporate governance reforms have brought about changes in the evaluation of shareholders within a context of obligations towards a wider set of stakeholders including employees (*Nikkei Shimbun* 2006). Yet, it seems that shareholder-oriented values prove to be highly controversial and not so easily adapted to 'the insider nature of Japanese management' (Dore 2007; Iwai *et al.* 2005).

References

Abu-Lughod, Lila. 1990. 'The Romance of Resistance: Tracing the Transformations of Power through Bedouim Women,' in *American Ethnologists*, 17 (1): 41–55.

Allison, Anne. 1994. *Nightwork: Sexuality, Pleasure, and Corporate Masculinity in a Tokyo Hostess Club*. Chicago: University of Chicago Press.

Ambaras, David R. 2005. *Bad Youth: Juvenile Delinquency and the Politics of Everyday Life in Modern Japan*. Berkeley, CA: University of California Press.

Aoki, Masahiko, Jackson, Gregory and Miyajima, Hideaki. eds. 2007. *Corporate Governance in Japan: Institutional Change and Organizational Diversity*. Oxford: Oxford University Press.

Appadurai, Arjun. 1996. *Modernity at Large: Cultural Dimensions of Globalization*. Minneapolis, MN: University of Minnesota Press.

Asad, Talal. 1987. 'Review: Are There Histories of Peoples Without Europe? A Review Article,' in *Comparative Studies in Society and History*, 29 (3): 594–607. Cambridge: Cambridge University Press.

Asahi Shimbun. 2007. *Gisō Ukeoi: Kakusa Shakai no Rōdō Genba* (*Disguised Ukeoi: the Labour Conditions of the Gap-widening Society*). Tokyo: Asahi Shimbun.

Bachnik, Jane. M. 1992. '*Kejime*: Defining a Shifting Self in Multiple Organizational Modes,' in *Japanese Sense of Self*, ed. Nancy R. Rosenberger. Cambridge: Cambridge University Press.

Bachnik, Jane M. and Quinn, Charles J. eds. 1994. *Situated Meaning: Inside and Outside in Japanese Self, Society and Language*. Princeton, NJ: Princeton University Press.

Bauman, Richard and Briggs, L. Charles. 1990. 'Poetics and Performance as Critical Perspectives on Language and Social Life,' in *Annual Review of Anthropology*, 19: 59–88.

Befu, Harumi. 1981. *Japan: An Anthropological Introduction*. Tokyo: Charles E. Tuttle.

Ben-Ari, Eyal. 1997. *Body Projects in Japanese Childcare: Culture, Organization and Emotions in a Preschool*. Richmond: Curzon.

Benedict, Ruth. 1946. *The Chrysanthemum and the Sword: Patterns of Japanese Culture*. Cambridge, MA: Houghton Mifflin.

Blanpain, Roger. 2004. 'Introductory Remarks: The Evolving Attitude Towards Temporary Agency Work,' in *Temporary Agency Work and the Information Society*, eds. Roger Blanpain and Ronnie Graham, International Conference on Temporary Agency Work and the Information Society (Brussels, Belgium). The Hague: Kluwer Law International.

Blanpain, Roger and Graham, Ronnie. eds. 2004. *Temporary Agency Work and the Information Society*, International Conference on Temporary Agency Work and the Information Society (Brussels, Belgium). The Hague: Kluwer Law International.

Bloch, Maurice. 1977. 'The Past and the Present in the Present,' in *Man* (n.s.) 12: 278–292.

Bourdieu, Pierre. 1991. *Languages and Symbolic Power*. Cambridge: Polity Press.

Brinton, Mary C. 1993. *Women and the Economic Miracle: Gender and Work in Postwar Japan*. Berkeley, CA: University of California Press.

Campbell, John C. 1996. 'Media and Policy Change in Japan,' in *Media and Politics in Japan*, eds. Susan J. Pharr and Ellis S. Krauss. Honolulu, HI: University of Hawaii Press.

Carrier, James G. 1996. 'Occidentalism,' in *Encyclopedia of Social and Cultural Anthropology*, eds. Alan Barnard and Jonathan Spencer. London: Routledge.

Chalmers, Norma J. 1989. *Industrial Relations in Japan: The Peripheral Workforce*. London: Routledge.

Cheater, Angela. ed. 1999. *The Anthropology of Power: Empowerment and Disempowerment in Changing Structures*. London: Routledge.

Clark, Rodney. 1979. *The Japanese Company*. New Haven: Yale University Press.

Clifford, James and Marcus, George E. eds. 1986. *Writing Culture: The Poetics and Politics of Ethnography*. Berkeley, CA: University of California Press.

Cohen, Abner. 1969. 'Political Anthropology: the Analysis of the Symbolism of Power Relations,' in *Man*, 4 (2): 215–235.

Crump, John. 2003. *Nikkeiren and Japanese Capitalism*. London: RoutledgeCurzon.

Dasgupta Romit. 2004. '"Crafting Masculinity": Negotiating Masculine Identities in the Japanese Workplace,' PhD thesis, Curtin University of Technology.

Dean, Meryll. 2002. *Japanese Legal System*. London: Cavendish.

Denys, Jan. 2004. 'Challenges for Temporary Agency Work in the Information Society,' in *Temporary Agency Work and the Information Society*, eds. Roger Blanpain and Ronnie Graham, International Conference on Temporary Agency Work and the Information Society (Brussels, Belgium). The Hague: Kluwer Law International.

Dore, Ronald. 1958. *City Life in Japan: A Study of A Tokyo Ward* (Section 3: pp. 91–120). London: Routledge and Kegan Paul.

Dore, Ronald. 1973. *British Factory, Japanese Factory: The Origins of National Diversity in Industrial Relations*. London: Allen & Unwin.

Dore, Ronald. 1976. *The Diploma Disease: Education, Qualification and Development*. London: The Institute of Education, University of London.

Dore, Ronald. 2007. 'Insider Management and Board Reform: For Whose Benefit?' in *Corporate Governance in Japan: Institutional Change and Organizational Diversity*, eds. Masahiko Aoki, Gregory Jackson and Hideaki Miyajima. Oxford: Oxford University Press.

Dore, Ronald and Mari Sako. 1998. [1989]. *How the Japanese Learn to Work*. London: Routledge.

Dresch, Paul and James, Wendy. 2000. 'Introduction: Fieldwork and the Passage of Time,' in *Anthropologists in a Wider World*, eds. Paul Dresch, Wendy James and David Parkin. New York: Berghahn.

Dumont, Louis. 1985. 'A Modified View of Origins: the Christian Beginnings of Modern Individualism,' in *The Category of the Person: Anthropology, Philosophy, History*, eds. Michael Carrithers, Steven Collins and Steven Lukes. Cambridge: Cambridge University Press.

Dumont, Louis. 1986. *Essays on Individualism: Modern Ideology in Anthropological Perspective*. Chicago: University of Chicago Press.

Eades, J. S., Goodman, Roger and Hada, Yumiko. eds. 2005. *The 'Big Bang' in Japanese Higher Education: The 2004 Reforms and the Dynamics of Change*. Melbourne: Trans Pacific Press.

Eccleston, Bernard. 1989. *State and Society in Post-War Japan*. Cambridge: Polity Press.

Edelman, Marc and Haugerud, Angelique. eds. 2005. *The Anthropology of Development and Globalization: From Classical Political Economy to Contemporary Neoliberalism*. Malden, MA: Blackwell.

Edwards, Walter. 1989. *Modern Japan through its Weddings: Gender, Person and Society in Ritual Perspective*. Sanford, CA: Stanford University Press.

EFILWC. 2006. *Temporary Agency Work in an Enlarged European Union* (http://www. eurofound.europa.eu).

Eriksen, Thomas Hylland. ed. 2003. *Globalisation: Studies in Anthropology*. London: Pluto.

Eriksen, Thomas Hylland. 2007. *Globalisation: The Key Concepts*. Oxford: BERG.

Evans, Harriet. 1997. *Women and Sexuality in China: Dominant Discourse of Female Sexuality and Gender since 1949*. Cambridge: Polity.

Evans-Pritchard, E. E. 1951. *Social Anthropology*. London: Cohen & West Ltd.

Evans-Pritchard, E. E. 1961. 'Anthropology and History,' a lecture delivered in the University of Manchester, Manchester University Press.

Feldman, Ofer. 1993. *Politics and the News Media in Japan*. Ann Arbor, MI: University of Michigan Press.

Firth, Raymond. ed. 1967. *Themes in Economic Anthropology*. London: Tavistock.

Forde, Chris and Slater, Gary. 2003. 'The Nature and Experience of Agency Working in Britain,' Discussion papers in Applied Economics and Policy. Nottingham: Nottingham Trent University.

Forde, Chris and Slater, Gary. 2004. 'Agency working in Britain: Character, Consequences and Regulation,' Discussion papers in Applied Economics and Policy. Nottingham: Nottingham Trent University.

Fox, Kate. 2004. *Watching the English: The Hidden Rules of English Behaviour*. London: Hodder.

Freeman, Laurie Anne. 2000. *Closing the Shop: Information Cartels and Japan's Mass Media*. Princeton, NJ: Princeton University Press.

Frühstück, Sabine. 2003. *Colonizing Sex: Sexology and Social Control in Modern Japan*. Berkeley, CA: University of California Press.

Fruin, Mark. W. 1980. 'The Firm as a Family and the Family as a Firm in Japan,' in *Journal of family History*, 5/4 (Winter).

Fujiwara, Masahiko. 2005. *Kokka no Hinkaku* (*The Nation's Dignity*). Tokyo: Shinchōsha.

Futagami, Nōki. 2005. *Kibō no Nīto: Genba kara no Messēji* (*NEET of Hope: Messages from the Field*). Tokyo: Tōyō Keizai Shinpōsha.

Geertz, Clifford. 1973. *The Interpretation of Cultures: Selected Essays*. London: Fontana Press.

Gellner, David N. 2001. *The Anthropology of Buddhism and Hinduism: Weberian Themes*. Oxford: University Press.

Gellner, David N. and Hirsch, Eric. eds. 2001. *Inside Organizations: Anthropologists at Work*. Oxford: BERG.

Genda, Yūji and Kosugi, Reiko. 2005. *Kodomo ga Nīto ni Nattara* (*When Children Become NEET*). Tokyo: NHK Shuppan.

Genda, Yūji and Maganuma, Mie. 2004. *Nīto* (*Not in Education, Employment, or Training*): *Furītā de mo Naku, Shitsugyōsha de mo Naku* (*NEET: Neither Freeters Nor the Unemployed*). Tokyo: Gentōsha.

Genda, Yūji and Rebick, Marcus. 2000. 'Japanese Labour in the 1990s: Stability and Stagnation,' in *Oxford Review of Economic Policy*, 16 (2).

Giddens, Anthony. 1979. *Central Problems in Social Theory: Action, Structure and Contradiction in Social Analysis*. Basingstoke: Macmillan.

Gill, Tom. 2001. *Men of Uncertainty: The Social Organization of Day Laborers in Contemporary Japan*. Albany, NY: SUNY Press.

Gill, Tom. 2003. 'When pillars evaporate: structuring masculinity on the Japanese margins,' in *Men and Masculinity in Contemporary Japan: Dislocating the Salaryman Doxa*', eds. James E. Roberson and Nobue Suzuki. London: RoutledgeCurzon.

Gillespie, Marie. 1995. *Television, Ethnicity and Cultural Change*. London: Routledge.

Goffman, Erving. 1959. *The Presentation of Self in Everyday Life*. Garden City, NY: Doubleday.

Goka, Kazumichi. 1999. *Koyō no Danryokuka to Rōdōsha Haken: Shokugyō Shōkai Jigyō (Employment Flexibility and Haken Workers: The Employment Introduction Business)*. Tokyo: Ōtsuki Shoten.

Goodman, Roger. 1990. *Japan's 'International Youth': The Emergence of a New Class of Schoolchildren*. Oxford: Clarendon Press.

Goodman, Roger. 2002. 'Anthropology, Policy and the Study of Japan,' in *Family and Social Policy in Japan: Anthropological Approaches*, ed. Roger Goodman. Cambridge: Cambridge University Press.

Goodman, Roger. 2006. 'Thoughts on the relationship between anthropological theory, methods and the study of Japanese society,' in *Dismantling the East-West Dichotom*, eds. Joy Hendry and Heung Wah Wong. London: Routledge.

Gordon, Andrew. 1985. *The Evolution of Labor Relations in Japan: Heavy Industry, 1853–1955*. Cambridge, MA: Harvard University Press.

Gordon, Andrew. 1993. 'Contests for the Workplace,' in *Postwar Japan as History*, ed. Andrew Gordon. Berkeley, CA: University of California Press.

Gottfried, Heidi. 2002a. 'Comment: Stability and Change: Typifying "Atypical" Employment in Japan,' in *ASIEN* (Juli 2002) 84, S. 31–33.

Gottfried, Heidi. 2002b. 'Commentaries: "Atypical" and "Irregular" labour in Contemporary Japan,' in *Social Science Japan Journal*, 5: 245–248.

Graaf-Zijl, Marloes de and Berkhout, Ernest E. 2007. *Temporary Agency Work and the Business Circle*, Discussion paper No. 51, SEO Economic Research, University of Amsterdam.

Graham, Fiona. 2003. *Inside the Japanese Company*. London: RoutledgeCurzon.

Graham, Fiona. 2004. *A Japanese Company in Crisis: Ideology, Strategy and Narrative*. Abingdon: RoutledgeCurzon.

Hamabata, Matthews. 1990. *Crested Kimono: Power and Love in the Japanese Business Family*. Ithaca, NY: Cornell University Press.

Hann, Chris. 2006. *"Not the Horse We Wanted!": Postsocialism, Neoliberalism and Eurasia*. Münster: LIT.

Hannerz, Ulf. 1992. *Cultural Complexity: Studies in the Social Organization of Meaning*. New York: Columbia University Press.

Hannerz, Ulf. 1996. *Transnational Connections: Culture, People, Places*. London: Routledge.

Harvey, David. 1989. *The Condition of Postmodernity: An Enquiry into the Origins of Cultural Change*. Cambridge, MA: Blackwell.

Harvey, David. 2005. *A Brief History of Neoliberalism*. Oxford: Oxford University Press.

Held, David, Goldblatt, David, Perraton, Jonathan and McGrew, Anthony. 1999. *Global Transformations: Politics, Economics and Culture*. Cambridge: Polity.

Hendry, Joy. 1981. *Marriage in Changing Japan*. London: Croom Helm.

Hendry, Joy. 1986. *Becoming Japanese: the World of the Pre-school Child*. Manchester: Manchester University Press.

Hendry, Joy. 1992. 'Individualism and Individuality: Entry into a Social World,' in *Ideology and Practice in Modern Japan*, eds. Roger Goodman and Kirsten Refsing. London: Routledge.

Hendry, Joy. 2003. [1989]. *Understanding Japanese Society*. London: RoutledgeCurzon.

Hobsbawm, Eric and Ranger, Terence. eds. 1983. *The Invention of Tradition*. Cambridge: Cambridge University Press.

Hook, Glenn D. and Takeda Hiroko. 2007. '"Self-responsibility" and the Nature of the Postwar Japanese State: Risk through the Looking Glass,' in *Japanese Studies*, 33 (1): 93–123.

Houseman, Susan and Osawa, Machiko. 2003. 'The Growth of Nonstandard Employment in Japan and the United States: A Comparison of Causes and Consequences,' in *Nonstandard Work in Developed Economies: Causes and Consequences*, eds. Susan Houseman and Machiko Osawa. Kalamazoo, MI: W.E. Upjohn Institute for Employment Research.

Hyodo, Tsutomu. 1997. *Rōdō no Sengoshi* (*The Post-war History of Labour*). Tokyo: The University of Tokyo Press.

Imai, Jun. 2004. 'The Rise of Temporary Employment in Japan: Legalisation and Expansion of a Non-Regular Employment', Working Papers on East Asian Studies, No. 62, Campus Duisburg, Germany.

Imai, Jun and Shire, Karen. 2006. 'Employment Deregulation and the Expanding Market for Temporary Labour in Japan,' in *The Changing Structure of Labour in Japan: Japanese Human Resource Management: Between Continuity and Innovation*, eds. René Haak and Markus Pudelko. New York: Palgrave Macmillan.

Inagami, Takeshi. 1989. *Tenkanki no Rōdō Sekai* (*The World of Work in Transition*). Tokyo: Yūshindō.

Ishida, Takeshi. 1986. 'The Introduction of Western Political Concepts into Japan: Non-western Societies' Response to the Impact of the West', Nissan Occasional Paper Series, No. 2. Oxford: Nissan Institute of Japanese Studies.

Ishii, Masayuki and Ishii, Kaori. 2005. *'Mitame' Izon no Jidai: 'Bi' toiu Yokuatsu ga Kaisōkashakai ni Hakusha wo Kakeru* (*The Appearance-obsessed Era: The 'Beauty' Oppression Accelerates the Stratified Society*). Tokyo: Harashobō.

Ishii, Kazumi and Jarkey, Narida. 2002. 'The Housewife is Born: The Establishment of the Notion and Identity of the *Shufu* in Moden Japan,' in *Japanese Studies*, 22 (1).

Ishii-Kuntz, Masako. 2003. 'Balancing Fatherhood and Work: Emergence of Diverse Masculinities in Contemporary Japan,' in *Men and Masculinity in Contemporary Japan: Dislocating the Salaryman Doxa*, eds. James E. Roberson and Nobue Suzuki. London: RoutledgeCurzon.

Iwai, Katsuhito, *et al.* 2005. *Kaisha wa Kabunushi no Mono Dewa Nai* (*The Company Is Not Owned by Shareholders*). Tokyo: Yosensha.

Jackson, Gregory. 2007. 'Employment Adjustment and Distributional Conflict in Japanese Firms' in *Corporate Governance in Japan: Institutional Change and Organizational Diversity*, eds. Masahiko Aoki, Gregory Jackson and Hideaki Miyajima. Oxford: Oxford University Press.

Jackson, Gregory and Miyajima, Hideaki. 2007. 'Introduction: The Diversity and Change of Corporate Governance in Japan,' in *Corporate governance in Japan: institutional change and organizational diversity*, eds. Masahiko Aoki, Gregory Jackson and Hideaki Miyajima. Oxford: Oxford University Press.

JASSA. 2002. *Jinzai Haken Hakusho: Jinzai Haken no Atarashī Nami* (*Personnel Dispatching White Paper: A New Wave of Personnel Dispatching*). Tokyo: Tōyō Keizai Shinpōsha.

JASSA. 2006a. *Rōdōshijyō no Kaseika ni Muketa Rōdōsha Hakenhō Bappon Kaikaku no Hōkōsei* ('Towards the Invigoration of Labour Markets: the Direction of Sweeping Reforms in *Haken* Law) (http://www.jassa.jp).

JASSA. 2006b. *Haken Rōdō to Kakusa Shakai* ('*Haken* Work and the Gap-widening Society') (http://www.jassa.jp).

JASSA. 2008. *Rōdōsha Haken wo Tadashiku Rikai Shitekudasai* ('Please Have a Proper Understanding of *Haken*') (http://www.jassa.jp).

JCGF. 1998. 'Corporate Governance Principles: A Japanese View (Final Report)' (http://jcgf.org).

JCGF. 2007. 'New Corporate Governance Principles'. (http://jcgf.org).

JILPT. 2007. *European Employment Strategy: Suggestion to Policy in Japan*. Tokyo: Rōdō Seisaku Kenkyū Kenshū Kikō.

Jyō, Shigeyuki. 2006. *Wakamono wa Naze San Nen de Yameru no ka?* (*Why do Young People Resign Within Three Years?*). Tokyo: Kōbunsha.

Just, Peter. 1992. 'History, Power, Ideology, and Culture: Current Directions in the Anthropology of Law,' in *Law and Society Review*, 26 (2): 373–411.

Kabashima, Ikuo and Broadbent, Jeffrey. 1986. 'Referent Pluralism: Mass Media and Politics in Japan,' *Journal of Japanese Studies*, 12 (2, Summer): 329–361.

Kadokura, Takeshi. 2006. *Wākingu Pua: ikura Hataraitemo Mukuwarenai Jidai ga Kuru* (*Working Poor: the Era of Unrewarded Efforts Arrives*). Tokyo: Takajimasha.

Kadokura, Takeshi. 2007. *Haken no Riaru: 300man Nin no Himei ga Kikoeru* (*Haken's Reality: Listening to the Cries of 3-million People*). Tokyo: Takajimasha.

Kariya, Takehiko. 2001. *Kaisōka Nihon to Kyōiku Kiki – Fubyōdō Saiseisan kara Iyoku Kakusa Shakai (Insentibu Dibaido) he* (*Stratified Japan and Education Crisis: From the Reproduction of Inequality to an 'Incentive Divide' Society*). Tokyo: Yūshindō Kōbunsha.

Kariya, Takehiko, Sugayama, Shinji and Ishida, Hiroshi. eds. 2000. *Gakkō, Shokuan to Rōdō Shijyō: Sengō Shinki Gakusotsu Shijyō no Seidoka Katei* (*School, Shokuan and Labour Market: the Institutionalisation of the Labour Market for New Graduates*). Tokyo: University of Tokyo Press.

Kasza, Gregory J. 1988. The *State and the Mass Media in Japan, 1918–1945*. Berkeley, CA: University of California Press.

Kawakita, Yoshinori. 2006. *Otoko no Hinkaku* (*Men's Dignity*) Tokyo: PHP Kenkyūjyo.

Keidanren. 2003. *The Current Labour Economy in Japan*. Tokyo: Keidanren.

Keidanren. 18 January 2006. *Korekara no Sekai Keizai to Nihon no Kadai* ('The Issues Regarding the Future World Economy and Japan') (http://www.keidanren.or.jp).

Keizer, Arjan B. 2007. 'Non-regular Employment in Japan: Continued and Renewed Dualities,' working paper No. 07/13. Bradford: Bradford University School of Management.

Kojima, Noriaki and Fujikawa, Keiko. 2003. 'Nonstandard Work Arrangements in Japan and the United States: A Legal Perspective,' in *Nonstandard Work in Developed Economies: Causes and Consequences*, eds. Susan Houseman and Machiko Osawa. Kalamazoo, MI: W.E. Upjohn Institute for Employment Research.

Kondo, Dorinne. 1990. *Crafting Selves: Power, Gender, and Discourses of Identity in a Japanese Workplace*. Chicago: The University of Chicago Press.

Kosugi, Reiko. ed. 2005. *Furītā to Nīto* (*Freeters and NEET*). Tokyo: Keisō Shobō.

Leach, Edmund. R. 1954. *Political Systems of Highland Burma: A Study of Kachin Social Structure*. London: G. Bell.

Leupp, Gary P. 1992. *Servants, Shophands, and Laborers in the Cities of Tokugawa Japan*. Princeton, NJ: Princeton University Press.

Lewis, I. M. ed. 1968. *History and Anthropology*. London: Tavistock.

Lindstorm, Lamont. 2002. 'Discourse,' in *Encyclopedia of Social and Cultural Anthropology*, eds. Alan Barnard and Jonathan Spencer. London: Routledge.

Lo, Jeannie. 1990. *Office Ladies, Factory Women: Life and Work at a Japanese Company*. Armonk: M.E. Sharpe.

Lukes, Steven. 1973. *Individualism*. Oxford: Basil Blackwell.

Lunsing, Wim. 2006. 'Quitting Companies: Individual Response to Changing Employment Patterns in Early 2000s Japan,' in *Perspectives on Work, Employment and Society in Japan*, eds. Peter Matanle and Wim Lunsing. Basingstoke: Palgrave Macmillan.

Lunsing, Wim. 2007. 'The Creation of the Social Category of NEET (Not in Education, Employment or Training): Do NEET Need This?' in *Social Science Japan Journal*, 10 (1): 105–110.

Mannari, Hiroshi and Befu, Harumi. eds. 1983. *The Challenge of Japan's Internationalization: Organization and Culture*. Tokyo: Kwansei Gakuin University and Kodansha International.

Martinez, Dolores P. 2004. *Identity and Ritual in a Japanese Diving Village: The Making and Becoming of Person and Place*. Honolulu, HI: University of Hawaii Press.

Maruyama, Shun. 2004. *Furītā Bōkokuron* (*The Theory of National Ruin Caused by Freeters*). Tokyo: Daiyamondosha.

Mathews, Gordon. 1996. *What Makes Life Worth Living?: How Japanese and Americans Make Sense of Their Worlds*. Berkeley, CA: University of California Press.

Mathews, Gordon and White, Bruce. eds. 2004. *Japan's Changing Generations: Are Young People Creating a New Society?* London: RoutledgeCurzon.

Matsunaga, Louella. 2000. *The Changing Face of Japanese Retail: Working in a Chain Store*. London: Routledge.

Mauss, Marcel. 1967. *The Gift: Forms and Functions of Exchange in Archaic Societies*, translated by Ian Cunnison. New York: W.W. Norton.

Mauss, Marcel. 1985. 'A Category of the Human Mind: the Notion of Person; the Notion of Self' (translated by W. D. Halls) in *The Category of the Person: Anthropology, Philosophy, History*, eds. Michael Carrithers, Steven Collins and Steven Lukes. Cambridge: Cambridge University Press.

MHLW. 2005. *Haken Rōdōsha Jittai Chōsa 2004* ('*Haken* Survey 2004') (http://www.mhlw.go.jp).

MHLW. 2007a. *Rōdōsha Haken Jigyō Hōkoku 2006* ('*Haken* Business Report 2006') (http://www.mhlw.go.jp).

MHLW. 2007b. *Rōdō Keizai Hakusho* ('Labour Economy White Paper') (http://www.mhlw.go.jp).

MHLW. 2008. *Rōdōsha Haken Jigyō no Tekisei na Unei no Kakuho oyobi Haken Rōdōsha no Shūgyō Jyōken no Seibi nado ni kansuru Hōritsu Nado no Ichibu wo Kaisei suru Hōritsuan ni tsuite* ('Revisions of Law for Ensuring the Proper Operation of *Haken* Business and Improved Working Conditions for *Haken* Workers') (http://www.mhlw.go.jp).

Mitarai, Fujio and Niwa, Uichiro. 2006. *Kaisha wa Dare no Tame ni* (*The Company Is For Whom*). Tokyo: Bungei Shunshū.

Mitchell, Richard. H. 1983. *Censorship in Imperial Japan*. Princeton, NJ: Princeton University Press.

Miura, Atsushi. 2005. *Karyū Shakai* (*Lower-Class Society*). Tokyo: Kōbunsha.

Miyajima, Tadashi. 2007. *Shūshoku Hyōgaki Sedai ga Shinsan wo Nametsuzukeru* (*The Generation in the Corporate Hiring Freeze Continue to Suffer Hardships*) or (*The Tragedy of Lost Generation*). Tokyo: Yōsensha.

Moeran, Brian. 1984. 'Individual, Group and *Seishin*: Japan's Internal Cultural Debate,' *Man*, 19 (2): 252–266.

Moeran, Brian. 2006. *Ethnography at Work*. Oxford: BERG.

MOL. 1995. *Rōdō Hakusho: Koyō Sōshutsu wo tsūjita Rōdō Shijyō no Kōzō Henka he no Taiō* (*Labour White Paper: Responses to the Structural Change of Labour Markets through Employment Creation*). Tokyo: Japan Institute of Labour.

MOL. 1999. *Rōdō Hakusho: Kyūsoku ni Henka suru Rōdō Shijyō to Aratana Koyō no Sōshutsu* (*Labour White Paper: Rapidly Changing Labour Markets and New Employment Creation*). Tokyo: Japan Institute of Labour.

Morris, Gillian. 2004. 'England,' in *Temporary Agency Work and the Information Society*, eds. Roger Blanpain and Ronnie Graham, International Conference on Temporary Agency Work and the Information Society (Brussels, Belgium). The Hague: Kluwer Law International.

Morris, Jonathan, Hassard, John and McCann, Leo 2006. 'New Organizational Forms, Human Resource Management and Structural Convergence? A Study of Japanese Organizations,' in *Organization Studies*, 27 (10): 1485–1511. London: Sage Publications.

Nagase, Nobuko. 2003. 'Standard and Non-standard Work Arrangements, Pay Difference, and Choice of Work by Japanese Mothers,' in *Nonstandard Work in Developed Economies: Causes and Consequences*, eds. Susan Houseman and Machiko Osawa. Kalamazoo, MI: W.E. Upjohn Institute for Employment Research.

Nakane, Chie. 1970. *Japanese Society*. London: Weidenfeld and Nicolson.

Nakano, Lynne and Wagatsuma, Moeko. 2004. 'Mothers and Their Unmarried Daughters: An Intimate Look at Generational Change,' in *Japan's Changing Generations: Are Young People Creating a New Society?* eds. Gordon Mathews and Bruce White. London: RoutledgeCurzon.

NHK. 2007. *Wākingu Pua – Nihon wo Mushibamu Yamai* (*Working Poor: The Disease Gnawing away at Japan*). Tokyo: Kabushiki Popula.

Nikkei Shimbun. ed. 2006. *Kaisha towa Nani ka* (*What Is Company*). Tokyo: Nihon Keizai Shimbun Sha.

Nikkeiren. 1995. *Shin Jidai no Nihonteki Keiei* (*Japanese-style Management for a New Era*). Tokyo: Nikkeiren.

Ogasawara, Yuko. 1998. *Office Ladies and Salaried Men: Power, Gender, and Work in Japanese Companies*. Berkeley, CA: University of California Press.

Ohnuki-Tierney, Emiko. 1984. *Illness and Culture in Contemporary Japan*. Cambridge: Cambridge University Press.

Ohta, Hajime. 2006. *'Sotomuki Sararīman' no Susume* (*Toward the 'Outward-looking Salaryman'*). Tokyo: Asahi Shimbun Sha.

Okano, Kaori and Tsuchiya, Motonori. 1999. *Education in Contemporary Japan: Inequality and Diversity*. Cambridge: Cambridge Press.

Okely, Judith and Callaway, Helen. eds. 1992. *Anthropology and Autobiography*. London: Routledge.

Okimoto, I. Daniel and Rohlen, P. Thomas, eds. 1988. *Inside the Japanese System: Readings on Contemporary Society and Political Economy*. Stanford, CA: Stanford University Press.

Ortner, Sherry. B. 1984. 'Theory in Anthropology since the Sixties,' in *Comparative Studies in Society and History*, 26: 126–166.

Osawa, Mari. 2001. 'People in Irregular Modes of Employment: Are they really not subject to discrimination?' *Social Science Japan Journal*, 4 (2): 183–199.

Ozasa, Yoshihisa. 2007. *Kaisha no Hinkaku* (*The Company's Dignity*). Tokyo: Gentōsha.

Parkin, David. 1978. *The Cultural Definition of Political Response: Lineal Destiny among the Luo*. London: Academic Press.

Parkin, David. ed. 1982. *Semantic Anthropology*. London: Academic Press.

Parkin, David. 1984. 'Political Language,' *Annual Review of Anthropology*, 29: 107–124.

Pharr, Suaan J. 1996. 'Media and Politics in Japan: Historical and Contemporary Perspectives,' in *Media and Politics in Japan*, eds. Susan J. Pharr and Ellis S. Krauss. Honolulu, HI: University of Hawaii Press.

Pocock, David F. 1971. *Social Anthropology*. London: Sheed and Ward.

Pocock, David F. 1994. 'The Idea of a Personal Anthropology,' in *Journal for the Anthropological Study of Human Movement*, 8: 11–28.

Polanyi, Karl. 1944. *The Great Transformation*. New York: Farrar & Rinehart.

Rebick, Marcus. 2002. 'Commentaries: "Atypical" and "Irregular" labour in Contemporary Japan,' in *Social Science Japan Journal*, 5: 243–245.

Rebick, Marcus.2005. *The Japanese Employment System: Adapting to a New Economic Environment*. Oxford: Oxford University Press.

Rebick, Marcus and Takenaka, Ayumi. eds. 2006. *The Changing Japanese Family*. Abingdon: Routledge.

Roberson, James E. and Suzuki, Nobue, eds. 2003. *Men and Masculinity in Contemporary Japan: Dislocating the Salaryman Doxa*. London: RoutledgeCurzon.

Roberts, Glenda S. 2002. 'Pinning Hopes on Angels: Reflection from an Aging Japan's Urban Landscape,' in *Family and Social Policy in Japan: Anthropological Approaches*, ed. Roger Goodman. Cambridge: Cambridge University Press.

Robertson, Jennifer. 1992. 'Doing and Undoing "Female" and "Male" in Japan: The Takarazuka Revue' in *Japanese Social Organization*, ed. Takie Sugiyama Lebra. Honolulu, HI: University of Hawaii Press.

Robertson, Jennifer.1998. *Takarazuka: Sexual Politics and Popular Culture in Modern Japan*. Berkeley, CA: University of California Press.

Rohlen, Thomas P. 1974. *For Harmony and Strength: Japanese White-collar Organization in Anthropological Perspective*. Berkeley, CA: University of California Press.

Rosenberger, Nancy R. ed. 1992. *Japanese Sense of Self*. Cambridge: Cambridge University Press.

Sakahigashi, Mariko. 2006. *Jyosei no Hinkaku* (*Women's Dignity*). Tokyo: PHP Kenkyūjyo.

Sakahigashi, Mariko. 2007. *Oya no Hinkaku* (*Parents' Dignity*). Tokyo: PHP Kenkyūjyo.

Satō, Hiroki. 2001. 'Atypical Employment: A Source of Flexible Work Opportunities?' *Social Science Japan Journal*, 4 (2): 161–181.

Satō, Hiroki, Osawa, Mari and Weather, Charles. 2001. '"Atypical" and "Irregular" Labour in Contemporary Japan: The Authors Debate,' in *Social Science Japan Journal*, 4 (2): 219–223.

Shipler, David K. 2004. *The Working Poor: Invisible in America*. New York: Knopf.

Shore, Cris and Wright, Susan. eds. 1997. *Anthropology of Policy: Critical Perspectives on Governance and Power*. London: Routledge.

Smith, Colin Scott. 2006. 'After Affluence: Freeters and the Limits of New Middle Class Japan', PhD thesis, Yale University, UMI.

Smith, Robert J. 1987. 'Gender Inequality in Contemporary Japan,' in *Journal of Japanese Studies*, 13 (1): 1–25.

Steven, Rob. 1983. *Classes in Contemporary Japan*. Cambridge: Cambridge University Press.

Suehiro, Akira. 2001. 'An Introduction to this Issue's Special Topic: "Atypical" and "Irregular" Labour in Contemporary Japan,' in *Social Science Japan Journal*, 4 (2): 159–160.

Sugimoto, Yoshio and Mouer, Ross E. eds. 1989. *Constructs for Understanding Japan*. London: Kegan Paul.

Suwa, Yasuo. 2000. 'Rōdō Shijyō Hō no Rinen to Taikei' ('The Ideas and Systems of Labour Market Law), in *21seiki no Rōdō Hō Dai Ni Kan Rōdō Shijyō no Kikō to Rūrū (Labour Laws in the 21st Century. Volume 2: The Structure and the Regulation of the Labour Market*), pp. 2–22. Tokyo: Yūhikaku.

Tachibanaki, Toshiaki. 2006. *Kakusa Shakai – Nani ga Mondai nanoka (The Gap-widening Society: What are the Problems?*). Tokyo: Iwanami Shoten.

Tachibanaki, Toshiaki. 2008. *Jyo Jyo Kakusa (Women/Women Divide)*. Tokyo: Tōyō Keizai.

Takanashi, Akira. 1985. *(Detailed Commentary on the Law of Dispatched Workers)*. Tokyo: Nihon Rōdō Kenkyū Kikō.

Takanashi, Akira. ed. 2001. *Dai 2-han Shōkai Rōdōsha Hakenhō (Second Edition: Detailed Commentary on the Law of Dispatched Workers)*. Tokyo: Nihon Rōdō Kenkyū Kikō.

Takeda, Hiroko. 2005. *The Political Economy of Reproduction in Japan: Between Nation-state and Everyday Life*. London: RoutledgeCurzon.

Takeyama, Akiko. 2005. 'Commodified Romance in a Tokyo Host Club,' in Mark McLelland and Romit Dasgupta eds. *Genders, Transgenders and Sexualities in Japan*, pp. 200–215. New York: Routledge.

Thomas, Nicholas. 1989. *Out of Time: History and Evolution in Anthropological Discourse*. Cambridge: Cambridge University Press.

Tobin, Joseph. 1992. 'Japanese preschools and the pedagogy of selfhood,' in *Japanese Sense of Self*, ed. Nancy R. Rosenberger. Cambridge: Cambridge University Press.

Trautmann, R. Thomas. 1992. 'The Revolution in Ethnological Time,' in *Man* 27 (2): 379–397.

Treanor, Paul. 2005. 'Neoliberalism: Origins, Theory, and Definition' (http://web.inter.nl.net/users/Paul.Treanor/neoliberalism.html)

Tsuchida, Michio. 2000. 'Kaisei Shokugyō Antei Hō no Igi to Kadai' ('The Meaning and Future Agenda of the Revised Employment Security Law'), in *The Monthly Journal of the Japan Institute of Labour*, 475: 36–47. Tokyo: Japan Institute of Labor.

Turner, Victor. 1967. *The Forest of Symbols: Aspects of Ndembu Ritual*. Ithaca, NY: Cornell University Press.

Turner, Victor. 1969. *The Ritual Process*. Chicago: Aldine.

Uno, Kathleen S. 1993. 'The Death of "Good Wife, Wise Mother"?' in *Postwar Japan as History*, ed. Andrew Gordon. Berkeley, CA: University of California Press.

Ujihara, Shōjirō. 1989. *Nihon Keizai to Koyō Seisaku (Japanese Economy and Employment Policy)*. Tokyo: University of Tokyo Press.

Van Maanen, John. 1988. *Tales of the Field: On Writing Ethnography*. Chicago: The University of Chicago Press.

Vogel, Ezra F. 1963. *Japan's New Middle Class: The Salary Man and His Family in a Tokyo Suburb*. Berkeley, CA: University of California Press.

Wakita, Shigeru. 1995. *Rōdō Hō no Kisei Kanwa to Kōsei Koyō Hoshō: Rōdōsha Haken Hō Unyō no Sōkatsu to Kadai (The Deregulation of Labour Laws and the Guarantee of Fair Employment: The Outline and Issues of the Application of Haken Law)*. Kyoto: Hōritsu Bunka sha.

Wallerstein, Immanuel. 1974. *The Modern World-system*. New York: Academic Press.

Watanabe, Shin. 2007. *Chūnen Dōtei – Shōshika Jidai no Renai Kakusa (Middle-age Virginity: Love Divide in a Low-fertility Era)*. Tokyo: Fusōsha.

Weathers, Charles. 2001. 'Changing White-collar Workplaces and Female Temporary Workers in Japan,' in *Social Science Japan Journal*, 4 (2): 201–218.

Weathers, Charles. 2009 'Nonregular Workers and Inequality in Japan,' in *Social Science Japan Journal*, January 30, 2009 (online edition).

White, Merry. 1993. *The Material Child: Coming of Age in Japan and America*. Berkeley, CA: University of California Press.

Wierzbicka, Anna. 1997. *Understanding Cultures through Their Key Words: English, Russian, Polish, German, and Japanese*. New York: Oxford University Press.

Wolf, Eric R. 1982. *Europe and the People Without History*. London: University of California Press.

Wolferen, Karel Van. 1989. *The Enigma of Japanese Power: People and Politics in a Stateless Nation*. London: Macmillan.

Yamada, Masahiro. 1999. *Parasaito Shinguru no Jidai (An Age of Parasite Singles)*. Tokyo: Chūkō Shinsho.

Yamada, Masahiro. 2004. *Kibō Kakusa Shakai – 'Makegumi' no Zetsubōkan ga Nihon wo Hikisaku (Society of Expectation Gaps: The Despair of 'Losers' is Tearing up Japan)*. Tokyo: Chikuma Shobō.

Yamada, Masahiro. 2006. *Shin Byōdō Shakai – Kibō Kakusa wo Koete (New Equal Society: Beyond Expectation Gaps)*. Tokyo: Bungei Shunshū.

Yamamoto, Beverley. 1999. 'A Gendered Analysis of the Teenage Pregnancy "Problem" in Japan: Pushing the Limits of "Good Girl" Behaviour,' PhD thesis, The University of Sheffield.

Yanagisako, Sylvia Junko. 1979. 'Family and Household: the Analysis of Domestic Groups,' in *Annual Review of Anthropology*, 8: 161–205.

Yoder, Robert Stuart. 2004. *Youth Deviance in Japan: Class Reproduction and Non-conformity*. Melbourne: Trans Pacific.

Yoroi, Takayoshi, Wakita, Shigeru and Goka, Kazumichi. eds. 2001. *Kisei Kanwa to Rōdōsha/Rōdō Hōsei (Deregulation and Labour/Labour Laws)*. Tokyo: Jyunpōsha.

Yuasa, Makoto. 2007. *Hinkon Shūrai (The Rushing Poverty)*. Tokyo: JRC.

Newspapers, magazines and online papers (last accessed in July 2009)*

Asahi Shimbun (http://www.asahi.com)
28 November, 2007
BBC News (http://www.bbc.co.uk)
22 February, 2008
6 October, 2008
Diamond 14 July, 2007
GIGAZINE (http://gigazine.net)

*Dates given are when the news/article was released online.

24 August, 2007
J-Read 2006 (http://www.videor.co.jp/service/newspaper/jread/index.htm)
Mainichi Shimbun (http://mainichi.jp)
1 February, 2006
Monthly Personnel Business (https://www.jinzai-business.net)
22 February, 2008
Nikkei Business (http://business.nikkeibp.co.jp)
6 February, 2007
2 April, 2007
7 August, 2007
25 October, 2007
Nikkei (Nihon Keizai Shimbun) (http://www.nni.nikkei.co.jp)
22 May, 2006
25 September, 2006
15 November, 2006
14 May, 2007
14 June, 2007
29 July, 2008
22 December, 2008
Nikkei Net (http://www.nikkei.co.jp)
1 February, 2006
Nikkei Weekly (http://www.nni.nikkei.co.jp).
12 February, 2007
3 March, 2008
Nikkei Woman January 2008
SPA!, 17 July, 2007
The Japan Times (http://www.japantimes.co.jp)
4 January, 2006
4 February, 2007
29 August, 2007
30 July, 2008
26 June, 2008
5 November, 2008
The Mainichi Daily News (http://mdn.mainichi.jp)
13 March, 2009
The New York Times (http://www.nytimes.com)
8 February, 2009
Yomiuri Weekly
21 January, 2007
2 December, 2007
27 January, 2008
2 March, 2008

Index

Note: page number is **bold** refer to illustrations.

168   *Index*

legislation: development of *haken* in
57–63; revisions 132
leisure interests, importance of 104–5
'licence system' 25
life pursuits, young women 112–14
lifestyle: choice of 20, 22, 113;
cultivation of 127–8; importance
of 125
lifetime employment: flourishing system
of 58; myth of 59; pros and cons of
67; protection of 64, 68; replacement
of 66, 132–3; state support for 99
Lindstorm, Lamont 5
'livelihood protection' 82, 84, 132, 142
Lo, Jeannie 11
long-term employment **19**, 55, **67**, 68, 69,
99, 132–3
long-term non-regular workers 55
low-skilled workers: contracts 38; income
levels 31; as *ukeoi* workers 60, 63;
unemployment 65
Lower-class Society (Miura) 124
Lunsing, Wim 133

male workers, experiences of 111–12
Mannari, Hiroshi 5–6
Manpower Japan 34, 61, 129
manufacturing and construction sector
28, **29**
Marcus, George E. 11
market-transferable skills 86
marketing strategies 128–9
'marketisation of public services'
scheme 37
marriage rates 123
marriage, women's desire for 107–8,
110–11, 117, 118–19
Martinez, Dolores P. 8
Maruyama, Shun 21
Marxism 80
Masahiro, Yamada 20
Mathews, Gordon 98, 112–13
Matsunaga, Louella 11, 19, 49–50, 55,
64, 106, 111, 113
Matsushita 38, 91, 131
Mauss, Marcel 3, 6, 14
'Me-Fetishism' 105
meaningful work, search for 97–119
mechanical design workers **32**
media 78–80; investigations of *haken*
87–96; reaction against 'freeters' 20
media announcers/presenters **33**
media workers, treatment of 100
Meiji modernisation 80

Meiji working-class society 57–8
merit-based pay systems 68
middle class 80–1, 89–90, 107, 113,
119, 122
Minimum Age Law 132
Ministry of Health, Labour and Welfare
2, 26–7, 33, 34, 63, 69–70; *Haken
Business Report* (2006) 25, 26, 32–3,
34; *haken* survey 26–8
Ministry of Internal Affairs and
Communications (MIC):
Employment Structure Survey 29,
31; Labour Force Survey 2007 23, 30
Ministry of Labour (MOL) 65, 67; White
Paper (1996) 103
Mitarai, Fujio 91, 100
Mitchell, Richard H. 79
Miura, Atsushi 124
Miura, Kazuo 36
Miyajima, Hideaki 85, 103, 133
Miyamoto, Michiko 85
Moeran, Brian 4, 5, 127
Morris, Gillian 68
motivation 47, 69–70, 107–15, 124, 132
Mouer, Ross E. 80
'multi-track' personnel system 65–6

Nakane, Chie 11, 49
national 'Big Five' newspapers 78–9
'NEETS' (Not in Employment, Education
or Training) 19–23, 36, 89
neoliberalism 21, 64–5, 67–8, 70, 72–6,
120, 129
'net-cafe refugees' 84–5, 92
Netherlands, temporary agency work **71**
'new poverty' 83–5
newspaper sales 78–9
Nihon Hōsō Kyōkai (NHK) 79, 82–7
Nihon Keidanren 122
*Nikkeiren, 'Japanese-style Management
for a New Era'* document 65–6
Niwa, Uichiro 100
non-executive employees, numbers of 23
non-regular employment: benefits of 94;
composition of 24; contrast with
regular workers 3, 93–6; emergence
of new category of 133–4; *haken* as
new breed of 17–23; public
perceptions of 18–23; types of 19
non-regular workers: differentiation/
relationship with regular workers
50–3, 124; maximising use of 66,
86; regular employment status 54–5;
as working poor 80–7

For Product Safety Concerns and Information please contact our
EU representative GPSR@taylorandfrancis.com Taylor & Francis
Verlag GmbH, Kaufingerstraße 24, 80331 München, Germany